THE SACRIFICIAL SYSTEM

THE SACRIFICIAL SYSTEM

JIMMY SWAGGART

JIMMY SWAGGART MINISTRIES

P.O. Box 262550 | Baton Rouge, Louisiana 70826-2550

Website: www.jsm.org | Email: info@jsm.org | Phone: 225.768.7000

ISBN 978-1-941403-03-7

09-126 | COPYRIGHT © 2014 Jimmy Swaggart Ministries®

14 15 16 17 18 19 20 21 22 23 / RRD / 10 9 8 7 6 5 4 3 2 1

TABLE OF CONTENTS

Introduction

Introduction

SOME WOULD ASK, *"Why should a book be written as it regards the Old Testament sacrificial system?"*

That's a good question!

There is at least one reason, and it is overwhelming in its significance and its scope.

The sacrificial system given by the Lord to Moses was meant to portray the one sacrifice of Christ, that is, when He would come. Considering how involved, how all encompassing, and how particular this system was, this tells us by the sheer weight of the Mosaic system just how important that the sacrifice of Christ actually was. To see something as involved as the Mosaic system, with all of its minute rules and regulations, and to see the space devoted to such by the Holy Spirit, we cannot help but grasp the fact that if this, in fact, did portray the one sacrifice of Christ, then this tells us in no uncertain terms just how important is the Cross.

THE CROSS OF CHRIST

That is the reason for this effort. If somehow we are made to understand the great sacrifice of Christ a little better by studying this, which was given to Moses, to be sure, it will be well worth our time. There is nothing in history and nothing in the world that is more important than the sacrifice of Christ, and there will never be anything more important than that. That's why Paul referred to the New Covenant, which, in effect, is the Cross of Christ, as *"the everlasting covenant"* (Heb. 13:20). Unfortunately, the modern church little grasps the significance of the Cross, much less the totality of the great sacrifice of Christ; however, that in no way diminishes its significance. Every single thing we receive from God, and I mean everything, all and without exception was paid for at the Cross of Christ. Jesus Christ is the New Covenant, and the Cross is the meaning of that covenant, the meaning of which was given to the Apostle Paul. The Cross of Christ was the single greatest exhibition of the wisdom of God that is known to man, greater than the creation of the universe and greater than anything else that God has done. The truth is, no believer matures beyond his understanding of the Cross. That's quite a statement, but it is true. If, in fact, that is true, then we begin to realize why the modern church accepts so many things which are obviously unscriptural.

MATURITY

Let us say it again: It is impossible for any believer, irrespective as to whom that believer might be, to rise above his understanding of the Cross. The truth is, every Bible doctrine is built on the foundation of the Cross. In fact, the Cross of Christ was the first doctrine, one might say, developed by the Godhead, which was carried out from before the foundation of the world (I Pet. 1:18-20). This means, as well, that one's understanding of the Word of God, which is the single most important exercise in the world, can rise no higher than one's understanding of the Cross of Christ. If the preacher is preaching something other than the Cross, he might be preaching about the Gospel, but he's not really preaching the Gospel.

Paul said, *"Christ sent me not to baptize, but to preach the Gospel: not with wisdom of words, lest the Cross of Christ should be made of none effect"* (I Cor. 1:17).

This I promise: If anyone will take the time to study the sacrificial system under the Mosaic Law, one will most definitely come away with a greater grasp and a greater understanding of the sacrifice of Christ, I believe, than ever before. If, in fact, that is the case, then, to be sure, your time involved will be well spent.

> *"God moves in a mysterious way*
> *"His wonders to perform:*
> *"He plants His footsteps in the sea,*
> *"And rides upon the storm."*
>
> *"Deep in unfathomable mines*
> *"Of never-failing skill,*
> *"He treasures up His bright designs,*
> *"And works His sovereign will."*
>
> *"You fearful saints, fresh courage take;*
> *"The clouds you so much dread*
> *"Are big with mercy, and shall break*
> *"In blessings on your head."*

"Judge not the Lord by feeble sense,
"But trust Him for His grace:
"Behind a frowning providence
"He hides a smiling face."

"Blind unbelief is sure to err,
"And scan His work in vain;
"God is His own interpreter,
"And He will make it plain."

1

Whole Burnt Offering

CHAPTER ONE

Whole Burnt Offering

"AND THE LORD called unto Moses, and spoke unto him out of the tabernacle of the congregation, saying" (Lev. 1:1).

The sacrifice or offering that we will address first is the whole burnt offering. It signified that God would give His all, which He did in the person of His Son and our Saviour, the Lord Jesus Christ. This alone would satisfy the demands of a thrice-holy God. In fact, God only accepted such offerings as He Himself ordained. In other words, as it regarded these sacrifices, everything said and done directly came from God.

When the offering was tendered, the worshipper — imperfect and sinful in himself — was accepted in the perfection of the offering. That is extremely important, and it has not changed to this moment.

When the believing sinner places his or her faith exclusively in Christ and what Christ has done at the Cross, the Lord accepts that person on the basis of the perfect sacrifice of Christ and the person's faith in Christ. In other words, in the sacrifices under the Mosaic Law, the priest didn't even really look at the sinner; he looked at the sacrifice. If the sacrifice was acceptable, then the believing sinner was acceptable as well. It has not changed from then until now.

And yet, the sacrifices under the Levitical system were, of necessity, imperfect. Therefore, the conscience of the offerer, being a reflection of the sacrifice, remained imperfect as well. And yet, at the same time, the sacrifice of Christ being perfect gives a perfected conscience and, therefore, a peace that nothing can destroy. That's the difference in the Mosaic sacrificial system and the perfect system under Christ. All of the old Levitical system was meant only to serve as a stopgap measure until the reality could come. Thank God, we have a much better sacrifice in Christ today than all the millions of lambs that were offered up over the many centuries.

Paul said, and rightly so: **"But now** *(since the Cross)* **has He** *(the Lord Jesus)* **obtained a more excellent ministry** *(the New Covenant in Jesus' blood is superior, and takes the place of the Old Covenant in animal blood),* **but how much also He is the Mediator of a better covenant** *(proclaims the fact that Christ officiates between God and man according to the arrangements of the New Covenant),* **which was established upon better promises.** *(This presents the New Covenant explicitly based on the cleansing and forgiveness of all sin, which the Old Covenant could not do.)*

"For if that first covenant had been faultless *(proclaims the fact that the first covenant was definitely not faultless; as stated, it was based on animal blood, which was vastly inferior to the precious blood of Christ),* **then should no place have been sought for the second** *(proclaims the necessity of the New Covenant)"* **(Heb. 8:6-7).**

COMMUNICATION

We find from Verse 1 that the Lord has now taken up abode in the tabernacle, actually, in the Holy of Holies, where He dwelt between the mercy seat and the cherubim. I think one can say without fear of contradiction that of the God-head, it was the Holy Spirit who occupied this place and position. Concerning the New Covenant, Paul said, *"Do you not know that you are the temple of God, and that the Spirit of God dwells in you?"* (I Cor. 3:16).

The Lord had spoken to Moses in various different means and ways, the last being in the giving of the Law on Mount Sinai. The fact that He now spoke to Moses from the tabernacle, and more specifically, the Holy of Holies, proclaims something of extreme importance.

The great plan has been advanced forward to a great degree. While the Law definitely was not the answer for man's dilemma, it would serve as a substitute until the solution would come, namely the Lord Jesus Christ. Inasmuch as the Law contained the great sacrificial system, which was a type and shadow of what Christ would do, such made it possible for God to dwell much closer to His people. In fact, the Cross, which would fulfill all of these types, would place the Lord into the very hearts and lives of all believers, and do so on a permanent basis (Jn. 14:16-17).

THE CALL OF GOD

It should be noted that the very first action of the Lord, as it regarded His taking up abode in the Holy of Holies, was to explain the sacrificial system to Moses and, thereby, to Israel.

We see then that the Cross of Christ is given preeminence. That's why Paul said, as it regarded the church, *"For I determined not to know anything among you, save Jesus Christ, and Him crucified"* (I Cor. 2:2). The emphasis must always be on the Cross, i.e., that which Christ did in order to redeem fallen humanity.

We must not allow this lesson to be lost on us. As it regarded the tabernacle, there were many functions that must be explained and observed; however, it was the sacrificial system which God broached first. By doing this, He was telling us that the sacrifice of Christ must always be preeminent. In fact, the Cross of Christ is a doctrine, not a mere doctrine, but rather the foundation of all doctrine. In other words, if we hold to any doctrine that is based on something other than the Cross, to the degree that it is separated from the Cross, to that degree will error be the result. In fact, the following will be the conclusion of such an effort: **"Now the Spirit** (*Holy Spirit*) **speaks expressly** (*pointedly*)**, that in the latter times** (*the times in which we now live*) **some shall depart from the faith** (*Jesus Christ and Him crucified*)**, giving heed to seducing spirits, and doctrines of demons"** (I Tim. 4:1).

I am positive that Jesus considered that His death on the Cross, with all of its implications, must be looked at as far more than a mere doctrine. No, as stated, the Cross is and, in fact, must be the foundation of all doctrine. The entirety of the Word of God bears this out, even as we now open our study of the Mosaic sacrificial system.

WORSHIP

As we go along, we will see the entirety of the process of the tabernacle unfold before our eyes, with its central focus, as stated, being the sacrificial system. We will find that all of these instructions were given in order that God's people could worship Him, their Creator. So, we find that there can be no suitable worship without the proper sacrifice. To be sure, that proper sacrifice is the sacrifice of Christ.

Let us say it again because it is so very, very important: Any supposed worship of God that's carried on outside of the Cross of Christ is worship that God will not accept. He will only accept worship that originates at the Cross, meaning that the believer understands that every single thing we receive from God, and I mean everything, comes by the way of the Cross of Christ. In other words, the price was paid for everything at the Cross.

FORGIVENESS

Without proper sacrifice, and again we refer to Christ, there can be no forgiveness.

To my knowledge, in all the religions of the world, with Christianity excepted, there is no teaching on the subject of forgiveness, and that is because there is no atonement. There are, in fact, whole races of men in whose vocabulary there is no word for forgiveness. The spirit of retaliation seems to be still as potent as ever, apart from the spirit of Christianity. One billionaire stated that the spirit of revenge must characterize our dealings with our fellow man. His great motto is, *"Get even!"* But Jesus said, *"You have heard that it has been said, An eye for an eye, and a tooth for a tooth: but I say unto you, that you resist not evil"* (Mat. 5:38–39). He evidently meant that men should curb the impetuosity of personal vindictiveness and leave their case in the hands of a more perfect Justice, namely the Lord.

To cut straight through to the chase, the less the believer knows about the Cross, the less he knows about forgiveness. If he properly understands the Cross, He will properly understand forgiveness and function accordingly. Someone has well said, and rightly so, *"The world is very slow to forgive, and the church forgives not at all!"*

That is tragic but true! The church little forgives, if at all, simply because it doesn't understand the Cross, which means that its trust and faith are little in the Cross, but rather other things.

MOSES

As well, we find that the great plan of God was revealed here to a man — Moses. This is the way that it still is, and the way it has always been.

This means that God doesn't actually deal with committees, boards, or such like. He always selects a man or a woman!

As well, the way of the Lord is not anchored in the democratic process. In other words, it's not a democracy. It is rather a theocracy, which means that God rules all, and does so through His appointed representative. Such a person cannot be elected by popular ballot and, in fact, is not elected by popular ballot. He is called of God, even as was Moses!

All of this pertains to the government of God, which is not at all like the government of this world. Unfortunately, far too often, the church adopts the government of the world, which means that in doing so, the government of God is abandoned. In fact, this is what ultimately destroyed the early church, and it will destroy any church.

In Old Testament times, we find that God guided His work primarily through prophets. In New Testament times, which include the present, He uses apostles.

Paul said: *"Now therefore you are no more strangers and foreigners, but fellow citizens with the saints, and of the household of God;*

"And are built upon the foundation of the apostles and prophets, Jesus Christ Himself being the chief corner stone" (Eph. 2:19–20).

THE OFFERING

"Speak unto the children of Israel, and say unto them, If any man of you bring an offering unto the LORD, you shall bring your offering of the cattle, even of the herd, and of the flock" (Lev. 1:2).

The sacrifices or offerings that were instituted here were not the beginning of the system, just the beginning as it pertained to the tabernacle. There is every evidence that the Lord explained to the first family how forgiveness could be obtained and fellowship could be enjoined, and we speak of the relationship of fallen man with God. It could only be by sacrifice of an innocent victim, namely a lamb, which would be a type of Christ. We are given this example in Genesis, Chapter 4, as it regarded Cain and Abel. The practice of offering up sacrifices was continued with Noah (Gen. 8:20), and greatly so with Abraham (Gen. 12:7–8; 13:4, 18). Isaac offered up sacrifices and so did Jacob (Gen. 26:25; 35:1, 7). So, the sacrificial system wasn't new but would now, under the Law of God, be regulated, thereby, expressing Christ even to a greater degree.

ANY MAN

There is no mention of any woman bringing an offering to the Lord as it regarded the sacrifice of an animal. This was always done by a man.

Why?

Even though Eve sinned first, it was Adam who dragged down the human race. God had given the first pair the power of procreation, even as He has given such to all human beings. However, the seed of that procreation is found in man and not in woman. The only seed that a woman has had was the Lord Jesus Christ (Gen. 3:15).

Due to Adam being the fountainhead of the human race, whatever happened to him would pass on to the entirety of the human race, even forever. In other words, every baby that would be born would be born in original sin, which means that the child is born as a fallen creature.

This is the reason that Jesus had to come as the last Adam, even as the Holy Spirit through Paul labeled Him (I Cor. 15:45). In other words, Jesus as the last Adam had to undo what the first Adam did, which refers to the plunging of the human race into spiritual darkness. As well, He had to do what the first Adam did not do, which was to fully obey God. That Jesus did in every capacity.

Although it is a moot point, if Eve alone had sinned, due to the fact that the seed of procreation did not reside within her, she could have asked forgiveness without her failure passing on to the human race. So, the man would have to bring the offering inasmuch as he was the cause of all failure.

A CLEAN ANIMAL

Certain animals were labeled by God as clean, which included the bullock, the heifer, the lamb, the ram, the goat, the dove, and the pigeon. Of these animals or fowls, the lamb was by far most offered and most epitomized Christ, who was to come. In fact, Jesus was referred to as *"the Lamb of God, which taketh away the sin of the world"* (Jn. 1:29).

A WHOLE BURNT OFFERING

"If his offering be a burnt sacrifice of the herd, let him offer a male without blemish: he shall offer it of his own voluntary will at the door of the tabernacle of the congregation before the LORD" (Lev. 1:3).

There were five types of sacrifices listed in the Levitical Law. Christ fulfilled all of them with His one sacrifice of Himself. We will list them but will give only a small amount of commentary at this time, addressing them more fully at a later time.

WHOLE BURNT OFFERING

The entire animal was burned on the altar, with the exception of the skin, which was given to the priests. It signified that God was giving His all and, in turn, would satisfy the demands of God, who was greatly offended. This offering set the standard and suggested the themes which are manifested by all the other Levitical offerings. It is thus a biblical type in the fullest sense of the word.

THE MEAT OFFERING

This was an offering of thanksgiving and contained no flesh. It almost always accompanied the whole burnt offering. Some of this offering was burned on the altar, with another part given to the priests. As well, the word *meat*, as it was used in Bible times, referred to all types of food, but not flesh. At the present, it refers only to flesh.

THE SIN OFFERING

The sin offering is linked to the stages of our Christian growth. When we start out with the Lord, there are many things we still need to learn. In fact, we commit sins of ignorance, or, to say it in a better way, we sin at times simply because we do not know or understand God's prescribed order of victory.

THE TRESPASS OFFERING

As the sin offering pertains to our Christian growth, the trespass offering relates to our Christian walk. This offering pertains more so to our sinning against our brother or sister in the Lord than anything else.

THE PEACE OFFERING

In offering up the other sacrifices, with the exception of the meat offering, most of the time, a peace offering would follow, meaning that the problem had been addressed, and the peace of God was now resident within the believer's heart.

It was the only offering of which the sinner could participate. Part was burned on the altar, with part given to the priests, and part was to be eaten by the offerer, who could call in his friends, if he so desired, for a feast.

A MALE

These animals were to be of the male species because they were types of Christ. Although Christ was fully God, at the same time, He was fully man. In fact, He was referred to as, *"the man Christ Jesus"* (I Tim. 2:5). As well, it was a man, Adam, who dragged down the entire human race.

As we've already stated, Jesus came as the last Adam (I Cor. 15:45). As *"the man,"* He would redeem the lost sons of Adam's fallen race, and He would do so by the giving of Himself in sacrifice on the Cross, of which these token sacrifices of the Levitical Law were symbols or types.

WITHOUT BLEMISH

The animal to be sacrificed (a lamb, a goat, etc.) had to be without blemish because again, it represented and symbolized Christ and what He would do regarding the salvation of souls.

Regarding the lambs which were offered at 9 a.m. (the morning sacrifice) and 3 p.m. (the evening sacrifice), it is said that the priests would kill the animal, which would be done by the slitting of its throat, with the blood caught in a basin, and then the skin would be stripped from the carcass. At that point, they would take a razor-sharp knife and cut the carcass down the backbone, in effect, laying it open. They would minutely inspect the flesh, and if there was a blemish of any kind, even a discoloration, that animal would be discarded and another chosen. It represented the One who was to come; therefore, the representation had to be correct.

These animals without blemish were but a type of the perfection of Christ, and a poor type at that, for what could adequately portray the Son of God? His perfection was total and complete in every respect. That's the reason He had to be born of the Virgin Mary. Had He been born as all other babies, of necessity, due to Adam's fall, He would have been born in original sin. Had that been the case, He would not have qualified to be a sacrifice that God would accept.

THE BIRTH OF CHRIST

Ironically, many of the Jews of His day, which even continues unto this hour, claimed that He was born illegitimately when, in fact, His birth was the only totally legitimate birth that there ever was. Joseph was not His father; God was His Father. In fact, He was not the product of Joseph's seed or Mary's egg, but rather of the Holy Spirit (Mat. 1:18; Lk. 1:35). This means that Jesus did not carry the traits of Joseph or Mary. What His appearance was, we aren't told; however, I think it is safe to say that He didn't look like His brothers or sisters but was totally different in every respect.

Being born without original sin, He also lived without sin of any nature (Heb. 7:26). This means that He never sinned in word, thought, or deed! He was perfect in every respect.

Actually, Jesus was a peasant. During His time, there was no such thing as a middle class. There were only peasants who were abysmally poor or those who were obscenely rich. So, this means that Jesus was not a part, not at all, of the aristocracy of Israel. He did not attend their schools, sit under their theologians, etc. As stated, He was a peasant.

This is what the great Prophet Isaiah was talking about when he said: *"Who has believed our report? and to whom is the arm of the LORD revealed?*

"For He shall grow up before Him as a tender plant, and as a root out of a dry ground: He has no form nor comeliness; and when we shall see Him, there is no beauty that we should desire Him.

"He is despised and rejected of men; a man of sorrows, and acquainted with grief: and we hid as it were our faces from Him; He was despised, and we esteemed Him not" (Isa. 53:1-3).

He was a carpenter by trade as was His foster father, which means that He worked with His hands and by the sweat of His brow. Josephus, the great Jewish historian, stated that He made plow yokes, which were done out of wood.

And yet, if the aristocracy of Israel had looked at the archives in the temple, they would have found that the foster father of Jesus, who was Joseph, went back to David through Solomon. They would have found that Mary, His mother, went back to David through another son of David, who was Nathan. In other words, His lineage or pedigree was perfect. However, the aristocracy of Israel had no regard for that. They wanted a messiah, but they wanted one of their own description, who would overthrow Rome and once again make Israel the leading nation in the world. In other words, they wanted deliverance, but not from their sins, which is what they desperately needed.

THE CROSS

Everything about Jesus was designed by the Holy Spirit. While there were many reasons, the main purpose of His coming to this earth was to go to the Cross. In fact, Peter said that His death on the Cross was *"foreordained before the foundation of the world"* (I Pet. 1:18–20).

Even before the world was brought back to a habitable state, and man was created, through foreknowledge, God knew that man would fall. To salvage His most noble creation, God would have to become man and would do so in order to redeem man, which was done at the Cross. God, being Spirit, cannot die, so in order to die, God would have to become man, as was prophesied also by Isaiah. He said, *"Therefore the Lord Himself shall give you a sign; behold, a virgin shall conceive, and bear a Son, and shall call His name Immanuel"* (Isa. 7:14).

Can you imagine what the scoffers thought whenever Isaiah gave forth this prophecy about a virgin conceiving? But yet, that's exactly what happened. In fact, His birth had to be of a virgin, otherwise, He would have been born in original sin like all other babies.

Of all the things that Jesus did in His Incarnation, the real purpose for His becoming man was to go to the Cross. The Cross was ever His destination. This means that it was not an accident, an incident, an assassination, or execution. His death on the Cross of Calvary was a sacrifice!

When He was placed on the Cross, He was perfect in every respect; therefore, God accepted His poured out life in the shedding of His precious blood as payment for all the sin of mankind—past, present, and future—at least for all who will believe (Jn. 3:16; Eph. 2:13–18). He was truly *"without blemish."*

WHOSOEVER WILL

The phrase, *"he shall offer it of his own voluntary will,"* would probably be better translated, *"he shall offer it for His acceptance."* According to the Pulpit Commentary, *"The animal, representing the offerer, was presented by the latter in order that he might be himself accepted by the Lord."* In other words, if the offering was accepted, then the one that was offering the sacrifice would likewise be accepted; however, if the offering or sacrifice was rejected, this meant that the one offering the sacrifice would be rejected also.

The animal was a substitute in the place of the offerer, symbolizing Christ, who was our substitute as well. In other words, God doesn't look so much at us as He does the object of our faith. If the object of our faith is anything other than Christ and the Cross, then it is rejected. Considering that there has been so little preaching and teaching on the Cross in the last several decades, this means that most of the efforts of Christian mankind are rejected by the Lord. The only thing that God will accept is the crucified Christ. So, if we are to be accepted, our faith, without fail, must be in Christ and Him crucified. That's why Paul said, *"But God forbid that I should glory (boast) save in the Cross of our Lord Jesus Christ, by whom the world is crucified unto me, and I unto the world"* (Gal. 6:14).

As one advances in the divine life, he becomes conscious that those sins that he has committed are but branches from a root, streams from a fountain; and moreover, sin in his nature is that fountain — that root. This leads to a far deeper exercise, which can only be met by a deeper insight into the work of the Cross. In a word, the Cross will need to be apprehended as that in which God Himself has *"condemned sin in the flesh"* (Rom. 8:3).

THE ROOT

In reading that passage in Romans, the reader should observe that it does not say, *"sins in the life,"* but the root from where these have sprung, namely, *"sin in the flesh."* This is a truth of immense importance. Christ did not merely die for our sins, according to the Scriptures, but He was made *"to be sin for us"* (II Cor. 5:21). This is the doctrine of the sin offering.

His being made *"to be sin for us"* refers to the fact that He, by His death, addressed the root cause of sin, which means that He became the sin offering. How did He do that?

NAILING IT TO HIS CROSS

Paul gave us the answer to the above question when he said: *"Blotting out the handwriting of ordinances that was against us, which was contrary to us, and took it out of the way, nailing it to His Cross;*

"And having spoiled principalities and powers, He made a show of them openly, triumphing over them in it" (Col. 2:14–15).

Breaking the Law of God, which refers to the Ten Commandments, is sin. The wages of that sin is death (Rom. 6:23).

In the burnt offering, with which the book of Leviticus opens, we have a type of Christ *"offering Himself without spot to God,"* hence, the position that the Holy Spirit assigns to it. Concerning this, C.H. Mackintosh said: *"If the Lord Jesus Christ came forth to accomplish the glorious work of atonement, His highest and most fondly cherished object in so doing was the glory of God. 'Lo, I come to do Your will, O God,' was the grand motto in every scene and circumstance of His life, and in none more markedly than in the work of the Cross. Let the will of God be what it might, He came to do it."* What was that will?

THE WILL OF GOD

Unequivocally, it was the offering up of Himself on the Cross, which paid the debt that man owed, which, incidentally, man could not pay. Man had forfeited life by his failure in the Garden of Eden, and we speak of the life of God. This, of course, brought death, which is separation from God, but which Jesus purchased back by the giving of His perfect life on the Cross. When He did this, He atoned for all sin, and that refers to past, present, and future (Jn. 3:16).

With this done, Satan and all of his cohorts of darkness were totally and completely defeated. Sin is the means by which Satan holds man in bondage. He has a legal right to hold sinful man accordingly. However, with all sin atoned, Satan's legal right is ended, at least if man will believe the Lord, thereby, trusting Christ.

In this manner, Satan and all demon spirits and fallen angels were totally defeated, which was done at the Cross.

HOW WAS CHRIST MADE SIN FOR US?

Paul said, **"For He** (*God the Father*) **has made Him** (*the Lord Jesus Christ*) **to be sin for us** (*a sin offering*)**, who**

knew no sin; that we might be made the righteousness of God in Him" (II Cor. 5:21).

God made Him to be sin for us in that He made Him a sin offering. The Prophet Isaiah said, *"Yet it pleased the Lord to bruise Him; He has put Him to grief: when You shall make His soul an offering for sin, He shall see His seed, He shall prolong His days, and the pleasure of the Lord shall prosper in His hand"* (Isa. 53:10).

Jesus became sin only in the sense of becoming the sin offering. If it is to be noticed, Paul didn't say, *"for He has made Him to be a sinner for us,"* but rather, *"to be sin for us."* To be a sinner, one has to sin, and Jesus did not sin in any capacity, but He did become a sin offering.

As we look at all the millions of lambs which were offered up under the Mosaic economy, those animals didn't sin, but they did bear the penalty of sin, which was death, and so did Christ, of whom they were a type.

JESUS DIED SPIRITUALLY IS NOT IN THE BIBLE

Our Word of Faith friends claim that Jesus became a sinner on the Cross, took upon Himself the nature of Satan, and died and went to Hell, and we speak of the burning side of Hell. They also state that He was tormented there for some three days and nights, with Satan thinking that He was defeated, whenever God finally said, *"It is enough,"* implying that it was His suffering in Hell that redeemed mankind. Jesus, they say, was then "born again," just like any sinner is born again, and then raised from the dead.

None of that is in the Bible because none of that happened. In fact, that entire scheme is an aberration of the Atonement, which means that if a person believes that, thereby, placing his faith in that, he is, in effect, trusting *"another Jesus,"* which means he forfeits his salvation.

Our salvation is 100 percent in Christ and what He did for us at the Cross. He paid the price by shedding His life's blood, which paid the debt we could not pay (Eph. 2:13–18).

While Jesus did go to the Paradise part of Hell, and while He even made an announcement to fallen angels who were locked up in the heart of the earth (I Pet. 3:19–20), there is no record whatsoever in the Bible that Jesus ever went to the burning side of Hell. The suffering of Christ was on the Cross and not in Hell (I Pet. 3:18).

Many of these Word of Faith preachers are prone to say, as they put Jesus in the burning side of Hell, *"it's not in the Bible, but that's what happened!"*

Now, stop and think about that for a moment. The greatest thing on the face of planet Earth—the redemption of man—and not a word of it is in the Bible! They are right about one thing: it is not in the Bible because it never happened. When Jesus went to the Cross, He served as a sin offering. While it is true that He went down into the heart of the earth, even Paradise, which is a part of Hell, there is no record in the Word of God that Jesus went into the burning side of Hell in any capacity. The work was completed on the Cross. He went down there for two reasons. First of all, He made an announcement to these fallen angels that had sinned terribly in the past and were now locked up, and yet, what He said to them, we aren't told.

He then went into Paradise, which was His chief reason for going there, and *"led captivity captive."* This means that all of those souls in Paradise, which included everyone who believed in the Lord before the Cross, was taken out of that place, where they would then transfer to Heaven. Since the Cross, when a believer dies, his soul and his spirit go to be with the Lord Jesus Christ in Heaven. The reason this could not be done before the Cross was because animal blood was insufficient to take away the sin debt (Heb. 10:4), but thank God, the Cross took all sin away.

AT THE DOOR OF THE TABERNACLE

The offerer of the animal sacrifice had to go to a designated place. When the Israelites were traveling through the wilderness, this place was wherever the tabernacle was. After the nation of Israel had been established, the offering place was in Jerusalem because that was where God had chosen to place His name.

Today, however, man does not have to go to a designated place to find God. He can find Him anywhere as he reaches out with his heart. However, let us see how this happy development came about, for it was no mere accident.

God once dwelt between the cherubim and the mercy seat, and He was to be found only where the tabernacle or the temple was. However, since Jesus Christ died on Calvary and broke down *the middle wall of partition*, it has become possible for man to approach God directly. The middle wall of partition, in a sense, spoke of both the wall that separated the Gentiles from the Jews, as it regarded the temple courts, and, as well, the partition that divided the Holy Place from the Holy of Holies, for the temple veil has been rent asunder. Now the approach can be made anywhere, anyplace.

However, we don't want to get ahead of ourselves. We need to think it through step-by-step. So, let us now go back several thousand years to where we will be in a position to see (thanks to the different perspective) how the present contract between God and man — the New Covenant — is based on much better promises.

When the Bible says, *"at the door of the tabernacle of the congregation before the LORD,"* it is pointing to a place where the Ark of the Covenant reposed. Let's look at this circumstance a bit more closely.

THE SACRIFICE

The offerer would come to the *"tent of meeting,"* or tabernacle, leading his sacrifice. If it was a bullock, a ram, a lamb, or a goat, he would, no doubt, be leading it by the neck or head. If he was a very poor individual and could only afford a turtledove or a pigeon, he would probably have it cradled within his hands.

The approach to the place of meeting with God would have been awesome to him, and it would have been to you and me as well. If he advanced toward the tabernacle in the daytime, then the offerer would have seen the cloud hovering over the place as it always did. If, however, he were approaching the tabernacle at night, then he would see the jagged forks of flames as they constantly played in the night air above the Holy of Holies, the tabernacle of the Lord.

THE DOOR

It would have been a fantastic, nearly stupefying sight. It would have struck terror in his heart. The sinner, the offerer of the sacrifice, would have known that right there was the living power of almighty God. So, if he did something wrong—once again, did something wrong—the consequences could be disastrous. So, he must follow to the letter Moses' instructions for all Israel. The sinner first had to come up to the fence that surrounded the tabernacle. There would be a door, like a gate, which led through the fence at the front of the tabernacle. Nearly 1,600 years later, Jesus would say, *"I am the door: by Me if any man enter in, he shall be saved, and shall go in and out, and find pasture"* (Jn. 10:9).

When Jesus uttered those words, every Jew there knew exactly what He was talking about. They knew that He was referring to the tabernacle gate of old. They knew He was referring to the fence that guarded the tabernacle from intruders. They knew that He was referring to the door that led the way to the brazen altar and the sacrifices, and that He was saying, *"I am the way, the truth, and the life: no man comes unto the Father, but by Me"* (Jn. 14:6).

THE BLOOD

Continuing our examination of the way in which the offerer experienced his personal sacrifice, the sinner would lead the animal through the gate with understandable fear and trembling. However, then the scene that would meet his eyes would be totally unlike anything our minds could ever imagine.

It was ghastly. Other contrite and ashamed sinners would, no doubt, be lined up with their animals. Our sinner would look around and see these other people, and he would also see the sharp knives of the Levitical priests flashing and the hot blood of the doomed animals flowing into the basins.

He would also see the priests as they were taking blood to the brazen altar. His eyes would witness other priests washing the blood off their hands and feet at the brazen laver. He would hear the bellowing of the animals as their throats were slit, and he would suddenly be half-sickened by the mingled scents of blood and entrails, and oily black smoke and burning animal flesh.

As I think would be obvious, this was no church picnic. This terrible place, however, was the very heart and center — the seat of true holiness.

CALVARY

Later, Calvary would afford no pleasant scene either. That hill would offer the most hideous, horrible spectacle that Heaven and earth would ever see.

"Now from the sixth hour there was darkness over all the land unto the ninth hour" (Mat. 27:45).

In fact, the scene of Calvary would be so horrible that even God would not look upon it. God literally pulled the blinds, as it were, on the most appalling bloody sacrifice that would ever be offered in all of human history; for of all the millions of animal sacrifices that had been offered through the centuries, the sacrifice on Calvary was to be the special one: *"the Lamb,"* Jesus Christ.

His beard would be pulled from His face. The soldiers would beat His face and head with their bare fists and with reeds until He would cease to look human. He would appear *"as an animal,"* as Isaiah had prophesied. Jesus' back would be cut to pieces by the lictor's lash. There is simply no way to describe the acute, awful suffering that He endured for you and me. The distance He dragged the Cross, He dragged it over a trail of bloody footprints.

Calvary, in short, would be a scene so hideous, so horrible, and so ghastly that God would attempt to hide it even from Himself with a curtain of nature's darkness.

Similarly, what the Hebrew offerer of the ordinary animal sacrifice would see would be a dreadful scene, too, because the scene would itself typify—actually predict, signal, and virtually announce—the terrible and shocking price that the coming Redeemer would have to pay in order to bring about the redemption, through grace, of sinful mankind.

As our sinner came, bringing the animal with him, with fear and trembling, he now approached the priest.

BEFORE THE LORD

All sin is against God. It is an insult to God, a willful, flagrant, disavowal of His Word, which is the highest insult to the Creator. So, inasmuch as all sin is committed against Him, it is before Him that we must come in order to have sin forgiven and cleansed.

This is at least one of the reasons that the Catholic way is so very wrong! It claims that man can forgive or make atonement for one's sins. Such does not lie within the domain of sinful, fallen man. Only the Lord can cleanse from sin (I Jn. 1:9).

Other than blaspheming the Holy Spirit, the greatest sin of all is rebelling against God's prescribed order of salvation and His prescribed order of victory. That prescribed order is the Cross, which should be overly obvious in these passages. So, what do I mean by one rebelling against the Cross?

If the unredeemed man and woman think they can be saved by any other method than trusting Christ and what He has done for us at the Cross, they are rebelling against God's prescribed order of salvation (Jn. 3:16). Of all the sins the unredeemed commit, and their lives are nothing but constant sin, this is the worst of all.

TRUSTING OTHER THAN THE CROSS

Jesus said: **"And when He is come** (*the Holy Spirit*)**, He will reprove** (*convict*) **the world of sin, and of righteousness, and of judgment:**
"Of sin, because they believe not on Me" (Jn. 16:8-9).

As it regards the Christians, of necessity, they have trusted Christ as it regards their salvation, but as it regards their sanctification, most are trusting other things. The Christians who are doing this are living in a state of *spiritual adultery* (Rom. 7:1-4), which means they are rebelling against God's prescribed order of sanctification.

Exactly as the believing sinner has to trust Christ and the Cross for salvation, the believing Christian has to trust Him in the same manner as it regards sanctification. The Cross plays just as much a part in our sanctification as it did our salvation (Rom. 6:3-14; 8:1-2, 11).

When Moses used the term, *"before the LORD,"* he was, in effect, saying that all sin is committed against the Lord, and all sin must be atoned by the Lord. It cannot be removed any other way.

ATONEMENT

"And he shall put his hand upon the head of the burnt offering; and it shall be accepted for him to make atonement for him" (Lev. 1:4).

As the man would lead the animal to the priest, he would then be told by the priest to put his hand upon the head of the animal which would shortly be a burnt offering.

Notice that Moses said, *"he shall put his hand upon the head of the burnt offering,"* which, in effect, treated the animal as if it was already dead. It was referred to as a burnt offering while still alive.

When Jesus came to this world, He came for but one purpose, and that was to go to the Cross. Listen to what John said, *"In the beginning was the Word, and the Word was with God, and the Word was God"* (Jn. 1:1).

This plainly tells us that Jesus Christ was the living Word and, as well, that He was and is God.

John then said, *"and the Word was made flesh, and dwelt among us"* (Jn. 1:14).

He was made flesh for one purpose and one reason only. Listen again to John — John the Beloved, quoting John the Baptist, said, *"Behold the Lamb of God, which takes away the sin of the world"* (Jn. 1:29).

So, in these three verses, we see the purpose and reason for which Jesus came. He came as the *"Lamb of God,"* and as the Lamb of God, He would *"take away the sin of the world."* If it is to be noticed, it used the word *"sin"* in the singular, meaning that he addressed the root cause of sin at the Cross.

THE BELIEVER'S IDENTIFICATION WITH CHRIST

The priest would have told the offerer to lay his hand on the head of the animal, which was expressive of full identification. By that significant act, the offerer and the offering became one. This oneness, in the case of the burnt offering, secured for the offerer all the acceptableness of his offering.

The application of this to Christ and the believer sets forth a truth of the most precious nature, and one largely developed in the New Testament, namely, the believer's everlasting identification with, and acceptance in, Christ.

"As He is, so are we in this world" (I Jn. 4:17).

"We are in Him who is true, even in His Son Jesus Christ" (I Jn. 5:20).

Nothing in any measure short of this could avail. The man who is not in Christ is still in his sins. There is no middle ground; you must be either in Christ or out of Him. There is no such thing as being partly in Christ.

Mackintosh said: *"If there is a single hair's breadth between you and Christ, you are in an actual state of wrath and condemnation; but, on the other hand, if you are in Him, then are you 'as He is' before God, and so accounted in the presence of infinite holiness. Such is the plain teaching of the Word of God."*

NO DEGREES IN JUSTIFICATION

All of this means that all stand in one acceptance, in one salvation, in one life, and in one righteousness. There are no degrees in justification. In other words, there is no such thing as one being partially justified, 50 percent justified, etc. One is totally justified, or one is not justified at all.

The person who has just come to Christ, in other words, a babe in Christ, stands in the same justification as the saint of 50 years' experience.

While there may be various degrees in the knowledge of the fullness and extent of justification, and even various degrees in the ability to exhibit its power upon the heart and life, as it definitely is, we must never confuse that knowledge with the degree of justification. Let us say it again: There are no degrees in justification. Everyone truly justified is 100 percent truly justified or not justified at all.

WORKS

This is what makes the Gospel of *"works"* so deadly. One's justification is judged by the amount of works or the validity of works, which is ludicrous. While good works will always follow proper justification, good works will never cause justification.

The church, at times, seems to believe in two justifications—one for the sinner and another for the saint. In other words, they understand and accept the sinner coming to Christ, being saved, and, thereby, instantly justified. However, when it comes to the saint, far too often the church attempts to mix works with faith.

Once justified, which takes place at the born-again experience, one is never unjustified, at least as long as one continues to believe in Christ. This means that the Christian who sins does not lose his justification, as awful as sin is. Were that the case, every single Christian on the face of the earth would lose their justification simply because there is no such thing as sinless perfection.

Because of this, upon hearing the great apostle speak of the grace of God, some of the Christians during Paul's time had come to believe that sin was not a big factor after all. In other words, if grace abounds more than sin, which it definitely does (Rom. 5:20), then sin is no big deal, so to speak.

THE ANSWER OF THE APOSTLE PAUL

Paul's answer to that was short and cryptic: *"Shall we continue in sin, that grace may abound?*
"God forbid. How shall we, who are dead to sin, live any longer therein?" (Rom. 6:1–2).

If sin is committed, the believer is to confess it before the Lord, who has promised *"to forgive us our sins, and to cleanse us from all unrighteousness"* (I Jn. 1:9). However, as bad as sin is, the Christian doesn't lose his justification at this time. But we must never forget, it is the business of the Holy Spirit to bring us to the place that the sin nature no longer dominates us (Rom. 6:14).

Let the Christian ever understand, and the entirety of the church for that matter, that if sin is committed, there is only one way that it can be forgiven, washed, and cleansed. That way is by continued faith in Christ and what He has done for us at the Cross. Works must never enter into this picture. For us to present any type of works before God as an atonement for sin insults Christ to the highest degree. In effect, we are saying, whether we realize it or not, that what He did at the Cross was not enough, and we need to add our two cents' worth. I think once we see this in the cold light of what it really is, we can thereby see how blasphemous that such action actually is. It is always by faith and never by works (Gal. 5:6).

ANOTHER WORD ON JUSTIFICATION

We should, as well, understand that there is no such thing as progress in justification. There certainly may be progress, and should be progress, in our understanding of justification, but the position itself doesn't change. The believer is no more justified today than he was yesterday, nor will he be more justified tomorrow than he is today. Any soul who is in Christ Jesus is as completely justified as if he were before the throne. He is complete in Christ. In fact, he is *"as Christ."*

Let us say it again: While there may be and certainly should be progress in the knowledge of justification, there can be no progress in justification itself.

We should understand that the manner in which we look at justification is the manner in which we look at Christ. He either paid it all, or He didn't! Either the Cross was enough, or it wasn't! In fact, as one views the Cross, one will view justification. This means that if we have a false understanding of the Cross, we will have a false understanding of justification, which can cause the believer untold problems.

Everything is based upon the divine protection of the work of Christ on the Cross.

IT IS ALWAYS THE SACRIFICE

Let the reader understand this: It was never a question of what the worshipper was; that was understood. It was always what the sacrifice was. That's what makes faith so important. Christ has done it, and we cannot do it, but our faith in Him grants us all that He has done. In other words, when we claim Christ, and do so by faith, God no longer looks at us but looks at Him.

If He looks at us at all, it is at our faith. That's why Paul said, *"Examine yourselves, whether you be in the faith; prove your own selves, know you not your own selves, how that Jesus Christ is in you, except you be reprobates?"* (II Cor. 13:5).

Sometime back, I was speaking with a preacher, and he mentioned to me how that a particular Pentecostal denomination functioned in the matter of discipline by punishing preachers who had done something wrong.

When he finished his statement, I said to him, *"Are they saying that what Jesus did at the Cross is not enough and that we have to add something to it?"*

He wheeled around and looked at me and never said anything for a few moments. Then he said, *"I've never thought of that."*

No, and I suspect the entirety of his denomination had not thought of it either. When we do anything that takes away from the Cross of Calvary, we sin greatly, and whatever it is that we have done, God cannot accept it.

THE HEAD

If it is to be noticed, the sinner was to put his hand on the head of the animal. This tells us several things.

It tells us that sin so warps the individual, so twists the individual, and so perverts the individual that the person doesn't think right, doesn't walk right, doesn't act right, and, in fact, is somewhat insane. There is an insanity to sin, typified by the head, which plays out to perverted actions on the part of the individual.

That's the reason for all the wars, man's inhumanity to man, criminal activity, crime, torture, and hurt in the world. Sin is the cause, and sin is a form of insanity! (Rom., Chpt. 3).

Of course, there are degrees of sinful insanity. For instance, some sins are worse than others. The entire world has looked on in astonishment at the followers of Islam, who commit suicide in order to kill those whom they consider to be their enemies. The truth is, the people they are trying to kill aren't their enemies, but, in reality, the Muslim religion itself is their enemy. However, they can't see that because they are blinded by spiritual insanity and conduct themselves accordingly.

Anyone who doesn't know the Lord lives in spiritual darkness, hence, the laying of hands on the head. That can be changed only in one way: Jesus Christ who is the Light of the World must be accepted, but He must be accepted as one's Saviour, which can only be brought about by what He did at the Cross. So, it's faith in Him and what He did at the Cross that saves the sinner, whether they understand such or not at the beginning!

MORE ABOUT ATONEMENT

The phrase, *"and it shall be accepted for him to make atonement for him,"* refers to the animal being accepted as a substitute on behalf of the sinner, which will make atonement for him.

The Jew was not taught that the death of the animal was accepted instead of his punishment, but he was instructed to look upon it as a foreshadowing of a perfect offering to come. This may not be apparent on a cursory glance in the writings of Moses (the Pentateuch), but the New Testament leaves no doubt on the question. *"It is not possible that the blood of bulls and of goats should take away sins"* (Heb. 10:4).

The first tabernacle was *"a figure for the time then present"*; *"the Law having a shadow of good things to come, and not the very image [or full revelation] of the things, can never with those sacrifices which they offered year by year continually make the comers thereunto perfect"* (Heb. 9:9; 10:1). This is not a contradiction of the Old Testament but an explanation of the Mosaic dispensation.

THAT WHICH WAS TO COME

All of this means that the Jews were never taught that the slaying or offering of the animal was an atonement in itself. They knew that it was a foreshadowing, an educating of the world for the appreciation of the one atonement which was to come in Christ.

In trying to explain the Atonement under the Old Testament economy, we cannot shut up the doctrine of the Atonement under the naked formula that man must be punished on account of his sins unless someone else can be found to be punished for him (that the justice of God must have suffering somewhere if man is not to suffer).

However, to provide suffering was not the one and only object of the Atonement; it was not merely to balance suffering against suffering that the one great sacrifice was offered.

To what then was satisfaction made? It was made on the basis of absolute justice, and we speak of the truth of God. It was made not only by the sufferings, but by the perfect life of Jesus as the perfect man in obedience to the Law. Justice — not retaliation — demands that what a man sows, that shall he reap. Man sows sin and reaps the necessary results: death, the forfeiture of God's presence. Man cannot be pardoned and restored on his own merits. The merits of another, consequently, are offered to him. The picture of atonement in the Old Testament is that of a covering of sins, and in the New Testament, is reconciliation of man to God.

THE BLOOD

"And he shall kill the bullock before the Lord: *and the priests, Aaron's sons, shall bring the blood, and sprinkle the blood round about upon the altar that is by the door of the tabernacle of the congregation"* (Lev. 1:5).

The man who offered up the sacrifice may not have understood all that took place. Likewise, we today do not really understand all that takes place when we come to the Lord Jesus Christ; but what we are actually doing, at that moment when we accept Jesus personally, is entering into a whole different order of life and being. It is the divine order — the order which operates in the spiritual life and, for that matter, in Heaven itself. We might think of this heavenly system of governance as the economy of grace.

Because of our fallen nature, it is necessary that we choose to live in this divine order. Sin, sad to say, is in all of us, and sin separates us from God, that is, unless proper steps are taken. On our own, we poor sinners cannot possibly be at one with God. So, atonement (the word means *"at-one-ment"*) positively must occur if our souls are to be made right with God during our earthly strivings, and if we are to be one with Him someday in Heaven.

Now, in the mind of God Himself, His fellowship with wrongdoers is restored by the shedding of innocent blood. Innocent blood cures the estrangement. It makes God and the sinner *"at one"* again.

Concerning the Old Testament sacrifices, we have often heard it said that the sins of the individual were covered by the atonement. That, in effect, is right; but it actually went further than that. Not only were the sins covered, but the sinner was covered as well, because, in reality, one cannot separate the sinner from the sin, or the sin from the sinner.

Now, in God's arrangement, not only is the sin treated, but the sinner is treated as well. This next area is subtle, however, and must be very carefully understood.

THE SHEDDING OF INNOCENT BLOOD

The only thing that stopped the wrath of God from being poured out on the sinner, as we have said, was the shedding of innocent blood. It was this sacrifice of blood that provided a facing, a covering, or a shield between the wrath of God and the sinner. In effect, the sin was still there. It was not taken away, and we continue to speak of Old Testament times; in other words, before the Cross, it was just covered over.

However, many centuries in the future, the Son of God would stand close to the River Jordan and John the Baptist would see Him coming and would say, *"Behold the Lamb of God, which takes away the sin of the world"* (Jn. 1:29).

When John uttered the words, *"Lamb of God,"* every Jew standing nearby understood exactly what he was talking about. They knew that millions of little sacrificial lambs had been offered up through the centuries—lambs that were types or symbolic predictions of the great Antitype, or unique One, who was to come and be the Messiah, the Saviour of Israel, and, as well, of the world. There by the Jordan, John was himself recognizing the Lamb of God, who would be the perfect sacrifice. However, it is the last part of John's statement that holds such a wealth of meaning for us.

SIN IS TAKEN AWAY

John said, *"which takes away the sin of the world."*

This was a startling revelation by the Baptist to all nearby, and it is to us today also. Whereas the offering of the sacrifices of old only covered the sin and the sinner, now the Lamb of God would not just cover the sin, He would actually *take it away!*

This Lamb, God's Lamb, would actually separate the sin from the sinner. Jesus would not only atone — in other words, satisfy the wrath of God — but He would make the person a brand-new creation (II Cor. 5:17). He would refer to the person as born again (Jn. 3:3).

John the Baptist, the prophet of the Highest, did not just say that the Lamb of God was going to take away sins. John didn't say *"sins"* in the plural form; he said *"sin"* in the singular, meaning generic sin — all sin. In other words, Jesus, at the Cross, dealt with the very cause of sin, even as we've already explained.

KILL THE ANIMAL

The sinner himself had to personally kill the animal. He would, no doubt, be supplied a knife by the priest, but due to the fact that he was the one who had sinned, he had to do the actual killing himself.

He would have to lay his hands on the head of the animal, thereby, transferring his guilt and his sin to this innocent victim — just as his guilt and sin would, later on, be transferred in turn to the Lord Jesus Christ.

That's what the great Prophet Isaiah meant when he said: *"Surely He has borne our griefs, and carried our sorrows: yet we did esteem Him stricken, smitten of God, and afflicted.*

"But He was wounded for our transgressions, He was bruised for our iniquities: the chastisement of our peace was upon Him; and with His stripes we are healed" (Isa. 53:4-5).

More than likely, the priest would hold back the head of the victim while the sinner slit the throat of the animal.

So, to make the application, here is what we too must understand: It was our sins that nailed Jesus Christ to the tree. Each and every one of us had our share in that horrible, bloody death that He had to suffer. The Lord Jesus did not die for His sins; He died for our sins.

Now when the offerer at the tabernacle would take the knife in his hand and put it to the throat of the animal, the thoughts that went through his mind must have been many. He knew this animal had done nothing amiss. He also realized that the animal was being made to pay the price that he should have paid himself.

He thus had to have a very sharp realization that his own sin was killing this little creature. In a sense, we did the same with the Lord Jesus Christ.

It is true, of course, that Christ the Lamb laid down His life willingly and that no man took His life from Him. However — each one of us, every human being who has ever lived — had a part in it: in the thorns upon His brow, in the beard plucked from His face, in the whip laid across His back, in the nails piercing His hands, and in the spear that entered His side.

One might say that we all had a hand in it. The crucifixion and death of the Lord Jesus was a horrible, bloody, gang killing. We all did it!

THE SPRINKLING OF THE BLOOD
ROUND ABOUT THE ALTAR

The assisting priest would catch in a basin the blood that poured from the slain animal's throat. He would then take the blood to the brazen altar and throw it around the bottom of the altar. In some respects, this was the most essential part of the ceremony, with the blood representing the life (Lev. 17:11), which was symbolically received at the hands of the offerer and presented by the priests to God. In the antitype, our Lord exercised the function of the sacrificing priest when He presented His own life to the Father as He hung upon the altar of the Cross.

As it regards this particular sacrifice — the whole burnt offering — we must bear in mind that the grand point set forth therein is not the meeting of the sinner's need, but the presentation to God of that which was infinitely acceptable to Him in order that the price be paid. This means that Christ, as foreshadowed by the burnt offering, is not for the sinner's conscience but for the heart of God. This is why, of all the sacrifices, the whole burnt offering was the foundation offering, so to speak, of the five presentation offerings. While each sacrifice played its part and served its purpose, even as

we shall see, it was the whole burnt offering that made everything possible simply because it satisfied the wrath of God.

Finally, atonement, as seen in the burnt offering, is not
merely commensurate with the claims of man's conscience,
but with the intense desire of the heart of Christ to carry out
the will and establish the counsels of God — a desire which
stopped not short of surrendering up His spotless, precious
life as a voluntary offering of sweet savour to God.

THE MEANING OF THE SACRIFICE OF CHRIST

In the entire debacle of sin that originated with the fall of
Lucifer, God's honor — the very fiber of His being, so to speak,
if we can refer to God accordingly — has been trampled in
the dirt. Lucifer dragged down one-third of the angelic host
with him and then onto man, God's most prized creation.
The latter has soaked this earth with blood and has brought
unmitigated sorrow. God's honor of goodness, grace, mercy,
compassion, longsuffering, and all of this in every capacity
had to be satisfied, and there was no one or nothing that
could fill this bill except that God would pay the price Himself. This is at least one of the reasons, actually, the primary
reason, that the Atonement is of such significance. While it
definitely met the need of sinful, fallen, depraved man — in
fact, the entire spectacle of Adam's fallen race — above all, it
satisfied the honour, justice, and character of God. We can
judge the worth of this sacrifice by the magnitude of God,
which, of course, is impossible for man to do!

That's the reason this great book of Leviticus is at least
one of the most important works in the entirety of the Word
of God. It goes into detail in explaining what Christ has done

for us as it regards the sacrifice of Himself on the Cross of Calvary, and does so by portraying and even detailing the sacrificial system of the Levitical Law.

THE PRIESTS

We must remember that it was the priests, Aaron's sons, who brought the blood and sprinkled it round about upon the altar that was by the door of the tabernacle of the congregation, of which we will have more to say in a moment.

In this, we must also remember that it is the blood of the burnt offering, and not of the sin offering, of which we speak. What does that mean?

It doesn't mean that we as convicted sinners enter into the value of the blood of the sin-bearer, as important as that is within its own right. In effect, it is as priests that we have anything to do with the burnt offering. As John said, we are *"kings and priests unto God"* (Rev. 1:6), but we are that because of what Jesus did for us at the Cross, where He *"washed us from our sins in His own blood"* (Rev. 1:5).

The truth is, we as believers are nothing at all; but in Christ, we are a purged worshipper. This means that we do not stand in the sanctuary, so to speak, as a guilty sinner, but as a worshipping priest, clothed in *"garments of glory and beauty."* In fact, to be occupied with guilt in the presence of God is not humility as it regards me, but unbelief as it regards the sacrifice. Please understand, this is something we don't want to do!

As stated, the burnt offering is not for the purpose of cleansing the conscience of the believer, that having already been done; it is to satisfy the justice and the character of God.

If I contemplate Christ as the sin offering, which we will do momentarily, I see atonement made according to the claims of divine justice with respect to sin. However, when I see atonement in the burnt offering, it is according to the measure of the willingness and ability of Christ to accomplish the will of God, which He did at the Cross. In fact, the burnt offering aspect of atonement is that about which the priestly household — the church of the living God — may well be occupied in the courts of the Lord's house forever.

THE DOOR

The brazen altar, on which the sacrifice was laid, and on which the blood was poured, was very near the door that led into the Holy Place of the tabernacle. Jesus plainly said of Himself, *"I am the door: by Me if any man enter in, he shall be saved, and shall go in and out, and find pasture"* (Jn. 10:9).

What the believer must know and understand is the great biblical truth, in fact, the foundational truth of the Word of God, that one cannot enter this door unless he goes by and through the brazen altar. This means that one cannot know Christ unless one comes by the way of the Cross. There is simply no other way.

That's the reason that the Apostle Paul was so strong as it regarded the Cross. That's the reason that he vehemently came against any doctrine that impugned the Cross in any way, as did, in his time, the Law/grace issue. That's the reason we presently take such a stand against the Word of Faith doctrine, which, in reality, is no faith at all simply because it demeans the Cross. It actually claims that salvation is brought about by one having faith in Jesus' suffering three days and nights in Hell, with Him dying spiritually, they claim.

Were that true, then sinners could suffer three days and nights in Hell and then be saved simply because such suffering would atone for their sin. Of course, we know that is foolishness!

However, the sinner can definitely be saved if He identifies with Christ on the Cross, even as Paul declared, and, in fact, it's the only way he can be saved (Rom. 6:3–5; Jn. 3:16; Eph. 2:8–9; Col. 2:14–15).

THE FLAYING AND THE CUTTING

"And he shall flay the burnt offering, and cut it into his pieces" (Lev. 1:6).

To flay means to take the hide off, usually through whipping. With this done, the sacrificer or sinful offerer and the priests or Levites assisting him needed to cut the animal into large pieces. The priests then took over by laying these pieces on the altar to be burned, thereby, following the Law that was set down regarding sacrifices.

In the grisly carving process, the head would be cut off, and the fat would be severed from the muscle, tissue, and skin. The animal needed to be cut into pieces like this to signify two things:

1. It signified how horrible and how deep a thing sin is. Sin is not merely exterior; it is interior. It is not just outward; it is inward. Sin is a disease of our vitals. It affects every single part of the human being.

You have heard it said, *"A man is not a liar because he lies; he lies because he is a liar,"* and similarly, *"A man is not a thief because he steals; he steals because he is a thief."*

IN THE HEART

In other words, at the time that he performs the sinful action, it is in his heart. Sin comes straight out of the vitals of a man or woman.

So, as an effect of this, sin and sinfulness cannot be dealt with by simply changing a person's clothing, environment, geography, or social situation. Sin can only be dealt with through a change of heart, and only God Himself can get to our hearts. We are by nature so dense and so thick, and we have so many twists, deceptions, and kinks as part of our sinful, inner beings that it takes God Himself, our Maker, to pierce right through into the very fiber of our individuality.

2. The cutting up of the animal in order to lay it on the brazen altar to be burned further emphasized the horror and deep effect of sin. There is no part of the human being that it does not corrupt, be it mental, physical, financial, or spiritual.

This is the reason that humanistic psychology is such a crock. It can only deal with the exterior, and really not that very well, and not at all the interior. So, why does the believer want to look to humanistic psychology when he has the Cross?

THE FIRE

"And the sons of Aaron the priest shall put fire upon the altar, and lay the wood in order upon the fire:

"And the priests, Aaron's sons, shall lay the parts, the head, and the fat, in order upon the wood that is on the fire which is upon the altar" (Lev. 1:7-8).

As it regards the fire, it would be well here to note that the Hebrew word that is rendered *burn* in the case of the burnt offering is wholly different from that which is used in the sin offering. The Hebrew word that is rendered *burn* in connection with the sin offering signifies *"to burn"* in general; however, the Hebrew word used in *burnt offering* signifies *"incense."*

Now, we cannot imagine for a moment that this distinction is a mere interchange of words, the use of which is immaterial. Concerning this, Mackintosh said, *"I believe the wisdom of the Holy Spirit is as manifest in the use of the two words as it is in any other point of difference in the two offerings."*

The idea is this, as we note in the concluding part of Verse 9, the phrase is used, *"of a sweet savour unto the Lord,"* which signifies that the honour and justice of Jehovah have been satisfied. This, of course, refers to it being satisfied in the Cross.

THE CROSS

As convicted sinners, we gaze on the Cross of our Lord Jesus Christ and behold therein that which meets all of our needs. The Cross, in this aspect of it, gives perfect peace to the conscience. However, then, as kings and priests, we can look at the Cross in another light, even as the grand consummation of Christ's holy purpose to carry out — even unto death — the will of the Father.

We should have a very defective apprehension of the mystery of the Cross were we only to see in it that which meets man's need as a sinner. There were depths in that mystery which only the mind of God could fathom. It is, therefore, important to see that when the Holy Spirit would furnish us with foreshadowings of the Cross, He gave us, in the very first place, one which sets it forth in its aspect Godward. This alone would be sufficient to teach us that there are heights and depths in the doctrine of the Cross which man never can reach. There is in the Cross that which only God could know and appreciate, hence, it is that the burnt offering gets the first place. It typifies Christ's death as viewed and valued by God alone.

THE CROSS AND RIGHTEOUSNESS

Strangely yet beautifully enough, from the Cross we might well say that the Father reaps His richest harvest of glory. In no other way could He have been so glorified as by the death of Christ. In Christ's voluntary surrender of Himself to death, the divine glory shines in its fullest brightness.

Creation never could have furnished such a basis. Moreover, the Cross furnishes a righteous channel through which divine love can flow. In that flow of love, every other gift from the Father comes our way, but it is all made possible by the Cross.

Finally, by the Cross, Satan is eternally confounded and *"principalities and powers made a show of openly."* These are glorious fruits produced by the Cross. When we think of them, we can see just why there should have been a type of the Cross exclusively for God Himself, and also a reason that type should occupy the leading place — in other words, should stand at the very top of the list, even as does the burnt offering. Lacking that, there would be a grievous blank in the page of inspiration.

WASH IN WATER

"But his inwards and his legs shall he wash in water: and the priest shall burn all on the altar, to be a burnt sacrifice, an offering made by fire, of a sweet savour unto the LORD*"* (Lev. 1:9).

Going back to Verse 7, the fire that was placed on the altar by the priests was to never go out. Twenty-four hours a day it was to burn, signifying two things:

1. God's anger against sin;
2. God's provision of mercy.

The phrase, *"burn all,"* is not the common term for destroying by fire, but rather it means, *"make to ascend."* The life of the animal has already been offered in the blood; now the whole of its substance is made to ascend to the Lord.

This means that the vapor that ascended was not something different from that which was burned, but the very thing itself — its essence. Having ascended, as previously stated, it was an *incense* providing a *"sweet savour unto the* LORD*,"* which means that it was acceptable and well-pleasing to Him.

The burnt offering, the meat offering, and the peace offering were sacrifices of a sweet savour. The expression was never used with regard to the sin offering and trespass offering.

A SWEET SAVOUR UNTO THE LORD

Paul applied it to the sacrifice of Christ in Ephesians 5:2: *"As Christ also has loved us, and has given Himself for us an offering and a sacrifice to God for a sweet-smelling savour,"* and then again in Philippians 4:18 where he said, *"having received of Epaphroditus the things which were sent from you, an odour of a sweet smell, a sacrifice acceptable, well-pleasing to God."* Two things are said here. They are:

1. How could the parts of an animal burning on an altar, with its greasy smoke ascending up to Heaven, be *"a sweet savour unto the Lord?"* It was so, simply because it portrayed the great victory that would be won at Cavalry's Cross by the Lord Jesus Christ which would be for the redemption of all of humanity, at least those who would believe. It was a sacrifice well-pleasing to Him.

2. The second way that the Holy Spirit used this phrase, *"a sweet savour unto the Lord,"* concerned an offering sent to Paul by the church at Philippi. Paul likened that gift, and all such gifts that placed preeminence on the Cross, as someway becoming a part of the sacrifice itself, which is well-pleasing to the Lord. For every person who doesn't know, Jesus died in vain. So, those who help take this Message of the Cross to a dying world are at the very height of pleasing God. In other words, there is nothing any higher than that.

The meat offering was a thank offering, which specified that we thank God for giving His only Son. The peace offering signified that all sin had been assuaged, and done so because the proper sacrifice had been made, and now peace was restored. All of this — Christ giving Himself to satisfy the honour and justice of God, the thanksgiving on our part, and the peace we obtain, all made possible by Christ and what He did — provides a sweet savour unto the Lord.

THE WASHING AND THE CROSS

The inwards typified the very being of Christ, while the legs typified His physical body. The washing signified the purity of Christ. Even though the animal was only a type, it had to be a type in every respect, and purity was an absolute requirement, hence, the washing. The parts would then be burned on the altar, given up as a sacrifice, and given up in totality.

When Jesus went to the Cross, He did so perfectly in every respect. In a spiritual sense, He was perfectly clean, in fact, as no human being had ever been clean. This was demanded by God because anything less than perfection could not be accepted.

This completely shoots down the theory that Jesus died spiritually (separated from God) on the Cross. The teachers of this blasphemy — and blasphemy it is — claim that Jesus became one with Satan while on the Cross, and had to do such in order to redeem humanity, which was completed in the burning side of Hell. Of course, all of this is made up out of whole cloth, meaning that there is not a shred of scriptural evidence to support these claims.

They teach that the fire on the altar symbolized the hell to which Jesus had to go, and where, after some three days and nights of torture, He would then be born again.

Scripturally, the fire symbolized the judgment of God and not hellfire. When the sacrifice was consumed completely, even the ashes were then moved away.

The ashes signified that all sin had been addressed, and there was nothing left, for everything had been atoned. When we think of something totally destroyed and consumed, we at times use the term, *"reduced to ashes."* It means that nothing is left.

So, when faith and trust are placed in Christ and what He did at the Cross, every sin is atoned, and nothing is left, in other words, *my sins are gone.*

The work of Christ on the Cross was a finished work (Heb. 1:3). This means that nothing remained to be done. This means that this finished work did not await the Resurrection, the Ascension, or the Exaltation for it to be complete. It was all done at the Cross. While these other things are of vast significance, as should be obvious, still, it's the Cross of Christ that made these other things possible, and everything else that comes from God for that matter.

THE LAMB

"And if his offering be of the flocks, namely, of the sheep, or of the goats, for a burnt sacrifice; he shall bring it a male without blemish.

"And he shall kill it on the side of the altar northward before the LORD: and the priests, Aaron's sons, shall sprinkle his blood round about upon the altar.

"And he shall cut it into his pieces, with his head and his fat: and the priest shall lay them in order on the wood that is on the fire which is upon the altar:

"But he shall wash the inwards and the legs with water: and the priest shall bring it all, and burn it upon the altar: it is a burnt sacrifice, an offering made by fire, of a sweet savour unto the LORD" (Lev. 1:10-13).

THE LAMB OF GOD

Those who could not afford a bullock could bring a lamb or a goat; and those who were not able to do that would be accepted by God, even if they brought only a turtledove or a pigeon.

So, the sacrificial system was made such that every single individual could participate, from the poorest to the richest, because all needed to participate, and all would be accepted, that is, if they followed the instructions given by the Lord.

It should be observable that the creatures chosen for sacrifice were most mild and gentle, but yet, the bullock, as would be obvious, was very strong as well.

All of this typified Christ, who was the strong of the strong, and we speak of the spiritual sense, as well as mild and gentle.

In fact, whether more lambs or pigeons were offered, we aren't told; however, lambs are mentioned more than anything else as it regards the sacrifices.

In fact, the lamb so typified Christ that the Prophet Isaiah said of Him, *"He is brought as a lamb to the slaughter"* (Isa. 53:7).

John the Baptist referred to Him as, *"the Lamb of God, which takes away the sin of the world"* (Jn. 1:29).

TURTLEDOVES OR YOUNG PIGEONS

"And if the burnt sacrifice for his offering to the LORD *be of fowls, then he shall bring his offering of turtledoves, or of young pigeons.*

"And the priest shall bring it unto the altar, and wring off his head, and burn it on the altar; and the blood thereof shall be wrung out at the side of the altar:

"And he shall pluck away his crop with his feathers, and cast it beside the altar on the east part, by the place of the ashes:

"And he shall cleave it with the wings thereof, but shall not divide it asunder: and the priest shall burn it upon the altar, upon the wood that is upon the fire: it is a burnt sacrifice, an offering made by fire, of a sweet savour unto the LORD*"* (Lev. 1:14-17).

A turtledove or a pigeon could be had for a pittance; consequently, we find that the Lord made it possible for the poorest of the poor to offer up sacrifices that would be accepted by God. The sacrifices would be accepted just as much as if they had been bullocks or lambs; therefore, no person in Israel, whatever the status in life, had any excuse for not obeying the Lord.

But yet, I think it would not be pleasing to the Lord if a person could afford to offer a bullock or a lamb but would instead offer a pigeon or a turtledove. The Lord, who sees and knows all things, would probably not accept such a sacrifice because it would be dishonest.

In fact, in later years, the prophets, as the Holy Spirit spoke through them, would greatly charge the people for bringing sick animals. (Mal. 1:13).

AN OFFERING TO THE LORD

Is it not the same presently when people give of their offerings to the Lord, and they give far less than they actually could give?

On my desk right now is a short note from a young couple in our church, who has just written a sizable check in order that we may use it for SonLife Broadcasting. In fact, this young couple has given a large portion of all that they have.

How does this measure up to those who are quite wealthy, and who give but a tiny, tiny portion of what they could actually give?

As we shall see, five different types of sacrifices were demanded, with even different sacrifices among the types. This means that no one type could fully present Him. We needed to have Him reflected in life and in death — as a man and as a victim, Godward and usward — and we have Him thus in the offerings of Leviticus.

"You are the everlasting Word
"The Father's only Son,
"God manifest, God seen and heard,
"The heavens' beloved One!"

"In You most perfectly expressed,
"The Father's Self does shine,
"Fullness of Godhead, too:
"The Blessed, Eternally Divine!"

"Image of Infinite Unseen,
"Whose Being none can know,
"Brightness of light no eye has seen,
"God's love revealed below!"

"The higher mysteries of Your fame
"The creature's grasp transcend;
"The Father only Your blest name
"Of Son can comprehend."

"Yet loving You, on whom His love
"Ineffable does rest,
"The worshippers, O Lord, above,
"As one with You, are blest."

"Of the vast universe of bliss,
"The center You, and Son!
"The eternal theme of praise is this,
"To heavens' beloved One."

2

The Meat Offering

CHAPTER TWO

The Meat Offering

"AND WHEN ANY will offer a meat offering unto the LORD, *his offering shall be of fine flour; and he shall pour oil upon it, and put frankincense thereon"* (Lev. 2:1).

Presently, meat refers to flesh; however, in Bible times, it just simply referred to food, mostly grains, which, of course, contain no flesh. In our interpretation presently, this offering could be labeled a food offering or a meal offering.

The Hebrew word for meat offering is *minchah,* and means *"a gift made by an inferior to a superior."* It actually was a gratitude or thanksgiving offering.

All the other sacrifices were bloody sacrifices, but this offering was a *vegetable sacrifice,* one might say!

While all of it refers to Christ, it does so in a different way. For instance, as the burnt offering typified Christ in death, the meat offering typified Him in life.

In this particular sacrifice, we find it a beautiful type of Christ as He lived, walked, and served down here on this earth. The pure and perfect manhood of our blessed Lord is a theme that must command the attention of every true Christian.

JESUS CHRIST, THE ONLY PERFECT MAN

This is very important when one considers that many do not properly understand Christ, and more so, do not understand the Incarnation, i.e., God becoming man. In fact, the expressions which one sometimes hears and reads are sufficient to prove that the fundamental doctrine of the Incarnation is not laid hold of as it ought to be, and as the Word of God presents it.

Considering that an entire Levitical sacrifice was appointed by God, which refers to the humanity of Christ — His life, living, and walk — we should realize how important this is. From the beginning, Satan has diligently sought to lead people astray in reference to this all-important aspect of our Saviour — His humanity.

Concerning this, Mackintosh said: *"The Lord Jesus Christ was the only perfect man who ever trod this earth. He was all perfect — perfect in thought, perfect in word, perfect in action. In Him every moral quality met in divine and, therefore, perfect proportion. No one feature was out of kilter. In Him were exquisitely blended a majesty which overawed, and a gentleness which gave perfect ease in His presence."*

THE FINE FLOUR

"His offering shall be of fine flour," presents the type of this perfect manhood. It formed the basis of the meat offering. There was not so much as a single coarse grain in this flour. This means there was nothing uneven, nothing unequal, and nothing rough to the touch. What does all of this mean?

It means that Christ, no matter what the pressure, was never ruffled by any circumstance or set of circumstances.

He never had to retrace a step or recall a word. Come what might, He always met it in that perfect response and repose, which are so strikingly typified by the fine flour.

Even though there have been godly men and women in history, in fact, some which portrayed Christ beautifully, none could even remotely match the perfection of the Son of God in any capacity, especially in the portrayal of life and living, with all of its difficulties, problems, and irritations. I think we could say without fear of exaggeration that while some stand out over other men, none even remotely approach Christ. In other words, that gap or chasm between Christ and man is uncrossable.

I FIND NO FAULT IN THIS MAN

As someone has well said, if a person could find on this earth the individual whom they think is the godliest, the kindest, the most Christlike, the one in whom the fruit of the Spirit functions to the greatest degree, upon close association with that individual, whomever he might be, one would quickly see the faults, flaws, and imperfections. The longer one stayed around that person, again, whomever that person might be, the more faults and flaws one would observe; however, the closer we get to Christ, the very opposite result is to be found. His perfection becomes even greater perfection, if such is possible. His attributes and qualities are enlarged upon the closer that we inspect the Man from Galilee. Truly, one has to say, even as the Roman governor of so long ago said, *"I find no fault in this man"* (Lk. 23:4), and no one else, at least if he is honest, has ever found any fault in this Man.

THE LAST ADAM

There has always been much discussion about Christ, concerning the question as to whether He could have sinned or not. Many take the position that inasmuch as He was God as well as man, in effect, the God-Man, Jesus Christ, He could not sin because God can't sin.

While it's certainly true that Jesus Christ was God, never ceased to be God, and, in fact, will always be God, still, when He became man, He forever laid aside the *expression* of His deity while, at the same time, retaining *possession* of His deity. In other words, even though He definitely is God, He functions as a man.

I would remind the reader that Jesus grew hungry, thirsty, and tired, which are all characteristics of the flesh. We know that God cannot get hungry, thirsty, or tired! So, we must come back to the position that even though Jesus is God, and always will be God due to the Incarnation, He now functions as a man and, in fact, will forever function as a man (Zech. 12:10; 13:6).

THE PURPOSE FOR JESUS
BECOMING THE LAST ADAM

The purpose for Jesus becoming man (the Incarnation) was that He may serve as the *"last Adam"* (I Cor. 15:45). In other words, He had to do what the first Adam did not do, which was to completely obey God, which He did. As well, He had to undo what the first Adam did, which was to plunge man into spiritual oblivion. He did the first by living a perfect life, which the meat offering typified. He did the second part, which was to effect the redemption of humanity, by dying on the Cross, typified by the burnt offering. In this, He was undoing what Adam had done, of course, the other offerings played into this, even as we shall see.

To answer the question as to whether Jesus could have sinned or not — to be the last Adam, He had to have the capacity to sin, or else He would not have fulfilled the type.

Satan is deluded, deceived, and demented, but as we think of such, he's no fool. He would not have spent all the time he did tempting Christ if there was no chance of success. The truth is, in the Incarnation, God becoming man, the Godhead reduced itself to its lowest possible denominator, one might say, which was *the* Man, Christ Jesus. In other words, everything was riding on Christ. Had He failed, which He had the capacity to do, it would have involved far more than the loss of humanity. It would have involved the loss of everything. In other words, Satan would have become the master of the universe; he would have taken the place of Jehovah, as god.

Concerning Christ, Paul said: **"That in the dispensation of the fullness of times, He** (*God the Father*) **might gather together in one all things in Christ** (*what Christ did at the Cross*), **both which are in Heaven, and which are on earth; even in Him"** (Eph. 1:10).

EVERYTHING WAS AT STAKE

This means that what Jesus did affected not only this earth but Heaven as well!

Paul was actually referring in this passage to a statement that he made in I Corinthians. He said: **"Then comes the end, when He** (*Christ*) **shall have delivered up the king-**

dom of God, even the Father; when He shall have put down all rule and all authority and power" (I Cor. 15:24).

This will take place at the conclusion of the Millennial Reign when Satan will be loosed out of his prison for a short period of time, and will make one more effort to take over the world. However, he will be totally and completely defeated and, as well, cast into the lake of fire along with all demon spirits and fallen angels (Rev. 20:7–15).

That will be the end of Satan's rebellion and will be the end forever. In other words, Satan and all sin — which refers to all who served him — will be forever locked away, actually in the lake of fire, where they will be forever and forever. Then Jesus will deliver up the kingdom to the Father, with the end result being that described in Revelation, Chapters 21 and 22.

Yes, in His earthly sojourn, Jesus could have sinned, but the facts are, He did not sin, whether in word, thought, or deed.

OIL

The phrase, *"and he shall pour oil upon it,"* refers to the oil being poured on the fine flour, which refers in type to Jesus being filled with the Holy Spirit beyond measure (Jn. 3:34). In fact, the Holy Spirit led and guided Him in all that He did (Lk. 4:18–19). We find that the oil was applied in two ways:

1. The fine flour was *mingled* with oil.
2. There was oil *poured* upon it.

This refers to the *conception* of Christ and then to His *anointing*, all by the Holy Spirit (Mat. 1:18–23; 3:16; Lk. 4:18–19).

We must ever understand that Christ never took our fallen nature into union with Himself. He didn't do it at His birth, not in His life and living, and not on the Cross, as some teach. At no point did He have a fallen nature. In fact, that was the reason for the Virgin Birth. Had He been born by normal pro-creation, He would have been born as all other babies — in original sin — which would have translated into a fallen nature. To escape that fallen nature, He was born of the Virgin Mary. In fact, had He had a fallen nature, this would have meant that He was a sinner and would have meant that He needed a saviour Himself, which, of course, is preposterous.

While Christ never unites with us in our fallen nature, we, in fact, do unite with Him in His divine nature, in which case, His divine nature becomes ours (II Pet. 1:4). How is this done?

THE CROSS

It was done totally and completely at the Cross. Paul said: **"But now in Christ Jesus you** *(Gentiles)* **who sometimes were far off are made nigh by the blood of Christ.**

"For He is our peace, who has made both one *(Jews and Gentiles)***, and has broken down the middle wall of partition between us;**

"Having abolished in His flesh *(His death on the Cross)* **the enmity, even the Law of Commandments contained in ordinances** *(the Ten Commandments)***; for to make in Himself of twain** *(both Jews and Gentiles)* **one new man** *(one church)***, so making peace;**

"And that He might reconcile both *(Jews and Gentiles)* **unto God in one body** *(the church)* **by the Cross, having slain the enmity thereby** *(removed the enmity by His death* *on the Cross)"* (**Eph. 2:13–16**).

As should be overly obvious in these passages, Jesus didn't do this by and through His resurrection, but rather through the Cross. While it is true that we are resurrection people, which means that we enjoy resurrection life, it is only because of what He did at the Cross.

Paul said, *"For if we have been planted together in the likeness of His death, we shall be also in the likeness of His resurrection"* (Rom. 6:5).

This plainly tells us that resurrection life is predicated solely on the *"likeness of His death"* and our part in that death (Rom. 6:3–4).

THE CROSS AND THE RESURRECTION

While we dare not minimize the great significance of the Resurrection, which should be overly obvious, at the same time, we must not place undue emphasis on that all-important work. The individual should ever be directed to the Cross, whether the sinner being saved or the saint being righteous. All are tied to the Cross, and the Cross alone!

The Resurrection was a foregone conclusion in that Jesus atoned for all sin. Had one sin been left unatoned (Rom. 6:23), Jesus could not have been raised from the dead. Inasmuch as all sin definitely was atoned, which means that redemption was completed at the Cross, the Resurrection was never in doubt.

Some Christians think of Christ as being raised from the dead by struggling with Satan, along with demon spirits, and finally breaking through them, and then walking out of the tomb. Nothing like that ever happened! To be factual, neither Satan nor any demon spirit wants anything to do with

Christ. In fact, they tremble in His presence.

The Holy Spirit, typified by the oil on the fine flour, could occupy Christ as He did simply because Christ was perfect. The Holy Spirit can function in us accordingly only because our faith is in a perfect Christ, who has afforded a perfect redemption. Our faith in Him gives us His perfection, which makes it possible for the Holy Spirit to work with us as He does, which, in fact, could only be done after the Cross (Jn. 14:17).

FRANKINCENSE

The phrase, *"and put frankincense thereon,"* has a spiritual meaning, as well, which should be obvious.

First of all, frankincense is white, which speaks of purity. The Holy Spirit could function in Christ as He did simply because Christ was perfectly pure, symbolized by the frankincense.

As well, frankincense was bitter, which speaks of the bitterness that Christ had to undergo, not only in His life and living but, as well, in His death on the Cross. Concerning His life, the Scripture says,*"He is despised and rejected of men"* (Isa. 53:3).

Concerning His death on the Cross, the Scripture also says, *"and the LORD has laid on Him the iniquity of us all (has laid on Him the penalty of our iniquity)"* (Isa. 53:6).

THE ALTAR

"And he shall bring it to Aaron's sons the priests: and he shall take thereout his handful of the flour thereof, and of the oil thereof, with all the frankincense thereof; and the priest shall burn the memorial of it upon the altar, to be an offering made by fire, of a sweet savour unto the LORD:

"And the remnant of the meat offering shall be Aaron's and his sons': it is a thing most holy of the offerings of the Lord *made by fire"* (Lev. 2:2-3).

So close was the union between the two sacrifices, and I speak of the burnt offering and the meat offering, that the burnt offering was never offered without the accompaniment of the meat offering (Num. 15:4).

When the meat offering was brought to the priests, and I speak of it being brought by Israelites who were offering up sacrifices, only about a handful was burned on the altar, along with the burnt offering, with the priests taking the remainder for themselves, for this is what was ordered by the Lord.

According to the Pulpit Commentary, for every handful of flour burnt on the altar, nearly a gallon went to the priests. They had to eat it within the precincts of the tabernacle, as was the case with all food that was *most holy*. This included the shewbread, and the flesh of the sin offering and of the trespass offering (Lev. 10:12). However, when the priests personally offered meat offerings, it was all wholly burnt, with none kept for themselves (Lev. 6:23).

THE MEMORIAL

The word *memorial* served a twofold purpose:

1. It pertained to the believer not failing to remember what the Lord has done for him, especially what Jesus has done for us.
2. As well, it pertained to the fact that God will not forget His promises. The Psalmist said, *"Remember all your offerings, and accept your burnt sacrifice"* (Ps. 20:3).

The first part is carried over into that sacred ordinance of the church, referred to as the Lord's Supper. Jesus said, *"Take, eat: this is My body, which is broken for you: this do in remembrance of Me."*

And then, *"This cup is the New Testament in My blood: this do you, as often as you drink it, in remembrance of Me"* (I Cor. 11:24–25).

The greatest promise that God made, and in which the meat offering was a type, was that He would send a Redeemer into the world to lift man out of this darkness. This one sent would be the perfect One. How much the Israelites understood this, we cannot actually tell. It was supposed to have been explained to them. To be sure, Moses would have been faithful to this task, but how much the people would have heeded what he said about all of these things is anyone's guess.

While Moses wrote all of this down, which constitutes the first five books of the Bible, still, how many of the Israelites, who were former slaves, could actually read, again, is anyone's guess. So, the instructions given to them would mostly have been given verbally.

A SWEET SAVOUR UNTO THE LORD

This offering was a sweet savour to the Lord, not so much because of the offering itself, but rather what, or more particularly, who it represented. It typified Christ in His perfection. So, we can understand how this would be a sweet savour. Correspondingly, this we must remember: In all of our doing, we must present Christ! In all of our believing, we must believe Christ! Nothing must come between us and

Christ, and nothing must take the place of Christ. Christ and Him crucified must always be the foundation of our faith. I think we can say without fear of contradiction that only Christ is a *"sweet savour unto the LORD."*

Consequently, how dare we offer anything else to the Lord except Christ! To be sure, the moment we offer something else, I think we can safely say that we have just incurred upon ourselves the wrath of God. Paul said: *"For the wrath of God is revealed from Heaven against all ungodliness and unrighteousness of men, who hold the truth in unrighteousness"* (Rom. 1:18).

MOST HOLY

The offerings, it seems, were placed in two classes:

1. That which was *less holy.*
2. That which was *most holy.*

The incense offering, the shewbread (Ex. 30:26; Lev. 24:9), the sin and trespass offerings (Lev. 6:25–28; 7:1, 6; 14:13), and the meat offerings, described here, belong to the *most holy* class. Among other things, this meant that these offerings could only be eaten in the court of the sanctuary by the priests alone.

UNLEAVENED

"And if you bring an oblation of a meat offering baked in the oven, it shall be unleavened cakes of fine flour mingled with oil, or unleavened wafers anointed with oil.

"And if your oblation be a meat offering baked in a pan, it shall be of fine flour unleavened, mingled with oil" (Lev. 2:4-5).

The meat offerings are mentioned after the burnt offerings. This means that all which pertained to the meat offerings are predicated on the burnt offering, which typifies the Cross and what Jesus did there to appease the wrath of God.

The price that God demanded was high, so high, in fact, that it beggars description. However, we have no argument, seeing that He paid the price Himself.

Only the spotless Lamb of God could pay the price, and the meat offering proclaimed the purity of Christ, in fact, a perfect purity.

All of the instructions concerning the meat offering were given for the children of Israel. There were several ways that the offering could be prepared, and instructions were given for each method.

The first type, as given in Verses 1 through 3, pertains to the uncooked offering; Verses 4 through 10 pertain to that which was prepared before it was brought to the priests.

LEAVEN

If they were going to prepare this offering fully, they must make certain that there be no leaven in any of the preparations.

In Hebrew life, leaven came to play an important part not only in breadmaking but also in law, ritual, and spiritual teaching. It was made originally from fine, white bran kneaded with the meal of certain plants, such as fitch or vetch, or from barley mixed with water and then allowed to stand until it turned sour. As baking developed, leaven was produced from bread flour kneaded without salt and kept until it passed into a state of fermentation.

In breadmaking, the leaven was probably a piece of dough retained from a former baking, which had fermented and turned acidic. This was then either dissolved in water in the kneading trough before the flour was added, or was *hid* in the flour (Mat. 13:33) and kneaded along with it. The bread thus made was known as *"leavened,"* as distinct from *unleavened* bread (Ex. 12:15).

The prohibition on leaven was possibly made because fermentation implies disintegration and corruption, and to the Hebrew, anything in a decayed state suggested uncleanness.

Doubtless for this reason it was excluded from the offerings placed upon the altar of Jehovah, which we are now studying.

However, two exceptions to this rule should be noted (Lev. 7:13). Leavened bread was an accompaniment of the thank offering, and leavened loaves were used also in the wave offering at the Feast of Pentecost, which we will study later.

THE ALTAR

"You shall part it in pieces, and pour oil thereon: it is a meat offering.

"And if your oblation be a meat offering baked in the frying pan, it shall be made of fine flour with oil.

"And you shall bring the meat offering that is made of these things unto the LORD: and when it is presented unto the priest, he shall bring it unto the altar.

"And the priest shall take from the meat offering a memorial thereof, and shall burn it upon the altar: it is an offering made by fire, of a sweet savour unto the LORD.

"And that which is left of the meat offering shall be Aaron's and his sons': it is a thing most holy of the offerings of the Lord made by fire" (Lev. 2:6-10).

The reader lacking in spirituality may grow weary at the tedious instructions given, wondering why all of this was necessary.

All of this represents Christ and the perfect life that He lived, who alone could serve as a perfect sacrifice; consequently, we should understand that anything that portrays Christ is of the utmost significance.

For instance, this offering could not have, as previously stated, any leaven mixed with its contents. As also stated, leaven represents decay and corruption, which, of course, was and is the opposite of Christ, who had no sin. So, the more we understand about these instructions given, the more we understand Christ.

To be frank, it's not really that difficult to understand, if we'll only take the time to carefully digest the contents. In giving all of this, the Holy Spirit most definitely intended that we make full use of all that is portrayed here.

NO HONEY

"No meat offering, which you shall bring unto the Lord, shall be made with leaven: for you shall burn no leaven, nor any honey, in any offering of the Lord made by fire.

"As for the oblation of the firstfruits, you shall offer them unto the Lord: but they shall not be burnt on the altar for a sweet savour" (Lev. 2:11-12).

Why was there no honey in this particular offering?

Honey, as leaven, can go into fermentation, as well; however, there is an added thought respecting honey.

Honey, as given here, represents all natural good, or at least that which man labels as good, which is in man outside of Christ. It would have something to do with the good part of the Tree of Knowledge of Good and Evil, with all of that tree being forbidden (Gen. 2:17). In fact, this *good* is not only the greatest problem of the unredeemed, it so happens to be the greatest problem of the redeemed as well!

The unredeemed man thinks that his *good* will save him, which it won't! Regrettably, the redeemed man often tries to live for God by the means of his so-called goodness. However, let it be understood that this particular good, whether in the unredeemed or the redeemed, cannot be accepted at all by God.

PAUL

Listen to what Paul said, *"For I know that in me (that is, in my flesh,) dwells no good thing"* (Rom. 7:18).

The only truly good that is within us, at least that which God will recognize, is that which comes exclusively by and through Christ, which refers to what He did at the Cross and our faith in that finished work. One of the fruits of the Spirit is goodness, but we must remember that it is a fruit of the Spirit and not of us (Gal. 5:22–23).

All of this means that all goodness that proceeds from our flesh is rejected by God, hence, no honey. Paul used the word *flesh* in the sense of our own efforts, strength, ability, and power. Of course, all of this is exhibited from our own person, which means that it did not originate with the Lord.

The idea is this: Man, even redeemed man, cannot originate anything that is good from his own strength and ability.

This is because of the Fall. Now, the problem with redeemed man is he thinks that because he is now a new creation in Christ — in essence, a son or daughter of God — he can produce good things. So, he sets about by his own strength and ability to produce those particular things. He is then chagrined when he realizes that God cannot use these efforts, which he will have to face sooner or later. This is why the Cross is so very, very important.

CRUCIFIED WITH CHRIST

The meat offering, as stated, typified the spotless, pure, perfect, and uncorrupted life of the Lord Jesus Christ. We make a great mistake when we look at that particular life and then try to imitate it by our own strength and ability. It cannot be done that way!

The only way that His perfect life can be ours, and the only way it is meant to be ours, is by and through what Christ did for us at the Cross. That's why Paul said, concerning this very thing: **"I am crucified with Christ** (*this takes us back to Romans 6:3–5*)**: nevertheless I live; yet not I, but Christ lives in me: and the life which I now live in the flesh I live by the faith of the Son of God, who loved me, and gave Himself for me"** (Gal. 2:20).

If it is to be noticed, all of Paul's life and living was predicated on the fact that he was crucified with Christ. To be sure, that's the only way that you and I are going to be able to give birth to goodness and exhibit the same. It is all in Christ and what He did at the Cross and our faith in that finished work, which gives the Holy Spirit the latitude to bring about these things. Otherwise, it is goodness and works which God cannot accept.

BURNT ON THE ALTAR

While leaven and honey could be offered to the Lord as an offering of thanksgiving, Verse 12 tells us that they cannot be offered if the oblation (something offered in worship or devotion) is to be *"burnt on the altar for a sweet savour."*

The altar represents the crucifixion of Christ and the price that He would pay there; consequently, this is a price that we couldn't pay, so our goodness, etc., is not to be added to the finished work of Christ.

SALT

"And every oblation of your meat offering shall you season with salt; neither shall you suffer the salt of the covenant of your God to be lacking from your meat offering: with all your offerings you shall offer salt" (Lev. 2:13).

Salt is a preservative and, therefore, serves as a type in the Old Testament of the Word of God.

As an example, after Elijah was taken up to Heaven, Elisha, now serving in his place, came to the city of Jericho, where the men of the city told him that the water was poisoned, and because of that, the ground was barren (II Ki. 2:19).

Elisha, no doubt, took this problem to the Lord, and then, doing what the Lord told him to do, told the men to **"bring him a new cruse** *(a new clay pot)***, and put salt therein."**

The Scripture then says, *"And he went forth unto the spring of the waters, and cast the salt in there, and said, Thus saith the* Lord, *I have healed these waters; there shall not be from thence any more death or barren land"* (II Ki. 2:20–21).

The new cruse was a type of the humanity of our Lord, and the salt in that new cruse was a type of the Word of God, by which the Master functioned in totality.

THE SALT OF THE COVENANT

In Verse 13, the Lord told Moses, *"With all your offerings you shall offer salt."* In fact, it is called *"the salt of the covenant,"* referring to the enduring character of the covenant. God Himself has so ordained it in all things, which means that nothing can alter it, and no influence can ever corrupt it because it is the unalterable, unchangeable, indescribable, eternal Word of almighty God.

The salt proclaims, *"thus saith the Lord,"* and, as such, runs at cross-purposes with men's desires. Every true preacher of the Gospel will have his message *"seasoned with salt"* (Mat. 5:13; Col. 4:6).

For instance, when Jesus ministered in the synagogue of Nazareth (Lk. 4:16–29), the people did *"bear Him witness, and wondered at the gracious words which proceeded out of His mouth."* However, when He proceeded to season those words with salt, which was so needful in order to preserve them from the corrupting influence of their national pride, they would have cast Him over the brow of the hill whereon their city was built had not the Holy Spirit intervened.

If there is anything that the church desperately needs today, it is the salt of the Word of God. Unfortunately, far too many in the modern church seek to bend the Word to their perfidious ways instead of conforming their ways to the Word of God. The trouble is, we've got too much honey in the modern gospel and not enough salt.

MEMORIAL

"And if you offer a meat offering of your firstfruits unto the LORD, you shall offer for the meat offering of your firstfruits green ears of corn *(grain)* dried by the fire, even corn *(grain)* beaten out of full ears.

"And you shall put oil upon it, and lay frankincense thereon: it is a meat offering.

"And the priest shall burn the memorial of it, part of the beaten corn *(grain)* thereof, and part of the oil thereof, with all the frankincense thereof: it is an offering made by fire unto the LORD" (Lev. 2:14-16).

As we have seen in this second chapter of Leviticus, there were several ways that the meat offering could be prepared. It speaks of being baked in an oven, baked in a pan, or baked in a frying pan. Now, the process of baking might suggest the idea of suffering. However, inasmuch as the meat offering is called *"a sweet savour,"* a term which is never applied to the sin offering or trespass offering, it should be evident that there is no thought of suffering for sin, no thought of suffering the wrath of God on account of sin, and no thought of suffering at the hand of infinite justice as the sinner's substitute. This means that the suggestion of suffering for sin is not intended here. Yes, suffering is intended, but not for sin.

In His earthly life and walk, Christ suffered for righteousness' sake, in which believers now endure the same (I Pet. 4:13).

However, when it came to suffering for sin, the Scripture plainly says, *"For Christ also has once suffered for sins"* (I Pet. 3:18). This means that whatever suffering that Christ endured, there was only one suffering which He endured for sins, and that was the Cross.

SUFFERING!

As the righteous servant of God, He suffered in the midst of a scene in which all was contrary to Him, which the preparation of the meat offering represented. However, this was the very opposite of suffering for sin. It is of the utmost significance to distinguish between these two kinds of suffering. The confounding of them will lead to serious error. Suffering as a righteous one standing among men on God's behalf is one thing, and suffering instead of man under the hand of God is quite another. The Lord Jesus suffered for righteousness during His life; He suffered for sin in His death.

During His life, man and Satan did their utmost, and even at the Cross, they put forth all their power. However, when all that they could do was done, and when they had traveled in their deadly enmity to the utmost limit of human and diabolical opposition, there lay, far beyond, a region of impenetrable gloom and horror into which the Sin-Bearer had to travel in the accomplishment of His work. In other words, Jesus underwent a suffering on the Cross when He suffered for sin — our sins, incidentally, and certainly not His own — which no human being will ever be able to comprehend.

SUFFERING FOR SIN

Here is the point I wish to make: While the believer may suffer because of sin (the sins of others or his own), there is no such thing as a believer suffering for his sins, and we refer to such suffering as being an atonement. To even think such, in effect, says that what Christ did at the Cross was not enough, and we, therefore, have to add to His atonement by suffering for sin as well. To think such, the believer might as well go to a Cross and attempt to hang himself on that wooden beam, which, of course, is ridiculous! But yet, sadly and regrettably, much of the church falls into the category of trying to make the meat offering into something it was never intended to be.

Let us say it again: While the believer will definitely suffer for righteousness' sake, and while the believer will definitely suffer at times because of the sins of others or even himself, he must ever understand that such suffering will never atone for sin.

PENANCE

The Catholic Church teaches penance, which, in effect, is an attempt to atone for sin and is a gross insult to Christ. Penance is an act of self-abasement or punishment of some kind, which is supposed to pay for sin.

But yet most in the Protestant world, while not quite as blatant, actually do the same thing.

One of my friends, a lawyer, incidentally, was conversing with some denominational leaders sometime back. The leaders, in speaking of a particular individual and concerning some things which had happened to him, made the statement, *"He has paid his dues and, therefore, we can accept him."*

After that meeting ended, he called me, and in relating this incident, said, *"Brother Swaggart, I soon realized that these men were advocating penance."*

He was right! That's exactly what they were advocating.

All of this stems from a lack of proper understanding as it regards the Cross and what Jesus accomplished there, or else, it evidences gross unbelief, which I am concerned is actually the case.

THE MEANING OF THE MEAT OFFERING

Getting back to the meat offering as it regards the suffering of Christ, there was absolutely nothing in His humanity or in the nature of His associations which could possibly connect Him with sin, wrath, or death. He was *made sin* on the Cross. There He endured the wrath of God, and there He gave up His life as an all-sufficient atonement for sin, but nothing of this finds a place in the meat offering. True, we have the process of baking — the action of fire — but this is not the wrath of God, at least in this instance. The meat offering was not a sin offering but a sweet savour offering. Thus, its meaning is definitely fixed, and, moreover, the intelligent interpretation of it must ever guard with holy jealousy the precious truth of Christ's spotless humanity and the true nature of His associations, which the meat offering represents.

When the Scripture speaks of our having fellowship with Christ's sufferings, it refers simply to His sufferings for righteousness — His sufferings at the hand of man. That was the meat offering.

When it came to suffering for sin, He did so on the Cross that we might not have to suffer for it. He endured the wrath of God that we might not have to endure it. There, He was the sin offering and the trespass offering.

THE MEAT OFFERING

Part of the meat offering was to be burned on the fire, with evidence that frankincense was to be poured only on the part that was burned by fire and not on the part given to the priests. Incidentally, the word *corn* is an unfortunate translation. There was no such thing as corn in that part of the world, being discovered as grown by the Indians in North America — a discovery that would not take place for some 2,000 years. It should have been translated *"grain."*

Inasmuch as part of the meat offering was burned in the fire and part eaten by the priests, we should understand that this symbolized Christ in His perfect life, but yet, a life that would be given on the Cross, hence, the burning of the meat offering on the altar. This signifies, as well, that Christ came to this world but for one purpose, and that was to go to the Cross. His life was perfect — His demeanor perfect, His way perfect, and His manner perfect — all for the purpose of being a perfect sacrifice.

So, the burnt offering symbolized Christ dying on the Cross, which was to appease the wrath of God, in other words, that part of His death was solely for God and not for man. The meat (food) offering symbolized His perfect life. If it is to be noticed, the grain that was to be offered was to be out of full ears, which alone could symbolize the perfection of Christ.

"Rejoice, the Lord is King;
"Your Lord and King adore!
"Rejoice, give thanks,
"And sing, and triumph evermore.
"Lift up your heart, lift up your voice!
"Rejoice, again I say, rejoice!"

"Jesus the Saviour reigns,
"The God of truth and love;
"When He had purged our stains,
"He took His seat above.
"Lift up your heart, lift up your voice!
"Rejoice, again I say, rejoice!"

"His kingdom cannot fail;
"He rules over earth and Heaven;
"The keys of death and Hell are to our Jesus given.
"Lift up your heart, life up your voice!
"Rejoice, again I say, rejoice!"

"Rejoice in glorious hope!
"Our Lord, the Judge, shall come,
"And take His servants up to their eternal home.
"Lift up your heart, lift up your voice!
"Rejoice, again I say, rejoice!"

3

The Peace Offering

CHAPTER THREE

The Peace Offering

"AND IF HIS oblation be a sacrifice of peace offering, if he offer it of the herd; whether it be a male or female, he shall offer it without blemish before the LORD" (Lev. 3:1).

Concerning the peace offering, Mackintosh said: *"There is none of the offerings in which the communion of the worshipper so fully unfolded as in the 'peace offering.' In the 'burnt offering,' it is Christ offering Himself to God. In the 'meat offering,' we have Christ's perfect humanity. Then, passing on to the 'sin offering,' we learn that sin, in its root, is fully met. In the 'trespass offering,' there is a full answer to the actual sins. But in none is the doctrine of the communion of the worshipper unfolded. This latter belongs to the 'peace offering.'"*

THE SIN NATURE

In both the peace offering and the trespass offering, we learn of the presence of the sin nature in the heart and life of the believer. However, we find out even more fully in the peace offering that even though the sin nature dwells in us, it is not to rule in us. In fact, Paul addressed this directly by saying, **"Let not sin** *(the sin nature)* **therefore reign** *(rule)* **in your mortal body, that you should obey it in the lusts thereof"** **(Rom. 6:12).** Were there no sin nature, there would have been no need for the peace offering or the trespass offering.

The more closely we view these offerings, the more fully we see the necessity of the five offerings in order that Christ be properly portrayed as it regards His finished work.

The peace offering portrays communion with God and the believer's place and position in Christ, due to what Christ has done for us at the Cross. It was the only offering in which the offerer could partake, which signified that peace had now been restored.

A MALE OR FEMALE

In the burnt offering, it had to be a male without blemish, whereas in the peace offering, it might be either a male or a female. Irrespective, whichever one was chosen, it had to be without blemish. As the peace offering was concerned with communion, a female was permitted as expressive of the incapacity of the worshipper to fully comprehend the unsearchable riches of Christ's nature and work. There was no such limitation on the part of God; hence, in the burnt offering, it was a male of the first year (Williams). Regarding the peace offering, there was no restriction regarding the age of the animal, only that it be without blemish. Of course, that was to portray Christ in all of His perfection, as would be obvious.

The peace offering was to be offered *"before the* LORD*"* (Lev. 3:1), *"unto the* LORD*"* (Lev. 3:3), and *"a sweet savour unto the* LORD*"* (Lev. 3:5).

THE SACRIFICE

"And he shall lay his hand upon the head of his offering, and kill it at the door of the tabernacle of the congregation: and Aaron's sons the priests shall sprinkle the blood upon the altar round about" (Lev. 3:2).

Much of the time, the sacrifices, whatever they were, were followed by a meat offering, which denoted thankfulness, and a peace offering, which referred to the fact that peace had been restored.

The male or female of the animals being allowed stipulated that all — both man and woman — could have fellowship and peace with God.

THE DOCTRINE OF SUBSTITUTION AND IDENTIFICATION

When the individual brought his animals for sacrifice, as he generally brought two, one would be for the peace offering. After the burnt, sin, or trespass offering had been presented, which was followed by the meat offering, it was now time for the peace offering.

He would then *"lay his hand upon the head of his offering,"* which portrayed the beautiful doctrine of substitution and identification. The animal became the substitute in the sinner's place, and by the laying of his hand or hands on the head of his offering, he identified with that substitute. That, in effect, is the heart of the Gospel. Christ became our substitute, and we identify with Him in all He did, but more particularly, what He did for us at the Cross. How do we do that?

THE MANNER OF SUBSTITUTION
AND IDENTIFICATION

It is always by faith. Paul said, *"For in Jesus Christ nei-ther circumcision avails anything, nor uncircumcision; but faith which works by love"* (Gal. 5:6).

This refers to the fact that identification cannot be made with Christ by works, but only by faith.

So, what did Paul mean when he said *"but faith,"* or, as it actually means, *"by faith?"*

BY FAITH

To properly understand faith, at least that which is given to us in the Word of God, we must understand the object of faith.

In truth, every human being in the world has faith, but only a tiny few have the right kind of faith. This refers to the correct object of faith, which is Jesus Christ and Him crucified (I Cor. 1:17–18, 21, 23; 2:2). In fact, the phrase, *Jesus Christ and Him crucified*, sums up the entirety of the Word of God all the way from Genesis 1:1 through Revelation 22:21.

So, as it regards the nonspiritual kind of faith, and even the spiritual kind that is not anchored in Christ and Him crucified, it is not recognized by God. Therefore, when we speak of faith, we must always understand that it's faith in Christ and His Cross. The Cross must never be divorced from Christ or Christ from the Cross. Now, by that, we're not meaning that Christ is still on the Cross. In fact, He is presently in Heaven, seated by the right hand of the Father (Heb. 1:3). As well, all true believers are seated with Him, spiritually speaking (Eph. 2:6).

The believer must understand that to properly have faith in the Word is to have faith in the Cross. If one doesn't have faith in the Cross, one cannot properly have faith in the Word. In fact, it is very important for the believer to understand that every single thing that we receive from God, and I mean every single thing, is all made possible by what Jesus did at the Cross.

Listen to John the apostle, *"In the beginning was the Word, and the Word was with God, and the Word was God"* (Jn. 1:1). This tells us that Jesus is the living Word!

He then said, *"And the Word was made flesh, and dwelt among us"* (Jn. 1:14). This speaks of the Incarnation of Christ — God becoming man.

John the Beloved then recorded the words of John the Baptist, who said, *"Behold the Lamb of God, which takes away the sin of the world"* (Jn. 1:29).

BAPTISM

As stated, all of this tells us that Jesus is the Word and that He, as God, became flesh, and did so for the purpose of going to the Cross, which alone could take away the sin of the world.

The manner in which faith is exhibited in Christ, which brings about peace with God, is that we are to understand that when Christ died, we were *"baptized into His death"* and were *"buried with Him by baptism into death."* Then, when Christ was raised from the dead by the glory of the Father, we were raised with Him *"in newness of life"* (Rom. 6:3–4).

Of course, as should be obvious, we were not there when Christ died. However, Paul was speaking of us having faith in what Christ did, which means to have faith in the Cross, which is the identification with our substitute. This is the key to all things. As should be obvious, this is something that one cannot earn by merit, so he has to come by this great and glorious life by faith. I trust that we have properly explained what faith actually is.

Also, in Romans 6:3–4, when Paul spoke of baptism, he wasn't speaking of water baptism, but rather the crucifixion of Christ. He used this word *baptism* because that was the strongest word that could be found to explain what actually happens in the mind of God when we evidence faith in Christ and what Christ did at the Cross. In God's mind, we are literally placed in Christ, and it means in what He did for us at the Cross as our substitute.

THE DOOR OF THE TABERNACLE

As well, the person who brought the sacrifice had to personally kill it because he — the one who had brought it — was the one who had sinned.

In doing this, he must have felt the pangs of what he had done which necessitated this action, realizing that an innocent victim was suffering in his stead. In fact, it was meant to portray this, in other words, it was meant to have a great effect because it portrayed Christ who was to come. It had to be done at the door of the tabernacle, even though the blood of this innocent animal couldn't get him through the door. That awaited Christ, whom the *Door* typified (Jn. 10:9).

When the sinner killed the animal, the priests caught the blood in a basin and then sprinkled or splashed it at the foot of the brazen altar, once again, typifying the blood that Jesus would shed. The Scripture says, concerning the peace offering: "**But now in Christ Jesus you who sometimes were far off are made nigh by the blood of Christ.**

"**For He is our peace, who has made both one** (*both Jews and Gentiles*)**, and has broken down the middle wall of partition between us ... And that He might reconcile both** (*Jews and Gentiles*) **unto God in one body by the Cross, having slain the enmity thereby**" (Eph. 2:13–16).

THE SHEDDING OF BLOOD

Of all the offerings, with the exception of the meal offering, the central core of the sacrifice was the shedding of blood, which was the life of the flesh. Eternal life had been forfeited in the Garden by the fall of Adam, and now for that life to be regained, a perfect life would have to be given, which could only be supplied by Christ. Fallen man was and is totally inadequate. This completely shoots down the erroneous doctrine (totally erroneous) of the Word of Faith people, who teach that any born-again man could have redeemed fallen humanity. Such portrays a complete lack of knowledge as it regards the Atonement, which is the worst error that can be believed.

THE ALTAR

"*And he shall offer of the sacrifice of the peace offering an offering made by fire unto the LORD; the fat that covers the inwards, and all the fat that is upon the inwards,*

"*And the two kidneys, and the fat that is on them, which is by the flanks, and the caul above the liver, with the kidneys, it shall he take away.*

"And Aaron's sons shall burn it on the altar upon the burnt sacrifice, which is upon the wood that is on the fire: it is an offering made by fire, of a sweet savour unto the LORD*"* (Lev. 3:3-5).

The first three offerings — the burnt offering, the meal offering, and the peace offering — are referred to as a *sweet savour.* The sin offering and the trespass offering are not referred to as such.

When we view Christ in the peace offering, we must remember that He does not stand before us as the bearer of our sins, as in the sin and trespass offerings, but (having already borne) as the ground of our peaceful and happy fellowship with God. If sin-bearing were in question, it could not be said, *"it is an offering made by fire, of a sweet savour unto the* LORD.*"*

THE VALUE OF THE BLOOD

Concerning this, Mackintosh said: *"Still, though sin-bearing is not the thought, there is full provision for one who knows himself to be a sinner, else he could not have any portion therein. To have fellowship with God, we must function 'in the light' (I Jn. 1:7). And to function or be 'in the light,' we must understand that only on the ground of that precious statement, 'The blood of Jesus Christ God's Son cleanses us from all sin,' can this be. The more we abide in the light, the deeper will be our sense of everything which is contrary to that light; and the deeper, also, our sense of the value of that blood which entitles us to be there."*

We must never forget that it is blood which is sprinkled on the altar round about. This means that fellowship with God must be encircled by atonement and only exists within it. Thus, God and the worshipper are brought into fellowship. Peace is established. Worship that's not based fully on the death of Christ is not worship that God will recognize.

Its eternal and unshakable foundation is not the worth of the worshipper but the preciousness of the sprinkled blood.

All the fat was wholly burnt upon the altar as a sweet savour. The fat and the blood symbolized the priceless life and the precious inward affections of the Lamb of God.

A SACRIFICE OF PEACE OFFERING

"And if his offering for a sacrifice of peace offering unto the Lord *be of the flock; male or female, he shall offer it without blemish.*

"If he offer a lamb for his offering, then shall he offer it before the Lord.

"And he shall lay his hand upon the head of his offering, and kill it before the tabernacle of the congregation: and Aaron's sons shall sprinkle the blood thereof round about upon the altar" (Lev. 3:6-8).

The lesson taught by the peace offering was the tremendous blessing of being in union with God as His covenant people, and the joys since this union, carried out by celebrating a festival meal. It was eaten reverently and thankfully, with a part being given to God's priests and a part symbolically consumed by God Himself. In simple terminology, it means that sin had been committed but a sacrifice had been offered — whether burnt, sin, or trespass offering had atoned. A peace offering was now sacrificed, of which the worshipper would receive a part, in which he, his family, and friends could celebrate. It was to be, as stated, a joyous occasion. The sin had been forgiven and atoned, brought about by the sacrifice, and now peace had been restored.

THE LORD JESUS CHRIST

Due to Christ not yet having come, these various sacrifices were instituted in order to symbolically proclaim to the people what Christ would do when He actually came. How much of this they understood is anyone's guess; however, the type beautifully portrayed Christ in all that He would do.

Jesus told the Pharisees, *"Search the Scriptures; for in them you think you have eternal life: and they are they which testify of Me."*

He then said, *"And you will not come to Me, that you might have life"* (Jn. 5:39–40).

The Master plainly tells us here that the Old Testament Scriptures, for that's what He was speaking of, testified of Him. To be sure, the sacrifices testified most of all!

So, this means that the children of Israel should have known.

THE FIRE

"And he shall offer of the sacrifice of the peace offering an offering made by fire unto the LORD; the fat thereof, and the whole rump, it shall he take off hard by the backbone; and the fat that covers the inwards, and all the fat that is upon the inwards,

"And the two kidneys, and the fat that is upon them, which is by the flanks, and the caul above the liver, with the kidneys, it shall he take away.

"And the priest shall burn it upon the altar: it is the food of the offering made by fire unto the LORD" (Lev. 3:9-11).

The fire spoke of the judgment of God. It spoke of judgment poured out on His only Son, with the sacrifice of the animal serving as the substitute. As the animal was totally consumed, in other words, reduced to ashes, the idea presented was that of our sins being reduced to nothingness. When anyone speaks of something being reduced to ashes, he is simply meaning that there is nothing left and nothing salvageable; it is totally consumed. So are our sins. Christ took the judgment for our sins, and how did He do that?

THE PRICE THAT WAS PAID

He paid the price, thereby, taking the judgment that, by all rights, was due us, and He did so by the giving of His life. This was accomplished by the shedding of His precious blood, for the life of the flesh is in the blood, hence, Peter saying: *"Forasmuch as you know that you were not redeemed with corruptible things as silver and gold ... But with the precious blood of Christ, as of a lamb without blemish and without spot"* (I Pet. 1:18–19).

The fire did not represent Hell, as some teach.

THE JESUS DIED SPIRITUALLY DOCTRINE

This teaching is propagated by the Word of Faith people, claiming that Jesus not only died physically on the Cross but, as well, died spiritually. By that, they mean that He actually became a sinner on the Cross, became one with Satan, died as a sinner, and went to Hell, and we speak of the burning side of Hell. They claim that He suffered there in the flames for three days and nights, with Satan thinking that he had won the day. At the end of that three days and nights, God the Father said, *"It is enough,"* and Jesus was then born again, even as any sinner is born again. According to their teaching, He was then raised from the dead.

There's not a shred of any of this in the Bible. In other words, it is pure fiction.

In the teaching of this subject, they belittle the Cross, claiming that it was the *"worst defeat in human history."* I quote one of their ministers verbatim. He said, *"The Cross is actually a place of defeat, whereas the Resurrection is a place of victory."* He went on to say, *"When you preach the Cross, you're preaching death."* This is derived from the April 2002 edition of his monthly magazine.

Some may claim that all of this is merely a matter of semantics, which is a play on words. In other words, they are claiming that we are both teaching the same thing about the Cross; he's just teaching it in another way. No, that is basely incorrect!

When one refers to the Cross as the *greatest defeat in human history*, that is clearly and plainly the very opposite of what the Bible teaches.

The Cross was the destination of Christ, which means that it was the supreme reason for which He came. In fact, the Cross was planned, as Peter said, from before the foundation of the world (I Pet. 1:18–20). The truth is, any individual who believes the doctrine of the Word of Faith teachers is believing gross error; and furthermore, it is the worst type of error, inasmuch as it is error concerning the Atonement. To have a hangnail is one thing, but to have heart problems is something else altogether. The hangnail won't kill you, but heart problems will! To be wrong about the Atonement is to be wrong about the very heart of the Gospel.

As well, the fire on the altar does not represent hellfire into which Jesus had to go, as they erroneously teach. Were that the case, then any sinner, upon going to Hell, could burn there for three days and nights, and his sin would then be atoned, and he would then be saved. No, the fire doesn't save anyone. It is what Jesus did at the Cross in the giving of His life by the pouring out of His precious blood that effects salvation, and that alone (Eph. 2:13–18; Col. 2:14–15)!

WHAT ACTUALLY HAPPENED BETWEEN THE CROSS AND THE THRONE?

Jesus became a sin offering while on the Cross. The great Prophet Isaiah said: *"Yet it pleased the LORD to bruise Him; He has put Him to grief: when You shall make His soul an offering for sin, He shall see His seed, He shall prolong His days, and the pleasure of the LORD shall prosper in His hand"* (Isa. 53:10).

The word *offering* in the Hebrew is *asham* and means *"a trespass offering"* and an *"offering for sin."* Offerings for sin, or guilt offerings, were distinct from sin offerings. The object of the former was satisfaction; of the latter expiation. The Servant of Jehovah was, however, to be both. He was both the sin offering and the guilt offering.

While Jesus definitely was a sin offering, He was not a sinner and did not become a sinner on the Cross. To have done so would have destroyed His perfection of sacrifice, which was demanded by God. In other words, the sacrifice had to be perfect, and He was perfect in every respect, and He never became imperfect at any point in time.

For a person to be a sinner, he has to sin, and Jesus did not sin. He could not become a sinner, but He could and did become a sin offering.

IN HELL?

David addressed this by saying, *"For You will not leave My soul in Hell; neither will You suffer Your Holy One to see corruption"* (Ps. 16:10).

The entirety of the underworld, including Paradise, is spoken of as *Hell.* While Jesus did go into the Paradise part of Hell, He never went to the burning side of Hell (Lk. 16:19-31).

For Jesus to have gone to the burning side of Hell when He died, at least His soul and spirit, this would mean that He saw corruption. The Scripture plainly says, *"neither will You suffer Your Holy One to see corruption."*

SO WHERE DID THE SOUL AND THE SPIRIT OF OUR LORD GO WHEN HE DIED ON THE CROSS?

Peter said, **"For Christ also has once suffered for sins** (*the suffering of Christ on the Cross was but for one purpose, and that was for sins; while we as believers might suffer because of sin, such is never in the realm of atonement; the price has been fully paid, which means there is nothing left owing*), **the just for the unjust** (*Christ was the perfect sacrifice, the One who was born without original sin, and who lived a perfect life, never failing even in one point; He* *alone was the Just)*, **that He might bring us to God** *(refers to the way being opened for sinful man to come into the very presence of God)*, **being put to death in the flesh** *(refers to the fact that Jesus died physically in order to serve as a sacrifice, which means He didn't die spiritually, as some claim!)*, **but quickened by the Spirit** *(raised from the dead by the Holy Spirit [Rom. 8:11])*:

"**By which also He went** *(between the time of His death and resurrection)* **and preached** *(announced something)* **unto the spirits in prison** *(does not refer to humans, but rather to fallen angels; humans in the Bible are never referred to in this particular manner; these were probably the fallen angels who tried to corrupt the human race by cohabiting with women [II Pet. 2:4; Jude Vss. 6-7]; these fallen angels are still locked up in this underworld prison)*;

"**Which sometime** *(in times past)* **were disobedient** *(this was shortly before the Flood)*, **when once the long-suffering of God waited in the days of Noah** *(refers to this eruption of fallen angels with women taking place at the time of Noah; this was probably a hundred or so years before the Flood)*, **while the Ark was a preparing** *(these fallen angels were committing this particular sin while the Ark was being made ready, however long it took, the Scripture doesn't say!)*, **wherein few, that is eight souls were saved by water.**" *(This doesn't refer to being saved from sin. These eight souls were saved from drowning in the Flood by being in the Ark)* **(I Pet. 3:18-20).**

Incidentally, those fallen angels are still there presently locked up and will be released only when they are cast into the lake of fire, which will take place at the conclusion of the kingdom age (Rev. 20:10-15).

When Jesus died, His soul and spirit also went down into Paradise and liberated everyone there and took them to Heaven with Him. Since the Cross, when a believer dies, his soul and spirit instantly go to Heaven to be with Jesus (Phil. 1:23).

Before the Cross, due to the fact that the blood of bulls and goats could not take away sins (Heb. 10:4), all the righteous souls went down into Paradise. While they were comforted there, they were still captives of Satan. It was not until the Cross, which satisfied the terrible sin debt, that they were delivered from this place, with it now empty.

Paul said: *"When He ascended up on high, He led captivity captive, and gave gifts unto men.*

"Now that He ascended, what is it but that He also descended first into the lower parts of the earth?" (Eph. 4:8-9).

Jesus stayed in the underworld some three days and three nights (Mat. 12:40). The only two things that the Bible said He did is what we related when addressing the fallen angels that were locked up (and still are) and then liberating all of those who were in Paradise.

Jesus never went to the burning side of Hell, for He is *"holy, harmless, undefiled, separate from sinners, and made higher than the heavens"* (Heb. 7:26).

As you will notice, the Scripture said, *"separate from sinners."*

THE FAT

All the fat, along with particular body parts, was to be burned on the brazen altar. This specified that God gave His best, as it regarded the giving of His only Son, and it also stated that all of our prosperity comes totally and completely from and through Jesus Christ and what He has done for us at the Cross.

THE GOAT

"And if his offering be a goat, then he shall offer it before the LORD.

"And he shall lay his hand upon the head of it, and kill it before the tabernacle of the congregation: and the sons of Aaron shall sprinkle the blood thereof upon the altar round about.

"And he shall offer thereof his offering, even an offering made by fire unto the LORD; the fat that covers the inwards, and all the fat that is upon the inwards" (Lev. 3:12-14).

The peace offering represented the blessedness and joyousness of communion between God and man. As someone has said, *"The character of these feasts cannot be mistaken. It was that of joyfulness tempered by solemnity, of solemnity tempered by joyfulness."*

Like the Passover, the peace offering at once commemorated a historical event and prefigured a blessing to come. The Passover, for instance, always looked backward to the deliverance from Egypt, but yet, forward to *Christ our Passover sacrificed for us.* In like manner, the peace offering commemorated the making of the covenant and prefigured the blessed state of communion to be brought about by the sacrifice of the Cross.

THE INTENT OF THE SACRIFICE

As is obvious, in this one chapter, the Lord portrays three different animals as potential offerings — the heifer, the lamb, and the goat. The instructions for the offering of each were basically the same.

This is to impress upon us the fact that even though the heifer was of greater value, as would be obvious, still, it was the intent of the sacrifice and what it represented, at least in the eyes of God, that really mattered.

More than likely, the goat was the least valuable of the three animals. But yet, this particular sacrifice had to be given the same attention as the sacrifice of the heifer.

The idea is this: All of these sacrifices, which necessitated the shedding of innocent blood, represented Christ. It was not so much what the animal was, providing it was one specified by the Lord, as to what was done with the animal as it regarded the sacrifice. Its blood was shed, which referred to the giving of its life, and all because sin had been committed.

I've had some to ask me the question, *"Are we saved because of who Jesus is, or what Jesus has done?"*

WHO JESUS WAS AND WHAT JESUS DID!

What was done, and I speak of the Cross, could not have been done by anyone other than Christ. So, it should go without saying that who He was, which refers to the God-Man, Jesus Christ, was an absolute necessity for redemption to be brought about. In other words, it was both — who He was and what He did!

The ridiculous idea put forth by the Word of Faith teachers that any born-again man could have redeemed humanity is worse than ridiculous; it borders on blasphemy. For a perfect sacrifice to be offered, only Jesus, the Son of God, could do such a thing.

However, I must remind the reader that Jesus has always been God. As God, He had no beginning — was not formed, was not made, was not created, and, in fact, has always been. However, I also remind the reader that as God, He did not redeem anyone. Now, think about that for a moment! If the mere fact of who He was would redeem people, then the Cross was unnecessary.

No, while it was definitely necessary that Christ be who He was, it was what He did, and I refer to the Cross, which brought about redemption. And yet, I say it again, only who He was made it all possible.

The Virgin Birth, as wonderful and necessary as it was, didn't save anyone. The miracles and healings of Christ, as wonderful and necessary as they were, didn't save anyone. For men to be saved, Christ had to go to the Cross and give Himself, which He did. Paul said, *"Who gave Himself for our sins, that He might deliver us from this present evil world, according to the will of God and our Father"* (Gal. 1:4).

THE OBJECT OF OUR FAITH

Almost all Christians talk about faith. When they do so, they are speaking of faith in the Word, faith in Christ, faith in the Lord, etc., which are all correct terms, at least as far as they go. In fact, *the object of our faith* and *"he correct object of faith* are terms that most Christians have little heard, if at all. But yet, there is nothing more important than the correct object of one's faith. What do we mean by that?

For faith to be that which God will recognize, it has to have the finished work of Christ as its object. In fact, to just merely say, *"I have faith in the Lord"* or, *"I have faith in the Word,"* and stop there, while correct as far as it goes, it really does not say, as stated, much of anything.

Most Christians have been taught that if they need something, whatever it might be, they should find two or three Scriptures that seem to apply themselves to that particular need, memorize them, and then quote them over and over. Somehow, at least according to this teaching, this is supposed to move God to action.

In truth, it doesn't move God to anything. While memorizing the Scriptures is wonderful and should be done by all believers, and while quoting the Scriptures is even more wonderful and should be done by all believers, our thinking that doing such in this fashion will bring about some positive results is actually white magic. This is the very opposite of black magic, which attempts to manipulate the spirit world of darkness in order to appease demon spirits or get them to do something positive for us. This has to do with witchcraft.

WHITE MAGIC

White magic is that which seeks to manipulate the spirit world of righteousness, to get the Lord to do something for you. Both, as should be obvious, are wrong!

The Lord responds to one thing only, and that is faith (Gal. 5:6), but it must be faith in the correct object, and that correct object is *Jesus Christ and Him crucified* (I Cor. 1:23).

Any other type of so-called faith that a person seeks to exhibit falls into the category of manipulation. It should be understood that God cannot be manipulated by anyone. He sees through whatever is on the surface, even to the very heart, and knows the motive behind all things. While our intention may not be to manipulate Him, still, if we are functioning in a wrong manner, it constitutes manipulation, whether we intend it or not, which God can never honor.

THE SACRIFICE OF CHRIST

The believer must ever understand that all faith, at least the type that God recognizes, must have as its object the sacrifice of Christ. The Lord dealt with Abraham, and the Scripture says that Abraham believed God, and God accounted it to him for righteousness. We must ask the question as to what Abraham believed.

Jesus answered that Himself by saying to the children of Israel, *"Your father Abraham rejoiced to see My day, and he saw it, and was glad"* (Jn. 8:56).

Abraham wasn't merely believing that there is a God; he was believing rather what God had said about redemption. In other words, through Abraham and Sarah, a child would be born, and somewhere in the future through this lineage, the Redeemer would be born into the world. He would give His life in order to bring about redemption for Adam's fallen race.

In effect, Abraham had placed his faith in Christ and Him crucified. Even though he might not have understood those terms, that's actually what he was doing.

In fact, if you as a believer properly understand the statement, *"Abraham believed God, and God accounted it to him for righteousness,"* you can understand, in effect, the entirety of the Bible. If you don't properly understand that term, you really cannot rightly understand the Word.

RIGHTEOUSNESS

This tells us that all righteousness comes entirely through one's faith and never by works. Paul said, *"I do not frustrate the grace of God: for if righteousness come by the Law, then Christ is dead in vain"* (Gal. 2:21).

This means that if anyone can earn righteousness in any manner, then Christ simply did not have to come down here and die on a Cross. Worse than that, His death was all in vain. However, what is actually happening?

What is actually happening pertains to the fact that most of the modern church is seeking to earn righteousness in some way. They think that by belonging to a certain church or a certain denomination, this will bring righteousness. Many think that being baptized in water, taking the Lord's Supper, joining the church, participating in any number of good works, etc., brings about righteousness. In fact, the list is long!

Even though these things may or may not be good in their own right, none of them bring about righteousness, for righteousness cannot be bought, purchased, or earned. The peace offering was a perfect representation of that.

HOW CAN ONE ATTAIN TO RIGHTEOUSNESS?

In other words, how can one be righteous?

There is only one way, and that is by one placing one's faith exclusively in Christ and what Christ has done for us at the Cross. Then, a perfect, pure, and spotless righteousness, the righteousness of God, is awarded to such a person. All it takes is faith, but it must be faith in Christ and the Cross.

Every believer should understand the following: Sin had been committed! A sin offering or trespass offering had been presented along with a meat (grain) offering. This atoned for sin because it represented Christ who was to come. With sin atoned, righteousness now was the sole object in the life of the believer. In recognition of that, a peace offering was presented. Part of it was burned on the altar, which meant it was given to God, part was eaten by the priests, who were types of Christ, and part was eaten by the sinner, his family, and his friends. It was a joyous occasion because peace had been restored, and had been restored because of what Christ would do at the Cross, which, of course, was then future.

All of this was fulfilled with Christ. Now, there is no need for animal sacrifices or grain sacrifices of any nature, with all having been fulfilled in Christ. Now, in order to obtain righteousness, as stated, all one has to do is simply express faith in Christ and what Christ has done for us at the Cross.

A PERFECT OFFERING TO COME

As previously stated, the Jew was not taught that the death of the animal was accepted instead of his punishment, but he was instructed to look upon it as a foreshadowing of a perfect offering to come. This may not be apparent with just a cursory glance at the Pentateuch, but the New Testament commentary leaves no doubt on the question. Paul said, *"It is not possible that the blood of bulls and goats should take away sins"*; and the first tabernacle was *"a figure for the time then present"*; and then, *"the Law having a shadow of good things to come, and not the very image"* (or full revelation). And finally, *"Of the things, can never with those sacrifices*

*which they offered year by year continually make the com-
ers thereunto perfect." As the writer said, "This is not a
contradiction of the Old Testament, but an explanation of
the Mosaic dispensation"* (Heb. 13:20; 10:1).

Jesus said to Israel, *"Had you believed Moses, you would
have believed Me: for he wrote of Me"* (Jn. 5:46). That the
sacrifices were nothing in themselves was a lesson constantly
brought before the Jews. Through the prophets, the Lord said
to them, *"To what purpose is the multitude of your sacrifices unto Me? saith the* LORD: *I am full of the burnt offerings of rams, and the fat of fed beasts; and I delight not
in the blood of bullocks, or of lambs, or of he-goats"* (Isa.
1:11). This meant, as should be overly obvious, that there
was nothing in the sacrifices themselves that was effective for
atonement. Israel's thinking that there was, was merely a per-
version of the truth.

Unfortunately, we seem to be doing the same thing presently by making the church, or some man-made rule or regulation, the object of our faith instead of Christ and Him crucified.
Righteousness can never be attained in this manner.

IS THE OBJECT OF FAITH THAT IMPORTANT?

I'll tell you how important it is!

Israel lost her way so badly that she didn't even know her
Messiah when He came, and it was all because the object of her
faith was moved from what the sacrifices represented, namely
Christ, to something else. It really didn't matter what the something else was, whether the sacrifices themselves, the ritual of
the Law itself, or whatever. Unless it was faith in Christ and
Him crucified, then it wasn't faith that God would recognize.

This is true, as well, as it regards the modern church. Satan tries to pull the faith of believers away from the Cross to other things, and he really doesn't care too very much what those other things are. They may be good in their own right, but still, if they become the object of one's faith, then that means the object of one's faith is not the Cross. This, in effect, puts that believer in a position of making war on God (Rom. 8:7).

THE CARNAL MIND AND THE SPIRITUAL MIND

Paul said, *"For to be carnally minded is death; but to be spiritually minded is life and peace"* (Rom. 8:6).

What did Paul mean by that?

Were I to ask most Christians what *carnally minded"* means, their answers would be mostly in this vein: They would claim that it refers to watching too much television, going fishing too often, being too interested in the stock market, or 101 other similar things.

The truth is, those things, which may or may not be harmful, have absolutely nothing to do with what Paul is addressing here as it regards being carnally minded.

To be carnally minded refers to the believer who is trusting in anything other than Christ and Him crucified. Without going into a lot of detail, let the reader understand that when we say *"anything,"* we are meaning *anything.* For our victory, our power, our strength, our holiness, our righteousness, our Christlikeness — and, in fact, every single thing that we receive from the Lord — we must ever understand that, without exception, it all comes through Christ and what He did at the Cross. When you understand that, believe that, and act upon that, that's being spiritually minded (Rom. 8:1–2). To believe something else, which means to make something else other than the Cross the object of one's faith, is being carnally minded.

ENMITY

Paul then said, *"Because the carnal mind is enmity against God: for it is not subject to the Law of God, neither indeed can be"* (Rom. 8:7).

The word *enmity*, as it is used here, refers to hatred or war. In other words, the carnal mind has declared war against God. That's a strong statement, but we must remember that the Holy Spirit is the One who has said this, using Paul as His instrument.

It is a shame when we realize that the majority of Christians, even those who truly love God and are sincerely trying to serve Him, are, in fact, at war with God. They are seeking to bring about nearness to Him through means other than simple faith in Christ and the Cross, which puts them at cross-purposes with God. In other words, as stated, whether they realize it or not, they have declared war on God, and that's a perilous situation for a believer to be in.

Let the believer understand that it's not so much what we do as what we believe. To be sure, what we believe is going to play out in what we do, but the correct doing cannot be brought about until we have correct believing (Jn. 3:16; Eph. 2:8–9; Rom. 6:3–14).

THE FAT AND THE BLOOD

"And the two kidneys, and the fat that is upon them, which is by the flanks, and the caul above the liver, with the kidneys, it shall he take away.

"And the priest shall burn them upon the altar: it is the food of the offering made by fire for a sweet savour: all the fat is the LORD's.

"It shall be a perpetual statute for your generations throughout all your dwellings, that you eat neither fat nor blood" (Lev. 3:15-17).

The fat, as stated, represented God giving His best, which was and is the Lord Jesus Christ. It also represented the prosperity of Israel and, as well, the saint presently. In other words, all true prosperity comes from the Lord and is made possible by what Christ did at the Cross, hence, the fat being burned upon the altar. Actually, this is what Jesus was speaking about when He said, *"Seek ye first the kingdom of God, and His righteousness; and all these things shall be added unto you"* (Mat. 6:33).

The true prosperity Gospel, and it definitely is prosperity, is Jesus Christ and Him crucified. The fat represented that. As well, it tells us how this prosperity is obtained, symbolized by the fat being burned on the altar, which was a type of Christ and His crucifixion.

The blood represented the price that Christ would pay in order for this prosperity to be brought about, whether spiritual or otherwise, hitherto the prohibition of eating fat or blood.

This prohibition was carried over into the New Covenant when James, the Lord's brother, stated: *"For it seemed good to the Holy Spirit, and to us, to lay upon you no greater burden than these necessary things;*

"That you abstain from meats offered to idols, and from blood, and from things strangled, and from fornication: from which if you keep yourselves, you shall do well" (Acts 15:28–29).

The prohibition given here against the eating of blood pertained, as well, to fat.

"I know not when the Lord will come,
"Or at what hour He may appear,
"Whether at midnight or at morn,
"Or at what season of the year."

"I know not what of time remains,
"To run its course in this low sphere,
"Or what awaits of calm or storm,
"Of joy or grief, of hope or fear."

"I know not what is yet to run
"Of spring or summer, green or sear,
"Of death or life, of pain or peace,
"Of shade or shine, of song or tear."

"The centuries have come and gone,
"Dark centuries of absence drear;
"I dare not chide the long delay,
"Nor ask when I His voice shall hear."

"I do not think it can be long,
"Till in His glory He appear;
"And yet I dare not name the day,
"Nor fix the solemn advent year."

4

The Sin Offering

CHAPTER FOUR

The Sin Offering

"AND THE LORD spake unto Moses, saying,

"Speak unto the children of Israel, saying, If a soul shall sin through ignorance against any of the commandments of the LORD concerning things which ought not to be done, and shall do against any of them:

"If the priest that is anointed do sin according to the sin of the people; then let him bring for his sin, which he has sinned, a young bullock without blemish unto the LORD for a sin offering" (Lev. 4:1-3).

This particular chapter represents the sin offering. Christ became a sin offering on the Cross (Isa. 53:10).

As we shall see, the words in the second verse, *"through ignorance,"* signify that a person cannot really know what sin actually is, irrespective of his knowledge of the Word of God. Oftentimes the church paints some sins as heinous, with others that are even more heinous being ignored altogether. All sin is heinous.

And yet, we find that man has a tendency to speak lightly of his own sin regardless of its dreadfulness. Actually, sin is a form of insanity.

The efficacy (effectiveness) of Christ's atonement for sin is not to be measured by man's consciousness of sin but by God's measurement of it. Sin is sin regardless of who commits it or when it is committed. So, according to Scripture, God deals with all who sin on the same basis.

In the burnt offering, the sinlessness of the victim was transferred to the worshipper. In the sin offering, the sinfulness of the sinner was transferred to the victim.

As we shall see, the sprinkling of the blood some seven times before the Lord portrays a perfect restoration, for the number seven proclaims the perfection, totality, and completeness of God.

In Verse 5, as we shall see, it says, *"and the priest who is anointed shall take,"* which refers to the high priest. Christ was anointed above all His fellows. He alone took the blood to the altar of worship, in a sense at Calvary, and sprinkled it before God, thereby, restoring fellowship. In fact, this is His high priestly role.

The *"blood upon the horns of the altar,"* speaks of the total dominion that Calvary brought about, which was brought about for believers. In other words, the Cross proclaims the fact that the believer can have victory over all sin. That doesn't speak of sinless perfection because the Bible doesn't teach such, but it does teach that sin is not to dominate us (Rom. 6:14).

IGNORANCE

"And the LORD spoke unto Moses, saying,
"Speak unto the children of Israel, saying, If a soul shall sin through ignorance against any of the commandments

of the LORD *concerning things which ought not to be done, and shall do against any of them"* (Lev. 4:1-2).

The burnt offering, the meal offering, and the peace offering were sweet savour offerings. The burnt offering portrayed Christ satisfying the demands of a thrice-holy God.

The meal offering was an offering of thanksgiving that would be presented along with the burnt offering, signifying thankfulness that the offering was accepted, and peace was restored.

The peace offering signified restoration and was almost always offered in conjunction with the burnt offering, as well as the sin or trespass offerings. All of these, as stated, were sweet savour offerings, but sacrifices for sin, which included sin offerings and trespass offerings, were not sweet savour offerings.

As we study the sin offerings, hopefully we will learn, at least as far as a human being can know, of the awfulness of sin and the price that was paid by the Saviour to rid us of this evil monster.

The sin offering typified the sacrifice of our Lord Jesus Christ upon the Cross as the great sin offering for mankind, whereby the wrath of God was propitiated (to appease or to conciliate), and an expiation (to pay the penalty; to atone) for the sins of man was wrought, bringing about reconciliation between God and man.

SINS OF IGNORANCE

The sins of ignorance addressed here portray to us amazing truths — truths we desperately need to know. When we think upon the atonement, what Jesus did for us, we soon find out that what was accomplished at the Cross addressed far more than the mere satisfaction of the conscience. In fact, even though the conscience may have reached a state of refined spirituality, which means that one is deep in the Lord and has an excellent understanding of His Word, still, this cannot be a guide as it regards the terrible problem of sin.

We know beyond the shadow of a doubt that the Cross of Christ addressed every aspect of sin in all of its horror and all of its effect. In fact, the Holy Spirit through Paul said, *"Knowing this, that our old man is crucified with Him, that the body of sin might be destroyed, that henceforth we should not serve sin"* (Rom. 6:6).

THE GUILT OF SIN

This tells us that not only was the power of sin broken at the Cross, but, as well, the guilt of sin was taken away.

Also, what Jesus did at the Cross not only addressed sin as it appears on this earth, especially in the hearts and lives of men, but it went to the very root of sin, which is Satan himself and all that he did in his revolution against God. Again, Paul said, *"That in the dispensation of the fullness of times He (God the Father) might gather together in one all things in Christ, both which are in Heaven, and which are on earth; even in Him"* (Eph. 1:10).

This tells us that the Cross not only addressed earth but Heaven as well!

So, the more we learn of the Cross, which these sacrifices teach us, the more we will learn of the horror of sin. The more we learn of that horror, the more we will learn that it was only the Cross that could address this monster. Man is foolish to think that his efforts to assuage sin can have any effect. Irrespective as to what he does, how much the intellect may address the problem, or how much money is thrown at the problem, the fact remains that all man can do is address the external, which really presents only the effects of sin. The core of sin began with Satan and has incorporated itself in the hearts of the unredeemed. It can only be addressed by the individual being born again. Jesus told Nicodemus, *"Verily, verily, I say unto you, except a man be born again, he cannot see the Kingdom of God"* (Jn. 3:3).

MAN'S STANDARD VERSUS GOD'S STANDARD

Concerning this, Mackintosh said, *"The holiness of God's dwelling place, and the ground of His association with His people, could never be regulated by the standard of man's conscience, no matter how high the standard might be. There are many things which man's conscience would pass over — many things which might escape man's cognizance — many things which his heart might deem alright, which God could not tolerate; and which, as a consequence, would interfere with man's approach to, his worship of, and his relationship with God.*

"Wherefore if the atonement of Christ merely made provision for such sins as come within the compass of man's apprehension, we should find ourselves very far short of the true ground of peace. We need to understand that sin has been atoned for, according to God's measurement thereof — that the claims of His throne have been perfectly answered — that sin, as seen in the light of His inflexible holiness, has been divinely judged. This is what gives settled peace to the soul. A full atonement has been made for the believer's sins of ignorance, as well as for his known sins."

GOD'S PRESCRIBED ORDER
FOR VICTORIOUS LIVING

The Cross deals not only with the salvation of the sinner but, as well, the sanctification of the saint. This is the great problem of the modern church. It has a modicum of understanding as it regards the Cross and salvation, but none at all as it regards the Cross and sanctification. We are talking about how we order our behavior, how we obtain victory over the world, the flesh, and the Devil, in other words, how we live for God. The truth is, the Cross of Christ plays as much of a part in our sanctification as it does our salvation; however, as stated, the church doesn't have a clue as to this of which I have just said.

Every single thing the believer has from God is made possible by the power of the Holy Spirit, according to what Jesus Christ did for us at the Cross, and I mean everything. In fact, almost every time Paul addressed the Cross, it was done so regarding believers (Rom. 6:1-14; 8:1-11; Gal. 6:14; I Cor. 1:17, 18, 23; 2:2; Col. 2:10-15). So, the Message of the Cross regards salvation from sin and victory over sin.

PLEASE NOTICE CAREFULLY

The following two diagrams will hopefully explain more fully what we are saying. The first is God's prescribed order:

- **Focus:** The focus of the believer must ever be on Christ and Him crucified (Rom. 6:3–14; I Cor. 1:23).

- **Object of faith:** With the focus being the Cross, the object of faith must always be the finished work of Christ (I Cor. 1:17–18; 2:2).
- **Power source:** If our focus is right, which means our object of faith is correct, our power source will then be the Holy Spirit, who works exclusively within the framework of the finished work of Christ, without whom we can do nothing (Rom. 8:1–2, 11).
- **Results:** With God's prescribed order followed, it will always bring victorious results and will do so perpetually. No, that doesn't mean sinless perfection, for the Bible doesn't teach such, but it does mean that sin will not have dominion over such a believer (Rom. 6:14).

THE DIRECTION OF THE MODERN CHURCH

Now let's look at this order that has been perverted, even as it has presently by the majority of the modern church because the church has had so little teaching on the Cross. The following is a diagram of defeat:

- **Focus:** The Cross is ignored, with works becoming the focus.
- **Object of faith:** With works now being prominent, our performance becomes the object of our faith.
- **Power source:** With the focus being on works and the object of faith now being our performance, the power source becomes self. The Holy Spirit will not function in such an atmosphere.

- **Results:** Trying to live this life in the fashion we've just described guarantees failure on every hand.

But yet, the far greater majority of the modern church is trying to live for God by functioning according to the second diagram. Most are doing this through ignorance.

THE MODERN SINS OF IGNORANCE

As repeatedly stated, God's prescribed order is Jesus Christ and Him crucified, meaning that our faith must ever be in the finished work of Christ, which then gives the Holy Spirit latitude to work within our lives. To try to function outside of this prescribed order is, pure and simple, rebellion against God, which, in effect, is a sin of the highest order. It is an insult to Christ. In effect, whether we realize it or not, it is actually saying that what He did at the Cross was not enough, and we need to add to His sacrifice. It puts us in the position of trying to do what no human being has ever done and, in fact, that which no human being can ever do. If man could somehow save himself, which refers to making himself holy or righteous, then Jesus would not have had to come down to this earth and die on a Cross. Paul bluntly said, *"If righteousness come by the Law, then Christ is dead in vain"* (Gal. 2:21).

REBELLION AGAINST GOD

Most people do not think of such action as sin. Actually, it is a declaration of war against God. This means it is not only sin, it is sin of the highest order and, as stated, rebellion against God. In fact, it is against the entirety of the plan of God. It is committing the same sin that Cain committed when he attempted to offer to God a sacrifice of the labor of his own hands instead of offering up that which God had demanded — an innocent victim, i.e., a lamb. Unfortunately, the problem didn't die with Cain; it remains with the human race unto this hour. In fact, the problem today is worse than ever. As we've said repeatedly, in the last several decades, the church has had so little teaching on the Cross that for all practical purposes, it is presently Cross-illiterate. Being in that condition, it has only one recourse, and that is to try to sail this ship alone, so to speak. That is sin against God because rebellion against His prescribed order, even though it's done in ignorance, is still sin, and it will still reap the terrible consequences that sin reaps.

Paul said: *"Because the carnal mind is enmity against God (war with God) for it is not subject to the Law of God, neither indeed can be.*

"So then they that are in the flesh cannot please God" (Rom. 8:7-8).

THE CROSS

Every iota of salvation, victory, blessings from the Lord, and worship as it regards the Lord — all and without exception pertain to the Cross. To the degree that we understand the Cross, to that degree will we have victory in all of these things mentioned, and many things not mentioned. To the degree that we do not understand the Cross, to that degree we will suffer!

That's one reason that Satan fights the Cross so hard and why all false doctrine has its roots, in some way, in opposition to the Cross.

During Paul's time, the great opposition to the Cross was the message of the Judaizers, which was the Law/grace issue. Teachers out of Jerusalem and Judea were pushing and promoting the Law while also professing Christ. In other words, they were trying to get Gentile believers to accept the Law of Moses, or at least parts of the Law. Paul, in answering this false message, said, **"Christ is become of no effect unto you, whosoever of you are justified by the Law** *(seek to be justified by the Law)*; **you are fallen from grace"** **(Gal. 5:4).**

While there have been many false doctrines down through the many centuries from the time of the early church to the present, perhaps the worst of all, because we're nearing the very end, is the so-called Word of Faith doctrine. The reader may not quite understand why we address this issue so very, very much. We do so because this doctrine bitterly opposes the Cross. In fact, one could only say as it regards its teachers and adherents, *"For many walk, of whom I have told you often, and now tell you even weeping, that they are the enemies of the Cross of Christ."*

The apostle went on to say, *"Whose end is destruction, whose God is their belly, and whose glory is in their shame, who mind earthly things"* (Phil. 3:18–19).

THE SIN OFFERING

"If the priest who is anointed do sin according to the sin of the people; then let him bring for his sin, which he has sinned, a young bullock without blemish unto the LORD *for a sin offering"* (Lev. 4:3).

The sin that was committed here, which was a sin of ignorance and was committed by a priest, in some way has a negative effect on the people. That is what is meant by the words, *"according to the sin of the people."* In some way, his sin caused them to sin; to do things wrong.

The priest was to select for a sin offering a young bullock, which was to be offered up to God. It was to be without blemish. Before we deal with this particular sin, let's first of all address ourselves to the sin offering per se.

Nothing can more forcibly express man's incompetency to deal with sin than the fact of there being such a thing as a sin of ignorance. Man's ignorance of sin proves his total inability to put it away.

To more fully understand the sin offering, perhaps it would be best to compare it with the burnt offering. In doing this, we will find the two very different aspects of Christ. Although these aspects may be different, it is still one and the same Christ; hence, the sacrifice in each case was to be without blemish.

In the burnt offering, Christ is seen meeting the divine demands; in the sin offering, He is seen meeting the depths of human need. In the former, we learn of the preciousness of the sacrifice; in the latter, the hatefulness of sin.

VOLUNTARY WILL

When considering the burnt offering, we observe that it was a voluntary offering. *"He shall offer it of his own voluntary will."* Now, the word *voluntary* does not occur in the sin offering.

In the sin offering, we have quite a different line of truth unfolding. The sin offering introduced Christ as the bearer of that terrible thing called sin and, as well, the endurer of all its appalling consequences. The sin offering alone furnished the fitting type of the Lord Jesus as the One who poured forth those accents of intense agony. In it alone do we find the circumstances which evoked such accents from the depths of His spotless soul. The young bullock signified Christ as a young man without sin, dying in man's place. In other words, He, *"without blemish unto the Lord,"* became a sin offering. In the burnt offering, the sinlessness of the victim was transferred to the worshipper. In the sin offering, the sinfulness of the sinner was transferred to the victim. So there was a vast difference in the burnt offering as a type of Christ, which it was, than the sin offering, which was also a type of Christ.

As we go further into the text, we shall see exactly how the sin offering so typified Christ.

THE SIN OF THE PREACHER

While there is no more office of the priest, that having been fulfilled in Christ, the church now has apostles, prophets, evangelists, pastors, and teachers (Eph. 4:11). When preachers or teachers wrongly explain to people how to live for God and how to walk in victory, which means that they direct them to that other than the Cross, such direction will cause the people to sin. The preacher is sinning when he gives them such false direction, and such false direction will always result in their sinning as well.

There is only one way to have dominion over sin, and that is by understanding the Cross and our part in that finished work (Rom. 6:3–5, 14).

While all of this — the sin committed by the preacher and the resultant sin of the people — is done in ignorance, it is still sin. It will still reap bitter results, and it must be washed by the blood and put away.

As well, the preacher giving such wrong direction is living a life of spiritual failure himself. It cannot be otherwise! If he knew and understood the Cross, he would be preaching the Cross (I Cor. 1:17–18, 21, 23; 2:2). However, not knowing and understanding the Cross, he preaches something else as the answer, which, of course, is no answer at all.

WORKS OF THE FLESH

But let all understand, such a preacher — even though God may be using him, and he, at the same time, may be very sincere before the Lord — without understanding the Cross, cannot live a life of spiritual victory. In some way, the works of the flesh are functioning through him. If he'll be honest with himself, which is not easy to do, he will admit that something is wrong (Gal. 5:19–21). There can never be settled peace upon this ground. There will always be the painful apprehension that there is something wrong underneath. If the heart be not led into settled repose by the Scripture testimony that the inflexible claims of divine justice have been answered, there must of necessity be a sensation of uneasiness. Every such sensation presents a barrier to our worship, our communion, and our testimony.

THE SETTLEMENT OF THE QUESTION OF SIN

The truth is, if one is uneasy in reference to the settlement of the question of sin, one cannot properly worship, cannot properly enjoy communion with God or His people, and cannot be an intelligent or effective witness for Christ.

The heart must be at rest before God as to the perfect remission of sin, or else we cannot worship Him in spirit and in truth. If there be guilt on the conscience, and most definitely, if the preacher is preaching something that's not scriptural, even though done in ignorance, there must be, at the same time, terror in the heart, even though one may try to cover such terror or even refuse to admit such.

It is only from a heart filled with that sweet and sacred repose, which the blood of Christ imparts, that true and acceptable worship can ascend to the Father.

THE HAND LAID ON THE HEAD

"And he shall bring the bullock unto the door of the tabernacle of the congregation before the LORD; and shall lay his hand upon the bullock's head, and kill the bullock before the LORD" (Lev. 4:4).

The *"priest that is anointed,"* as given in Verse 3, refers to the high priest. If he sinned through ignorance or otherwise, it was required of him that a bullock be sacrificed. While all sin is terrible, and while it is a terrible thing for anyone to sin, the sin of a leader, as typified here by the high priest, causes far more damage to the work of God, as certainly would be obvious. To be sure, the remedy for his sin is the same as the remedy for all others, even as there can be no other remedy. The most valuable of all the clean animals that could be offered for sacrifice was a bullock; therefore, a bullock was demanded to be offered in order that the import of such a sin might be known and understood.

For instance, when David sinned by committing adultery with Bath-sheba and then murdering her husband Uriah, the impact on the work of God, not to speak of David, was awful to behold. Many others in Israel, no doubt, committed the same sin at one time or the other. Although the sin was just as heinous, irrespective as to who would have committed it, still, the impact was far greater when committed by David. But yet, the blood of the lamb was David's recourse just as it is with all others (Ps. 51).

THE DOOR

The door stood for the tabernacle proper but included the brazen altar and even the brazen laver. It actually pertained to the entire apparatus of the plan of God.

The door, as given here, was a type of Christ (Jn. 10:9). This means that it is through Christ and Christ alone that sin can be addressed, washed, cleansed, and put away. Of course it is done, even as we shall see, by and through what Christ did at the Cross.

While our Lord is God and, in fact, has always been God and always will be God, it is not as God per se that He gives us all these things. It is as the Man, Jesus Christ, that all of this is done (Jn., Chpt. 10). More particularly, it is the reason that He became a man, which was to go to the Cross, which He did, that makes all these things possible. When I say all these things, I am referring to every single thing the Lord does for us, irrespective as to what it might be, but most particularly, I'm referring to sin.

SIN

Sin cannot be addressed, cannot be cleansed and removed, and cannot be handled correctly except by and through Jesus Christ and what He has done for us at the

Cross. Concerning this, Paul said: **"But this man** (*the Lord Jesus Christ*), **after He had offered one sacrifice for sins** (*the only sacrifice that God would accept, which was the sacrifice of Himself*) **forever, sat down on the right hand of God** (*which refers to the task being completed and thereby accepted*)" (**Heb. 10:12**).

Through and by this great sacrifice, Paul went on to say, *"From henceforth expecting till His enemies be made His footstool"* (Heb. 10:13).

This means that Calvary has defeated every single enemy, irrespective of what it might be. This means that you, through Christ, which refers to faith in His Cross, can vanquish every enemy. Paul also said, *"And has put all things under His feet, and gave Him to be the head over all things to the church, which is His body, the fullness of Him who fills all in all"* (Eph. 1:22–23).

In other words, the church, and I speak of the true church, is the body of Christ. Understanding that the feet are on the body, this means that Christ overcame at the Cross in order that we might be the overcomers that we must be. This can only be by and through faith in Christ and what He has done for us in His great sacrifice.

Unfortunately, most of the modern church, the Pentecostal varieties included, are telling people to take their sins to psychologists, i.e., the psychological way.

Let me give you an example. The Assemblies of God and the Church of God, the two largest so-called Pentecostal denominations, have gone the psychological way. This probably includes most, if not all, the other denominations, as well. In these Pentecostal denominations, if a preacher has a problem with sin of any nature, before he can be accepted in good standing, he must be signed off by a psychologist, which demands several months of so-called psychological therapy.

AN INSULT

There could be no higher insult to Christ than this abominable practice. Humanistic psychology is a lie from beginning to end. It holds no answer, has no help, and can provide no satisfaction whatsoever as it regards victory over sin. It is humanistic wisdom, which James said is *"earthly, sensual, and devilish"* (James 3:15).

Such a direction can be construed as none other than ungodly! For such to be demanded, in effect, is a vote of no confidence as it regards Christ and His Cross. It must ever be understood that one cannot have both. The Cross cancels out psychology while psychology cancels out the Cross. As stated, one cannot have both.

Jesus said: *"No man can serve two masters: for either he will hate the one, and love the other; or else he will hold to the one, and despise the other. You cannot serve God and mammon"* (Mat. 6:24).

The problem is, most of the church doesn't understand at all what the Cross means as it regards the sanctification of the saint. This refers to how one is to live for God. As I have stated in one way or the other over and over in this volume, the church, for all practical purposes, seeks to live for God in all the wrong ways. In other words, it simply doesn't know how to live for the Lord. The reason for that is that it doesn't understand the Cross as it regards sanctification. Once again, please bear with my repetition.

The entirety of Paul's teaching centers up on this very subject, and is done so in all of his 14 epistles. The following is very abbreviated but is basically what the great apostle taught, even as it was given to him by Christ (Gal. 1:12).

THE CROSS

Paul said: *"Don't you know, that so many of us as were baptized into Jesus Christ were baptized into His death?*

"Therefore we are buried with Him by baptism into death: that like as Christ was raised up from the dead by the glory of the Father, even so we also should walk in newness of life.

"For if we have been planted together in the likeness of His death, we shall be also in the likeness of His resurrection" (Rom. 6:3–5).

This, along with so many other passages, tells us that everything comes to us by the Cross. Salvation is made possible by and through the Cross alone, even as is everything else.

So, the believer should settle the fact in his or her mind that every single thing we receive from the Lord, irrespective as to what it is, is all made possible in totality by Christ and what He did for us in the sacrifice of Himself. This means that the believer should be zeroed in on the Cross at all times, actually making that his emphasis, which, of course, is the work of Christ.

That's why Paul also said, *"For Christ sent me not to baptize, but to preach the Gospel: not with wisdom of words, lest the Cross of Christ should be made of none effect"* (I Cor. 1:17).

The apostle was not demeaning water baptism, but rather making the point that the emphasis must always be on the Cross and nothing else, even as important as the other things might be in their own right. Incidentally, in Romans 6:3-5, Paul is not speaking of water baptism, but rather using the word *baptism*, figuratively speaking, to describe what Christ did on the Cross and how that we by faith are literally in *Him* as it refers to that great work.

FAITH

The apostle also said, *"Likewise reckon you also yourselves to be dead indeed unto sin, but alive unto God through Jesus Christ our Lord"* (Rom. 6:11). This refers to faith. In other words, Jesus Christ and Him crucified must ever be the object of our faith.

Even as we have said over and over again, the object of faith is all-important. If Satan trips up the believer, this is where he does it most of all.

The Evil One tries to get our faith moved from the Cross of Christ to other things. He doesn't much care what the other things are, just as long as it isn't the Cross of Christ.

Once we begin to question Christians, we can quickly find out what the object of their faith actually is, and you would be surprised simply because it covers the waterfront, so to speak.

Without going into all types of detail, let the reader understand that the object of faith must always be the Cross of Christ, which, at the same time, is the same as saying that it's faith in the Word simply because the story of the Bible is the story of Jesus Christ and Him crucified. As stated, this is where Satan fights the hardest. That's why Paul again said, *"Fight the good fight of faith, lay hold on eternal life, whereunto you are also called"* (I Tim. 6:12).

Actually, in the original text, the definite article is placed in front of the word faith, making it read *"the* faith," which refers to the body of faith, not so much the act of faith. In fact, the term *the faith* refers to Jesus Christ and Him crucified, just as the term *in Christ* refers to the same.

The idea is, if your faith isn't anchored in the Cross of Christ, then what you have might be faith, but it's not the faith. So, the Cross of Christ must always, and without exception, be the object of our faith.

THE HOLY SPIRIT

Listen again to Paul: **"But if the Spirit** *(Holy Spirit)* **of Him** *(God the Father)* **who raised up Jesus from the dead dwell in you, He who raised up Christ from the dead shall also quicken your mortal bodies by His Spirit who dwells in you"** (Rom. 8:11).

This is not speaking of the coming resurrection, although it certainly does include that. It is rather speaking of the working of the Holy Spirit within our hearts and lives to help us live the life we ought to live.

This means that the same power that raised Jesus from the dead is available to us and is available at all times. Now, if we properly understand that, we certainly should realize that victory should be ours in every respect.

The Holy Spirit doesn't demand a lot of us, but He does demand that our faith be anchored in Christ and what Christ did for us in the sacrifice of Himself.

Jesus said of the Holy Spirit, *"He shall glorify Me: for He shall receive of Mine, and shall show it unto you"* (Jn. 16:14).

The Holy Spirit alone can make us what we ought to be in Christ; however, He works one way and one way only, and that is by the Cross of Christ. In other words, it is the Cross that gave and gives the Holy Spirit the legal means to do all that He does within us and for us. He doesn't require much of us, but He does require one thing, and that is that our faith be exclusively in Christ and the Cross (Rom. 8:2). With our faith properly placed and properly maintained, the Holy Spirit, to be sure, can then work unhindered within our hearts and within our lives, which He most definitely will, and which He strongly desires to do. If the believer places his or her faith in anything other than the Cross of Christ, and it doesn't really matter what the other thing might be, the Holy Spirit will not honor such.

SPIRITUAL ADULTERY

When the believer places his or her faith in something other than Christ and Him crucified, this means that such a believer is being unfaithful to Christ, which God looks at as spiritual adultery (Rom. 7:1-4). One can well imagine the damage that physical adultery causes in a marriage, and it is the same with spiritual adultery. But yet, sadly, this is where most believers presently are. Not understanding the Cross as it refers to our everyday living for God, they place their faith in something else, which, as stated, is spiritual adultery. To be unfaithful in any capacity is bad, but to be unfaithful to Christ is the worst of all.

What I have given you in a very abbreviated way is, in fact, God's prescribed order of victory. I might quickly add, it is His only prescribed order of victory. Other than the Cross of Christ, He has no other because no other is needed!

SHALL LAY HIS HAND UPON THE BULLOCK'S HEAD

This act was common both to the burnt offering and the sin offering, but in the case of the former, even as we've already stated, it identified the offerer with an unblemished offering. In the case of the latter, it involved the transfer of the sin of the offerer to the head of the offering.

What, then, is the doctrine set forth in the laying on of hands?

In the words of Mackintosh, it is this: *"Christ was 'made sin for us, that we might be made the righteousness of God in Him' (II Cor. 5:21). He took our position with all its consequences, in order that we might get His position with all its consequences. He was treated as sin upon the Cross, that we might be treated as righteousness in the presence of infinite holiness. He was cast out of God's presence for a short period of time, because He had sin on Him by imputation, that we might be received into God's house, and into His bosom because we have a perfect righteousness by imputation. He had to endure the hiding of God's countenance that we might bask in the light of that countenance. He had to pass through three hours of darkness, that we might walk in everlasting light. He was forsaken by God for a short period of time, that we might enjoy His presence forever."*

WHAT IS IMPUTATION?

The word *impute* or *imputation* means to lay the responsibility or blame for something on someone when they do not rightly deserve it. For instance, God imputed the penalty of all of our sins on Christ, even though He had never sinned and did not deserve such, as would be obvious. As well, He imputed the righteousness of Christ upon us, even though we were sinners and did not at all deserve such righteousness.

In the biblical account, it refers to setting to one's account or reckoning something to a person.

For instance again, it is said in Genesis 15:6 that God reckoned righteousness to believing Abraham, which means that He gave Abraham something that Abraham did not have within himself and, in fact, did not deserve. Paul quoted this passage in arguing man's justification by God through grace alone. If Abraham had been able to justify himself by works, he might boast, but man is unable to save himself.

TRUST IN GOD

The meaning is not that God accepted Abraham's faith instead of perfect righteousness as the meritorious ground for his justification. It is rather that God accepted Abraham because he trusted in God rather than in anything that he could do. To make it simple, God imputed righteousness to Abraham, even though Abraham didn't deserve such and, in fact, could not do anything to attain such, at least as far as works were concerned. This means that the righteousness that Abraham had, God had to impute it unto Him just exactly as He does with us presently.

In fact, this reckoning, or imputation, of righteousness to the believer lies at the heart of the biblical doctrine of salvation.

Paul used the phrase *righteousness of God* nine times (Rom. 1:17; 3:5, 21; 10:3; II Cor. 5:21). In most of these instances, it was mentioned in order to teach that God grants the sinner a new legal standing, i.e., he is counted righteous even while a sinner.

Men are not righteous within themselves; consequently, we need God's righteousness, which has been made manifest in Christ, and in Christ alone. Paul also said, *"Not having a righteousness of my own, based on law, but that which is through faith in Christ, the righteousness from God that depends on faith"* (Phil. 3:9).

This righteousness is imputed, or reckoned, so that while, strictly speaking, it is not our own, yet God reckons it to us so that we are justified, even though we certainly do not deserve such.

The imputation of the righteousness of God to the sinner lies at the heart of the doctrine of salvation (Gen. 15:6).

THE LORD JESUS CHRIST

The second sense in which the word imputation is used in Christian doctrine is the reckoning of man's sin to Jesus Christ. This is exemplified in the sin offering. The sinner would lay his hand on the head of the bullock just before he killed the animal, in effect, imputing his sin to the innocent animal, which was a type of Christ, and would be fulfilled in Christ when He died on the Cross. Whenever the believing sinner evidences faith in Christ and what Christ did at the Cross, he is, in effect, transferring his sins from himself to Christ, the same as the Israelite did in Old Testament times. Of course, the difference is very great.

The blood of bulls and goats could not take away sins but only cover them in a sense, while our faith in Christ takes our sins completely away, and in every respect.

However, when this happens, even as we've already stated, not only are our sins imputed to Christ, which refers to their penalty, but, as well, His perfect righteousness is in turn imputed to us.

The imputation of our sin to Christ is not that Christ actually becomes a sinner, for all of the Gospel contradicts that position. It is rather that by virtue of His identification with the human race that sin is reckoned to Him. Although it is not explicitly said in Scripture that sin is reckoned or imputed to Christ, the meaning is clear.

It is said that He bore our sins in His body on the tree (I Pet. 2:24), that *"the LORD has laid on Him the iniquity of us all"* (Isa. 53:6), and that He was made to bear the iniquities of His people (Isa. 53:11; Heb. 9:28).

Each of these passages of Scripture has in mind the Old Testament institution of sacrifice, in which guilt was symbolically and ceremoniously transferred to an animal with the laying on of hands to the head of the victim. Applied to Christ, to whom the sacrifices of the Old Testament pointed, the teaching is that He bore the punishment of our sin vicariously (to suffer in place of another), its guilt having been imputed to Him.

PAUL

The same teaching is set forth graphically by Paul in Galatians 3:13, where Christ is said to have *become a curse for us*. The meaning is that He bore the penalty for human sin that, as Luther declared, God dealt with Him as though He were the greatest of sinners. Sin was imputed or reckoned to Him so that man might be forgiven. Imputation is thus bound together with the teaching of the vicarious salvation.

All of this completely refutes the modern teaching that Jesus died spiritually.

Even though we have already dealt with the following subject once, due to the importance of the matter, please allow us at least some repetition.

THE ERRONEOUS JESUS DIED SPIRITUALLY DOCTRINE

This teaching claims that Jesus not only died physically on the Cross but, as well, died spiritually. This means that He died as a lost sinner, actually became one with Satan, and took upon Himself the satanic nature. Of course, dying as a sinner, He then went to the burning side of Hell, where, they teach, He was tortured for some three days and nights in the burning flames. After three days and nights of punishment in Hell, they then teach that God said, *"It is enough,"* and Jesus was then born again, even as any sinner must be born again. He was then raised from the dead. That's the reason that they also teach that any born-again man could redeem humanity.

This teaching is pure fiction and, as one might say, made up out of whole cloth, meaning that none of it is in the Bible.

This teaching completely abrogates the Cross and the shed blood of Jesus Christ, making it of no effect. In fact, one of their brightest lights somewhat speaks out of both sides of his mouth, while in one breath, claiming the veracity of the shed blood of Christ, and in the next breath, denying its effectiveness.

He states that the day Jesus died on the Cross, thereby, shedding His life's blood, hundreds of others died on crosses in the Roman Empire, as well, thereby, reckoning the shed blood of Christ as no different than any other man. He then goes on to state that it was necessary for Christ to go to the burning side of Hell and be tortured there for three days and nights for the redemption process to be completed. So, as is obvious, he is claiming one thing while contradicting it in the next breath.

THE PERFECT SACRIFICE

What he seems to fail to realize is, while it is true that many others died that day on crosses, those others were not Jesus Christ. He alone was the perfect sacrifice because He was perfect in every respect, a sacrifice which God could accept and, in fact, did accept.

Listen again to Paul: **"But now in Christ Jesus you who sometimes were far off are made near by the blood of Christ** *(notice that he said it was by the blood of Christ, and not by Christ burning in hellfire)* **... Having abolished in His flesh** *(the word flesh means that He died physically, and not spiritually, as these false teachers claim)* **the enmity** *(hatred)*, **even the Law of Commandments contained in ordinances** *(Jesus satisfied the claims of the broken Law by and through His death)*; **for to make in Himself of twain one new man** *(the body of Christ)*, **so making peace;**

"And that He might reconcile both *(Jews and Gentiles)* **unto God in one body** *(the church)* **by the Cross, having slain the enmity thereby"** (Eph. 2:13–16). Again, notice that Paul said this was done by the Cross, which means it was not done in Hell.

In short, the Jesus Died Spiritually doctrine is blasphemy! It is an attack on the Atonement and, as well, an attack that is so serious that it strikes at the very heart of the salvation plan, which is the Cross. In other words, if one believes that doctrine, one cannot be saved. To believe that doctrine means that one is preaching another Jesus, whom Paul did not preach, which means it has been received by another spirit, which is not the Holy Spirit, which translates into another gospel, which cannot be accepted (II Cor. 11:4).

KILL THE BULLOCK BEFORE THE LORD

The sin was committed before the Lord, as all sin is committed before the Lord, which refers to sin being an affront to God. Consequently, the animal had to be killed before the Lord, which referred to the fact that the sinner acknowledged his guilt, and that the One this sacrifice represented, namely Christ, was his only hope. That hope lay completely within its death.

Concerning this, George Williams said: *"Directly the sinner laid his hand upon the substitute it was put to death; but in the burnt offering it was not so (Lev. 1:4). The burnt offering was indeed also put to death; but before being killed the words 'It shall be accepted for him to make an atonement, (i.e., a covering) for him,' are introduced. These two passages explain substitution. In the burnt offering the sinlessness of the victim is transferred to the worshipper; in the sin offering, which we are now studying, the sinfulness of the sinner is transferred to the victim. Personal identification with Christ brings peace; for it means the taking away of sin and the reception of righteousness."*

THE BLOOD SPRINKLED SEVEN TIMES

"And the priest that is anointed shall take of the bullock's blood, and bring it to the tabernacle of the congregation:

"And the priest shall dip his finger in the blood, and sprinkle of the blood seven times before the LORD, before the veil of the sanctuary" (Lev. 4:5-6).

The *"priest that is anointed"* refers to the high priest, who was a type of Christ. Christ was anointed above all His fellows. At the Cross, He alone took the blood to the altar of worship and sprinkled it before the Lord, thereby, restoring fellowship.

The blood sprinkled seven times before the Lord speaks of a complete restoration, of a complete redemption, and of a complete relationship. For a Christian not to know that his sin is gone, and gone forever, is to cast a slight upon the blood of his divine sin offering. It is to deny that there has been the perfect presentation — the sevenfold sprinkling of the blood before the Lord.

BEFORE THE VEIL OF THE SANCTUARY

This latter phrase of Verse 6 pertains to the altar of incense, which sat immediately before the veil that separated the Holy Place from the Holy of Holies.

If we are to notice, the blood was sprinkled seven times on the altar of incense (the altar of worship) before it was then poured out at the base of the brazen altar, exclaimed in Verse 7. Why was it done this way?

It was done in this manner that we might know and understand that when we as believers sin, as bad as that sin is, we do not have to get saved all over again for relationship to be restored. But yet, even as Verse 7 proclaims, all that pertains to the altar of incense — which speaks of our relationship with Christ and His intercessory work on our behalf—is based strictly on what had transpired originally at the brazen altar. This speaks of the whole burnt offering, which typified the death of Christ. The Cross of Christ, typified by the brazen altar, is the foundation of all that we are in Christ and all that we ever shall be. In other words, everything is based on that finished work.

THE SIN OFFERING

Mackintosh said, concerning the sin offering: *"The full assurance of sin put away ministers, not to a spirit of self-confidence, but to a spirit of praise, thankfulness, and worship. It produces, not a spirit of self-complacency, but of Christ-complacency, which, blessed be God, is the spirit which shall characterize the redeemed throughout eternity. It does not lead one to think little of sin, but to think much of the grace which has perfectly pardoned it, and of the blood which has perfectly canceled it. It is impossible that anyone can gaze on the Cross — can see the place where Christ died — can meditate upon the sufferings which He endured — can ponder on those three terrible hours of darkness, and at the same time think lightly of sin."*

He then went on to say: *"When all these things are entered into, and the power of the Holy Spirit, there are two results which must follow, namely, an abhorrence of sin in all its forms, and a genuine love for Christ, His people, and His cause."*

THE HORNS AND THE BRAZEN ALTAR

"And the priest shall put some of the blood upon the horns of the altar of sweet incense before the LORD, which is

in the tabernacle of the congregation; and shall pour all the blood of the bullock at the bottom of the altar of the burnt offering, which is at the door of the tabernacle of the congregation" (Lev. 4:7).

We learn several things from this particular verse.

The blood applied to the four horns of the altar of incense speaks to the fact that even though forgiveness for believers is available at all times, which the sin offering proclaims, the horns, which speak of dominion, testify to us that we, in fact, should have dominion over all sin. However, it also testifies to the fact that such dominion cannot come about except by the Cross of Christ and our faith in that finished work, typified by the blood applied to the horns.

Salvation is not a sinning and repenting, sinning and repenting, spectacle. It is rather one of dominion over sin. Paul plainly told us, **"For sin** *(the sin nature)* **shall not have dominion over you: for you are not under the Law, but under grace"** **(Rom. 6:14).**

In effect, the apostle was definitely telling us that if we attempt to have dominion over sin by law — rules and regulations, works, etc. — victory will never be obtained in this manner. It can only be obtained under grace. Now, what does that mean?

GRACE

Grace refers to the goodness of God extended to undeserving believers. It actually refers to all the work the Holy Spirit performs within our hearts and lives, which He alone can do. We obtain this, not by works of the Law, but by simply believing in Christ and what Christ has done for us at the

Cross. If we try to function through law, we will find ourselves committing spiritual adultery, with which the Holy Spirit will have no part (Rom. 7:1–4).

The idea is this: The believing sinner is saved by trusting in Christ and what Christ has done at the Cross (Jn. 3:16). He, in fact, may understand very little about Christ, or what Christ has done, but if he believes at all, thereby, calling on the Lord, he will be saved (Rom. 10:13).

After the believing sinner comes to Christ, in order to maintain his salvation, and even to grow in grace and the knowledge of the Lord, he must, as well, maintain his faith in the Cross of Christ, even that which saved him. However, the problem is, after being saved, many Christians transfer their faith from the Cross to other things. As stated, this makes one a spiritual adulterer.

WHAT IS SPIRITUAL ADULTERY?

In brief, it is the Christian being unfaithful to Christ. How can a Christian do that?

It refers to trusting in things other than Christ, whatever those things might be. Let us explain: In Romans 7:1–4, Paul uses, as an example, a woman who is married to a particular man and then, at the same time, marries someone else. The apostle said, *"She shall be called an adulteress."* He then said, *"but if her husband be dead, she is free from that law; so that she is no adulteress, though she be married to another man"* (Rom. 7:3).

He then stated, in effect, that we are married to Christ, and we are, therefore, to trust Him for all things. We are dead to the Law, meaning that what we were, we are no more. We died with Christ (Rom. 6:3–14). We are raised a new man and are married to Christ. Consequently, we are to trust Him for everything (Rom. 7:4).

If we place our faith in our works, we have gone back to Law, which means that we are now living the life of a spiritual adulterer, meaning that we are being unfaithful to Christ. Of course, the Holy Spirit will not help us in such a situation, as should be obvious, because we are functioning under law and not under grace. In fact, if one functions in any manner, no matter what it is, other than faith in Christ and the Cross, such a believer is being unfaithful to Christ.

The sad fact is, most modern Christians are spiritual adulterers because they are not trusting Christ and what He has done for us at the Cross, but rather other things.

WHAT DOES IT MEAN TO FULLY TRUST CHRIST?

I suppose that almost every Christian would claim that he is trusting Christ, and doing so fully, but the sad fact is, at least for most, this is actually not the case.

For one to fully trust Christ, one must trust in what Christ has done for us at the Cross. The Cross was the very reason that Jesus came. Peter said that Christ, in the mind of God, was given up to the Cross even before the foundation of the world (I Pet. 1:18–20).

The destination of Christ, despite all the other things that He did, was ever the Cross. His Virgin Birth, although necessary, couldn't save anyone. His healings and miracles, although necessary, couldn't save anyone. It took the Cross, for which He came, in order for man to be redeemed.

So, for a believer to fully trust Christ, that believer must place his faith totally and completely in what Christ has done, which refers to the Cross. He must understand that not only did his salvation come by that means, but, as well, his sanctification did also! Even as these sacrifices of the Old Testament economy point out over and over in every way possible — everything hinges on the Cross.

That's why Paul said, *"But God forbid that I should glory, save in the Cross of our Lord Jesus Christ, by whom the world is crucified unto me, and I unto the world"* (Gal. 6:14). This is all proven by our next point.

THE BLOOD POURED OUT AT
THE BASE OF THE BRAZEN ALTAR

The effectiveness of the blood applied to the horns of the altar of incense, which speaks of dominion over sin in every capacity, is all based upon the fact that a whole burnt offering had been originally offered on the brazen altar, which means that everything is predicated on that (Lev. 4:18).

In the redemption of the transgressor, the priest did everything; the man did nothing. He stood, he looked, he listened, and he believed! Like action today in relation to Christ on the Cross ensures conscious salvation.

Let the believer ever understand that the Cross is the key to everything. It is what Jesus did there.

Satan will do everything within his power to push the faith of the believer away from the Cross to other things. He doesn't much care what these other things are because he knows that within themselves, as right as they may be in their own place, faith placed therein will not bring about victory. Only the Cross can do that.

This means that the modern Christian placing his faith in his confession, in his denominational ties, or anything for that matter that is not the Cross, will bring no victory. In fact, all of these other things are merely the result of a carnal mind. Paul plainly said concerning that, *"For to be carnally minded is death; but to be spiritually minded is life and peace"* (Rom. 8:6).

WHAT DID PAUL MEAN BY BEING CARNALLY MINDED OR SPIRITUALLY MINDED?

To be carnally minded is to place one's faith in anything except the Cross. To be spiritually minded is to place one's faith exclusively in the Cross of Christ.

When we speak of the Cross, we aren't speaking of the wooden beam on which Jesus died, but rather to what He there accomplished. What did He do on the Cross? (Col. 2:10-15).

He atoned for all sin — past, present, and future — at least for all who will believe (Jn. 3:16). Sin is the legal means that Satan has to hold man captive, but with all sin atoned, that legal means has been taken from him. So, that being the case, how does he continue to hold man captive?

He can hold man captive simply because man, whether redeemed or unredeemed, will not take advantage of what Christ has done for him at the Cross. In other words, his faith is in something else other than Christ and the Cross, which gives Satan the ability to continue holding that person in bondage. Sadly, at this very time, the far greater majority of Christians around the world are in bondage to Satan in some way. I am speaking of those who truly are born again, with many of them Spirit-filled and even used of God, but yet, still in bondage. It's because they are being unfaithful to Christ and are trusting in something other than the Cross of Christ.

Always remember this: There is only one answer for sin, and whenever we look at the situation, whatever it is, we find it is sin. There is only one answer for sin, and that is Christ and the Cross.

When most Christians think of being carnally minded, they think it refers to watching too much television, being too interested in sports, or anything of that nature for that matter.

While those things may or may not be wrong, they have nothing to do with what Paul was speaking about here.

Likewise, most Christians, when they think of being spiritually minded, think of one reading so many chapters a day in the Bible, praying so much each day, witnessing to a certain number of souls each day, etc.

While those things are spiritual, that's not what Paul was speaking of. In fact, the entire gist of Paul's discussion in Romans, Chapters 6, 7, and 8, refers to the Cross.

As well, all of this is beautifully typified, even as we are attempting to explain, in these Levitical sacrifices.

THE FINAL DESTRUCTION OF ALL THAT IS SINFUL

"And he shall take off from it all the fat of the bullock for the sin offering; the fat that covers the inwards, and all the fat that is upon the inwards,

"And the two kidneys, and the fat that is upon them, which is by the flanks, and the caul above the liver, with the kidneys, it shall he take away,

"As it was taken off from the bullock of the sacrifice of peace offerings: and the priest shall burn them upon the altar of the burnt offering.

"And the skin of the bullock, and all his flesh, with his head, and with his legs, and his inwards, and his dung,

"Even the whole bullock shall he carry forth without the camp unto a clean place, where the ashes are poured out, and burn him on the wood with fire: where the ashes are poured out shall he be burnt" (Lev. 4:8-12).

As we shall see, the carcass of the slain animal was not to be burned upon the brazen altar, but rather taken to a place without the camp and burned there. Why?

THE SIN OFFERING

This means that when the Christian sins, as bad as it is, the Christian doesn't have to get saved all over again. In the sin offering, we see the means and the manner by which relationship is restored.

If it was commanded that the animal, constituting the sin offering, was to be burned on the altar, as was the animal of the whole burnt offering, this would mean that the person would have to get saved all over again every time he sinned. Of course, the Bible doesn't teach that, and graphically illustrates the very opposite in the sin offering and the way it was handled.

But yet, even as we have previously studied, the blood of that slain animal had to be sprinkled seven times on the altar of incense, as well as smeared on its four horns, and then poured out at the base of the brazen altar. This signified that the crucifixion of Christ, even though accomplished many centuries ago, has continuing results. The Crucifixion constituted the shedding of His precious blood, which paid for all of the sin of humanity, at least for all who will believe. In fact, these results will never be discontinued. The blood of Christ continues to avail today exactly as it did 2,000 years ago, or whenever! However, even as all of this typifies, the believer must maintain his faith in that shed blood, which means that he must ever maintain his faith in the Cross.

THE FAT

And yet, the fat, plus some of the physical organs of the animal, such as the kidneys and the caul (intestines), were to be burned on the brazen altar. Why this and not the whole bullock?

The fat constituted the prosperity of Christ, while the organs constituted daily living.

This means that as believers, if we do not approach sin in the right manner, meaning that the sacrifice of Christ alone can handle sin, we will lose our spiritual prosperity, which will greatly affect in a negative way our daily living.

This is one of the reasons that Jesus said: **"If any man will come after Me, let him deny himself** (*deny his own strength and ability*) **and take up his cross daily, and follow Me** (*this means to trust daily in the benefits that come to us from the Cross, and the Cross alone*).

"For whosoever will save his life shall lose it (*try to live outside of the Cross of Christ*)**: but whosoever will lose his life for My sake, the same shall save it** (*will place his life exclusively in Christ*)**" (Lk. 9:23-24).**

WHERE THE ASHES ARE POURED OUT

After the items mentioned above were removed from the carcass of the animal and burned upon the altar, the remainder of the carcass, which constituted almost all of it, was to be taken *"without the camp unto a clean place, where the ashes are poured out."* There it was to be burned and consumed.

As we've already stated, the carcass of the animal being burned outside of the camp signified that the believer doesn't have to be saved all over again when he sins. However, he definitely does have to confess his sin before the Lord, typified by the sin offering (I Jn. 1:9), and then renew his faith in Christ and what Christ has done for him at the Cross. This was typified by the animal being slain and its blood poured out at the base of the brazen altar. Fellowship was restored by the blood being sprinkled seven times on the altar of incense and smeared on the four horns, but all, as stated, is predicated on what was done originally at the brazen altar.

The animal being burned without the camp signified that while the believer, because of his sin, should, in fact, be banned without the camp, instead, the sins were taken without the camp and banished. The animal being burned signified that God cannot abide sin in any form, and it must be totally and completely eradicated. In fact, this typified the final removal of sin from God's kingdom and the final destruction of all that is sinful.

Paul stated in Hebrews that one of the points in which our Lord was the antitype of the sin offering was that He suffered without the gate that He might sanctify the people with His own blood (Heb. 13:12).

SIN COMMITTED THROUGH IGNORANCE

"And if the whole congregation of Israel sin through ignorance, and the thing be hid from the eyes of the assem-

bly, and they have done somewhat against any of the commandments of the LORD concerning things which should
not be done, and are guilty;

"When the sin, which they have sinned against it, is known,
then the congregation shall offer a young bullock for the sin,
and bring him before the tabernacle of the congregation.

"And the elders of the congregation shall lay their hands
upon the head of the bullock before the LORD: and the bullock shall be killed before the LORD.

"And the priest that is anointed shall bring of the bullock's blood to the tabernacle of the congregation" (Lev.
4:13-16).

Verses 13 through 21 make it clearly known that when sin
has been committed through ignorance but is now found out,
it must be immediately addressed.

God, being just, passes over sin until it is made known by
the conscience, the Word, and the Holy Spirit. Then He holds
sinners responsible and will judge and punish them if the sin
is allowed to continue (Jn. 16:7-11; Rom. 2:12-16).

We will see in the following commentary how that sins of
ignorance are committed presently.

We have already touched upon this, but because it is so
very, very important, I think it would be profitable to address
the subject again of sinning through ignorance.

The modern believer may well understand how Israel of
old could do such a thing, and even do it as a corporate body,
considering all the many rules and regulations contained in the
Law of Moses. It would be very easy to miss one or more, or
more particularly, to misunderstand what was said.

However, let the reader understand that even though the
infraction was committed in ignorance, God still labeled it as sin.

So, how is it that modern-day Christians can sin through ignorance?

MODERN CHRISTIANS AND THE SIN OF IGNORANCE

If the Christian doesn't understand the Cross as it regards sanctification, through ignorance, that Christian will attempt to live for God through and by his own strength and ability, which are always woefully inadequate. To rebel against God's prescribed order, which is Jesus Christ and Him crucified, is sin, even though done in ignorance, even as it is by most. Paul plainly said: **"Because the carnal mind is enmity (war) against God: for it is not subject to the Law of God, neither indeed can be.**

"So then they who are in the flesh cannot please God" **(Rom. 8:7–8).**

As we've already explained, the carnal mind is the effort by the individual to live for God outside of total dependence on Christ and the Cross.

A PERSONAL EXPERIENCE

This of which I speak, I have lived. I know what it is to understand the Cross as it regards salvation but understand it not at all as it regards sanctification. Regrettably, almost all of the modern church presently falls into the latter category. It has no understanding of the Cross as it refers to our everyday living before God, i.e., our walk. That being the case, the believer will attempt to live for the Lord in all the wrong ways.

Even in this state (as are most Christians) the Lord was using me mightily. We were seeing literally hundreds of thousands of souls brought to a saving knowledge of Jesus Christ, the fruit of which remains unto this hour, and I exaggerate not!

FUNCTION AND FAITH

The call of God on a person's life regards their function, in other words, what He has called them to do. Even if that person doesn't understand sanctification as it was taught by Paul, the Lord will still use him as it regards his function. Many Christians misunderstand this. They think if the Lord is using someone, and it is obvious that He is doing so, this means that such a preacher is close to perfect. Regrettably, that's not the case at all.

It doesn't matter how much the Lord is using a person, and He will definitely do so, that is, if the person is truly called of God and truly believes Him. If that preacher (or whomever) doesn't understand the Cross as it regards sanctification, then, in some way, that preacher is going to be living a life of spiritual failure — despite the fact that God is using him (or her)! However, the following must quickly be said.

THE CHILD OF GOD CAN
NEVER OUTGROW THE CROSS

Without understanding the Cross as it regards sanctification, no matter how sincere, no matter how earnest, and no matter how honest, such a Christian simply will not be able to live a life of spiritual victory, at least on a perpetual basis. God has made one provision for sin, which includes victory over sin, and that is the Cross of Christ. It pertains, as should be obvious, to the sinner being saved and the saint being sanctified.

The child of God can never outgrow the Cross, hence, Paul referring to it as *"the everlasting covenant"* (Heb. 13:20). However, as stated, the moment the believer seeks to live this life outside of the Cross of Christ, that believer is rebelling against God's prescribed order of victory, and even though it is done in ignorance, it is sin and will reap bitter results. In fact, there are untold millions at this very moment who are struggling, and have been struggling for years, trying to overcome a problem or problems within their hearts and lives, but have been unable to do so. In fact, despite all of their struggles, the problem has grown steadily worse. As we've said, we'll say again — the problem, for the most part, is ignorance.

UNBELIEF

However, I have found in dealing with many people, especially preachers, that the problem for many is not ignorance, but rather unbelief. And yet, with those who function in ignorance, when many of them hear the truth, they simply will not believe. In other words, they simply do not believe that what Jesus did at the Cross is the answer for mankind. Why?

It is like Abraham. He did not at all enjoy giving up Ishmael, even though God said he must do so. Ishmael was the fair work of his flesh, and he loved the young man. While Abraham definitely obeyed, there are many who do not obey.

They love the labor of their hands, the works of their flesh, and, in fact, they have invested much into these particular works, and they do not take kindly to being told that they must give them up, and give them up completely.

In fact, many preachers would have to change their entire ministry if they looked to the Cross instead of their own efforts. Let me give you an example.

DELIVERANCE MINISTRY

Most of the ministries which go under the guise of a *deliverance ministry*, for the most part, work under the auspices of the laying on of hands. While the laying on of hands is certainly scriptural, at least for healing and for blessing, it will do no good as it regards deliverance from bondages of sin and darkness.

And yet, that statement needs some qualification. If, in fact, the preacher understands the means and the way in which true deliverance does come, and also, if the person coming for deliverance understands, as well, then the laying on of hands will definitely be of benefit to the individual. Otherwise, it won't! Let me explain.

Jesus said, *"You shall know the truth, and the truth shall make you free"* (Jn. 8:32). In other words, manifestations, as scriptural as they might be in their own right, will not set anyone free. Momentarily, I will explain what the truth actually is.

If it is to be noticed, Jesus also said, *"The Spirit of the Lord is upon Me, because He has anointed Me to ... preach deliverance to the captives"* (Lk. 4:18).

If it is to be noticed, He didn't say that the Holy Spirit had anointed Him to deliver the captives, but rather to preach deliverance to the captives. It is a subtle difference, but very important!

He was actually saying that one cannot truly be delivered until the truth is given to that particular person. Now, what is the truth?

THE TRUTH

The truth is *"Jesus Christ and Him crucified"* (I Cor. 2:2). It is explained in detail in Romans, Chapter 6. In fact, some have spoken of this chapter as the mechanics of the Holy Spirit, with Chapter 8 of Romans spoken of as the *dynamics* of the Holy Spirit. In other words, Chapter 6 of Romans tells us what we are in Christ and how we obtained it, which is through faith in what Christ did at the Cross. Once the Cross of Christ is the object of our faith, which it must ever be, then we will witness what the Holy Spirit will do within our lives, as outlined in Chapter 8 of Romans. It is *how He does it* in Chapter 6 and w*hat He does, once we know how He does it* in Chapter 8.

The person can truly experience deliverance only if he understands Christ and what Christ has done for him at the Cross. That's the reason that Paul also said: **"I am crucified with Christ *(Paul takes us back to Rom., Chpt. 6)*: nevertheless I live; yet not I, but Christ lives in me: and the life which I now live in the flesh I live by the faith of the Son of God, who loved me, and gave Himself for me"** (Gal. 2:20).

THE SAME REMEDY

"And the priest shall dip his finger in some of the blood, and sprinkle it seven times before the LORD, even before the veil.

"And he shall put some of the blood upon the horns of the altar which is before the LORD, that is in the tabernacle of the congregation, and shall pour out all the blood at the bottom of the altar of the burnt offering, which is at the door of the tabernacle of the congregation.

"And he shall take all his fat from him, and burn it upon the altar.

"And he shall do with the bullock as he did with the bullock for a sin offering, so shall he do with this: and the priest shall make an atonement for them, and it shall be forgiven them.

"And he shall carry forth the bullock without the camp, and burn him as he burned the first bullock: it is a sin offering for the congregation" (Lev. 4:17-21).

The only difference in this ritual, as it regards the priests who had sinned and the entirety of Israel, as described in Verses 13 through 21, was that instead of the priest laying his hand on the head of the bullock before it was killed, thereby, transferring his sins, the elders were to perform that task as it regarded the whole nation of Israel.

As it regarded the elders of Israel, there were 70 of these men, so we know that a representative group had to perform this task. It is said that it was ordained that during the second temple, three of their members should lay their hands upon the sacrifice. Besides this sin offering, there was only one other congregational offering upon which there was this laying of hands, which was the scapegoat (Lev. 16:21).

The rest of the regulations are exactly the same as those prescribed in the sin offering for the high priest himself, as described in Verses 5 through 12.

THE REMEDY IS THE SAME

"When a ruler has sinned, and done somewhat through ignorance against any of the commandments of the LORD his God concerning things which should not be done, and is guilty;

"Or if his sin, wherein he has sinned, come to his knowledge; he shall bring his offering, a kid of the goats, a male without blemish:

"And he shall lay his hand upon the head of the goat, and kill it in the place where they kill the burnt offering before the LORD: it is a sin offering.

"And the priest shall take of the blood of the sin offering with his finger, and put it upon the horns of the altar of burnt offering, and shall pour out his blood at the bottom of the altar of burnt offering.

"And he shall burn all his fat upon the altar, as the fat of the sacrifice of peace offerings: and the priest shall make an atonement for him as concerning his sin, and it shall be forgiven him" (Lev. 4:22-26).

The ruler of Verse 22 refers to a king, but, as well, it could probably refer to members of the Sanhedrin — the highest Jewish court — or even to lesser courts, and most likely, as well, to anyone of the 70 elders. Incidentally, there was a political Sanhedrin and a religious Sanhedrin, with the latter mostly made up of priests; therefore, the former would have probably been included, with the latter excluded. If it is to be noticed, the remedy was basically the same for sin, irrespective as to who committed it, with the exception of some minor particulars.

Irrespective as to who sins, ultimately the person must be led to the Cross because the Cross is the only answer. There is no other!

THE SHED BLOOD

As we shall see, there were some differences in the ritual, but the ultimate point is, it was the shed blood that brought about forgiveness of sin, all pointing to the coming Christ.

The difference in the ritual, as it regarded a ruler, the priest, or congregation, was that the blood of the sin offering was put on the four horns of the altar of burnt offering, instead of the altar of incense, as it regarded the other two.

Why this difference?

It is the same with the sin of the common people, as we will study in Verses 27 through 35. The blood there, as well, was applied to the horns of the brazen altar instead of the altar of incense.

The first two included the priest and the entirety of the congregation of Israel. The latter two included rulers and the common people.

The priest was a type of Christ, with the entirety of the nation consisting of God's plan. The latter two pertained to individuals among the people, which would pertain even to a king.

Inasmuch as the priest represented Christ — and the entire nation represented His plan — the blood had to be sprinkled seven times on the altar of incense and then applied to the four horns, with the remainder taken to the brazen altar and poured out at its base. Intercession was at stake with the first two because of who they were, and intercession pertains to the altar of incense. So, for the first two, intercession and atonement were required. For the latter two, only atonement was required, which in their cases, would automatically include intercession, but which evidently was not automatic with the first two.

COMMON PEOPLE

*"And if any one of the common people sin through
ignorance, while he does somewhat against any of the commandments of the LORD concerning things which ought not
to be done, and be guilty;*

*"Or if his sin, which he has sinned, come to his knowl-
edge: then he shall bring his offering, a kid of the goats, a
female without blemish, for his sin which he has sinned.*

*"And he shall lay his hand upon the head of the sin offer-
ing, and slay the sin offering in the place of the burnt offering.*

*"And the priest shall take of the blood thereof with his
finger, and put it upon the horns of the altar of burnt offering, and shall pour out all the blood thereof at the bottom of
the altar"* (Lev. 4:27-30).

As is obvious here, in the eyes of God, sin is sin, irrespective as to who commits it. It must be addressed and, in
essence, addressed the same way, even if it's a common person, a ruler, a priest, or even the entirety of the nation of Israel.

The fat of the sin offering for a common person was
burned upon the altar for a sweet savour. This is not said of
the offering for the priests, for the congregation, or for the
ruler. If Christ's death for a multitude is sweet to God, His
death for an individual sinner of the common people is especially sweet. Such is grace!

As it regards a common person, a female animal was to
be brought. Evidently, the others required were to be males.
Why a female?

All the priests were men and types of Christ. A ruler was,
as well, a man, or almost always! Also, the nation of Israel as

a whole was looked at in the same capacity. However, when it came to the common people, it must include, of necessity, both males and females. So, a female animal was demanded in this instance, which would cover both men and women, for both at times sinned. However, only the men were allowed to bring the animals for sacrifice.

SIN IS SIN

As we have stated, and as in this explanation of the sin offering, God cannot abide sin in any capacity, which is overly obvious. Whether it was the high priest, who was a type of Christ, the nation as a whole, a king, or now, the common people, sin is sin and must be dealt with. Furthermore, it can only be dealt with in one manner and that is by the sacrificial, atoning death of Christ on the Cross, of which these sacrifices were a type.

As we've already stated, Israel wasn't washed, cleansed, and forgiven because of these animal sacrifices simply because the blood of animals was woefully insufficient, but rather by what the sacrifices represented, namely the Lord Jesus Christ and what He would do at the Cross on behalf of Adam's fallen race. While their understanding of this would have been dim, still, the original command had pointed to the seed of the woman, which was to come, and who would bruise Satan's head (what Jesus would do at the Cross), even though Satan would bruise His heel (what Jesus would suffer at the Cross) (Gen. 3:15). In fact, this had been graphically spelled out in Genesis, Chapter 4, as it regards the episode of Cain and Abel.

TURNING THE SACRIFICES INTO A RITUAL

Unfortunately, in later years, Israel turned the sacrifices into a ritual, completely ignoring what and who they represented, which, in essence, made the sacrifices ineffectual.

Christ and Him crucified is the subject of the entirety of the Bible from Genesis 1:1 through Revelation 22:21. The idea ever was that He would come as the second man, i.e., *"the last Adam"* (I Cor. 15:45–50), and do what the first Adam failed to do, which was to render perfect obedience to God but, as well, to address the broken law, of which every man was guilty. This Christ did at the Cross. In fact, God, through foreknowledge, planned all of this, even before the foundation of the world (I Pet. 1:18–20).

Paul tells us that under the Old Covenant, which we are now studying, the animal sacrifices could not salve the conscience, even though they were a type of Christ and what He would do at the Cross.

He said: **"Which was a figure for the time then present** *(which pertained to the old Levitical system, including the sacrifices),* **in which were offered both gifts and sacrifices, that could not make him who did the service perfect, as pertaining to the conscience"** (Heb. 9:9).

So, how could one know under the old Levitical Law that one was saved?

THE BLOOD AND THE WORD

The knowledge that he was saved was founded upon two facts outside of himself:

1. The value of the blood shed for him.
2. The trustworthiness of the Word spoken to him.

In fact, on this divine foundation — the blood and the Word — not only rested the Jew under the old economy but, as well, is where the Christian's peace rests also. The knowledge that Christ's blood is of infinite value to cleanse all sins, which declares that whoever trusts that Saviour shall never be confounded, is trustworthy and, as stated, is the divine foundation. This double knowledge establishes assurance of salvation.

So, one can see that the object of faith was identical in Old Testament times as it is presently — the Cross. But yet, the result of that faith, and I now speak of Old Testament times, was not nearly as glorious as it is presently because of the weakness of animal blood by comparison to the blood of Christ.

PAUL

Listen again to Paul: *"How much more shall the blood of Christ, who through the eternal Spirit offered Himself without spot to God, purge your conscience from dead works to serve the living God?"*

Paul went on to say: **"And for this cause He** *(Christ)* **is the mediator of the New Testament** *(the New Covenant)***, that by means of death** *(the Cross)***, for the redemption of the transgressions that were under the first testament** *(the Cross addressed itself also to all the sins of Old Testament times)***, they which are called might receive the promise of eternal inheritance."**

And then: "**And almost all things are by the Law** (*Old Testament Law*) **purged with blood; and without shedding of blood is no remission** (*meaning there is no remission of sin*)" (Heb. 9:14–15, 22).

So, when any one of the people of Israel sinned, and this sin was called to their attention, in other words, they knew they had sinned, they were to take a kid of the goats (a baby goat), a female without blemish, or a lamb (Lev. 4:32), and offer it up in sacrifice. He was, as well, to lay his hand upon the head of the sin offering, thereby, transferring his sin to this innocent victim, which was a type of Christ. Then he was to personally kill the animal, with the priest then carrying out the balance of the ritual.

The blood would be applied with the finger of the priest upon the four horns of the altar of burnt offering, which was the brazen altar. Those four horns signified not only dominion, but that salvation was the same for all, even as the horns pointed in all directions: north, south, east, and west. The problem for all of mankind is the same — sin — and the solution for mankind is the same — Christ and Him Crucified — of which the altar was a type.

THE SWEET SAVOUR

"*And he shall take away all the fat thereof, as the fat is taken away from off the sacrifice of peace offerings; and the priest shall burn it upon the altar for a sweet savour unto the LORD; and the priest shall make an atonement for him, and it shall be forgiven him.*

"*And if he bring a lamb for a sin offering, he shall bring it a female without blemish.*

"And he shall lay his hand upon the head of the sin offering, and slay it for a sin offering in the place where they kill the burnt offering.

"And the priest shall take of the blood of the sin offering with his finger, and put it upon the horns of the altar of burnt offering, and shall pour out all the blood thereof at the bottom of the altar:

"And he shall take away all the fat thereof, as the fat of the lamb is taken away from the sacrifice of the peace offerings; and the priest shall burn them upon the altar, according to the offerings made by fire unto the LORD: *and the priest shall make an atonement for his sin that he has committed, and it shall be forgiven him"* (Lev. 4:31-35).

There is one difference in this which the priest did for the common person than he would do for the others.

The Scripture says that when he burned the fat upon the altar, it went up before the Lord as a sweet savour, which was not said concerning the others.

REDEMPTION

Why did it use the term *sweet savour* here without relating such when the fat was burned regarding sins of ignorance concerning the priests, the nation of Israel, and rulers?

Of course, as would be obvious, the far, far greater number of sacrifices were offered for the common people than for the others. As a result, the grace of God was portrayed to a greater extent, a far greater extent!

This signified the fact that when Jesus died on the Cross, His death was so effective that it paid for all sin—past, present, and future—at least for all who would believe (Jn. 3:16). In fact, there are several Greek words for redemption used in the New Testament, but there are three that are more prominent. They are:

1. **Garazo:** to purchase out of the slave market.
2. **Exgarazo:** to purchase in such totality and with such finality that the subject will never again be offered as a slave.
3. **Lutroo:** the price that was paid, which was the blood of Christ, was so sufficient that no creature in eternity past, eternity present, or eternity future will ever be able to say that it was insufficient. So, it is a *"sweet savour unto the Lord."*

"One day when Heaven was filled with His praises,
"One day when sin was as black as could be,
"Jesus came forth to be born of a virgin,
"Dwelt among men, my example is He."

"One day they led Him up Calvary's mountain,
"One day they nailed Him to die on the tree;
"Suffering anguish, despised and rejected;
"Bearing our sins, my Redeemer is He."

"One day they left Him alone in the garden,
"One day He rested, from suffering free;
"Angels came down o'er His tomb to keep vigil;
"Hope of the hopeless, my Saviour is He."

"One day the grave could conceal Him no longer,
"One day the stone rolled away from the door;
"Then He arose, over death He had conquered;
"Now is ascended, my Lord evermore."

"One day the trumpet will sound for His coming,
"One day the skies with His glory will shine;
"Wonderful day, my beloved ones bringing;
"Glorious Saviour, this Jesus is mine!"

5

The Trespass Offering

CHAPTER FIVE

The Trespass Offering

"AND IT SHALL be, when he shall be guilty in one of these things, that he shall confess that he has sinned in that thing:

"And he shall bring his trespass offering unto the LORD *for his sin which he has sinned, a female from the flock, a lamb or a kid of the goats, for a sin offering; and the priest shall make an atonement for him concerning his sin.*

"And if he be not able to bring a lamb, then he shall bring for his trespass, which he hath committed, two turtledoves, or two young pigeons, unto the LORD; *one for a sin offering, and the other for a burnt offering"* (Lev. 5:5-7).

The trespass offering was provided to atone for trespass against God and trespass against man, for any sin against man is also, at the same time, a sin against God.

The words in Verse 7, which we will get to momentarily, *"And if he be not able to bring a lamb,"* then go on to say that he can bring *"two turtledoves, or two young pigeons."* God always makes it possible for anyone to meet His terms of reconciliation. This is why He permitted different kinds of offerings for the rich, poor, and the very poor — from rams to turtledoves, and pigeons to a handful of flour.

The Cross of Christ alone is the means by which any and all — red, yellow, brown, black, white, old, young, rich, poor, great, and small — can come to the Lord the same way. In other words, there isn't a different way for different people.

Jesus said, *"I am the way, the truth, and the life: no man comes to the Father, but by Me"* (Jn. 14:6).

This is what sets the Cross apart from every effort of man. For anything that man comes up with, as it regards salvation or victory in Christ, while certain ones may accomplish the task, many others cannot.

Sometime ago, a preacher wrote a book, in essence, saying that if one would fast 21 days, that would give one victory over sin, the flesh, and the Devil. Unfortunately, there are many people who cannot fast 21 days. In other words, they would die. It is only what God produces that makes it possible for anyone to come.

The great Prophet Isaiah said: *"Ho, everyone who thirsts, come you to the waters, and he who has no money; come you, buy, and eat; yes, come, buy wine and milk without money and without price"* (Isa. 55:1).

THE GREAT INVITATION

With Chapter 53 of Isaiah proclaiming the great price that was paid at Calvary, and Chapter 54 of Isaiah proclaiming the coming grand and glorious Kingdom Age, now the inhabitants of the entirety of the world are invited to come and partake of the One who guarantees entrance into that kingdom.

Three times in this one passage the word *come* is used. It corresponds to Revelation 22:17; it is used there three times as well! The triple invitation corresponds to the Trinity: God the Father, God the Son, and God the Holy Spirit. All are participants in the great salvation plan.

The four articles of purchase, as are outlined in Verses 1 and 2 of Chapter 55 of Isaiah — water, bread, wine, and milk — express the plentitude of grace in the Saviour as exhibited in the Four Gospels.

The word *buy* is used, and yet, the purchase price is not money. Were it so, most would never obtain the treasure. Therefore, the price that is demanded is the heart of man! (Rom. 10:9-10).

Then the phrase is used, *and eat.* Men must partake of Christ before they can become a part of Christ, which can be done only by faith in Christ and what He has done for us at the Cross.

We find in all of this that despite some claims to the contrary, there are lingering defilements and trespasses adhering to man, even though he be justified, consecrated, and in fellowship with God.

INIQUITY

Verse 1 reads, *"And if a soul sin, and hear the voice of swearing, and is a witness, whether he has seen or known of it; if he do not utter it, then he shall bear his iniquity"* (Lev. 5:1).

There are many who claim that the first 13 verses of this chapter should have been included in the previous chapter because it is claimed that they pertain to the sin offering and not the trespass offering. That may very well be correct; however, I think not!

First of all, the trespass offering has to do with sins against God and man, even as Verse 1 of this chapter proclaims. As well, Verse 6 mentions the trespass offering.

SIN

Joseph Seiss said, *"With all his efforts, prayers, and joys, the best Christian is still very faulty."*

He went on to say: *"Christ has taught us to pray daily, 'Forgive us our trespasses;' but why continue praying for forgiveness if we have not continual trespasses to be forgiven? I know and preach that 'the blood of Jesus Christ cleanses from all sin.' That is a precious truth to me. But did He not continue a priest forever, daily presenting His atoning blood anew in our behalf, we should most certainly come into condemnation. It is only because 'He continues ever,' that He is 'able to save them to the uttermost who come unto God by Him, seeing He ever lives to make intercession for them.' If He did not ever live to make intercession for us, we could not stand for a single day."*

Men tend to attempt to put sins into categories. While some sins are most definitely worse and greater than others, let it ever be understood that the Catholic teaching of venial sins and mortal sins has no scriptural validity. While men may talk of little sins, God never does. However small they may be, they are big enough to sink the soul to everlasting death if not canceled by the Saviour's blood.

Let me quote Seiss again, *"And there is not a Christian on earth, however eminent, who does not, every day he lives, accumulate guilt enough to ruin him forever, were it not that he has 'an advocate with the Father, Jesus Christ the Righteous.'"*

BLOOD

As we have already seen and will continue to see, there are literal rivers of blood demanded from the slaughter of innocent animals, which would serve as a stopgap measure regarding the sins of the people. Until Christ came and shed His life's blood, the problem of sin was not totally addressed. The blood of bulls and goats simply could not take away sins.

A PERSONAL EXPERIENCE

While we now have a state-of-the-art recording studio at the ministry, for years I recorded in Nashville. On one particular session, when the backup singers came in, one of the young girls, who happened to be Jewish, complained that many of the songs were about the blood. She remarked as to how this was somewhat gruesome.

Our producer recalled to her the Old Testament sacrificial system, which was originated by the Lord, and how that it was actually given to the Jewish people. Evidently she had not studied the Word of God at all, but she did have enough knowledge to understand what was being told her and then answered accordingly.

OFFENDED

It is easy to understand how some people will be offended by the continual displays of blood, blood, blood, as these accounts are given in the Old Testament. They conclude all of this as unworthy of God and repulsive to man. However, they do this simply because they do not understand the terrible power of sin and the price that had to be paid, which, incidentally, God paid Himself. The price was the shedding of innocent blood, and I now speak of the blood of God's Son, the Lord Jesus Christ (Eph. 2:13–18).

Though there is a constant recurrence of blood in the Old Testament, as well as in the New Testament, it is all full of great significance. It tells of guilt, death, and ruin merited by that guilt. It tells of our condemnation and of the way in which that condemnation is removed in Christ Jesus. It shows us the awful penalty that we have incurred, and how our Saviour undertook to bear it in His own body on the tree.

When we begin to understand this, then we begin to see that the reason for the blood is because of our sins, from which we could never be saved were it not for the ever efficacious (effective) blood of the Lamb of God who was slain for us.

BEARING THE INIQUITY

The last phrase of Verse 1 says, *"Then he shall bear his iniquity."* This proclaims the fact that each individual will have to answer for his own personal sin. I cannot answer for the sins of another, and neither can you, but the Holy Spirit, through Moses, is definitely telling us here that we must answer for our own sins. No one is exempt! How do we answer?

That's what all of this instruction is all about. Under the Mosaic Law, the individual who had sinned had to bring a particular animal to the tabernacle or temple, when the latter would ultimately be constructed. Of course, our Lord has now totally fulfilled the Mosaic Law, which means it's not incumbent upon us anymore.

While he was to be given instruction as to what type of animal was to be brought, which would be according to who he was and the type of sin committed, that was actually all that he was required to know. The priests, after questioning him as to the type of sin committed, would then carry out the necessary ritual concerning the blood and the disposal of the carcass, according to the instructions given to them by Moses. As is obvious, it was a very cumbersome process and was very costly and very time-consuming because sin is such a terrible business.

THE NEW COVENANT

Incidentally, under the New Covenant, which is based upon much better promises, as should be obvious, the procedure is entirely different (Heb. 8:6-7).

When a Christian sins presently, he is to simply confess that sin before the Lord, for which he is then promised forgiveness (I Jn. 1:9). In order for this to be done, he doesn't have to go to a church, a priest, a preacher, or anyone else for that matter, only to the Lord.

When Jesus Christ died on the Cross of Calvary, he fulfilled in total all of the sacrificial system, making it no longer necessary. He died on the Cross, shedding His life's blood, and the one sacrifice of Himself was and is totally sufficient and, in fact, will ever be sufficient.

Paul said, **"But this man** *(the Lord Jesus Christ),* **after He had offered one sacrifice for sins forever** *(which was* *the sacrifice of Himself)*, **sat down on the right hand of God"** (Heb. 10:12).

AN UNSCRIPTURAL TEACHING

Some are presently claiming that if a Christian sins, he does not have to confess it to the Lord in any way or fashion. They claim it is automatically forgiven.

Now, that's strange because John wrote, *"If we confess our sins, He is faithful and just to forgive us our sins, and to cleanse us from all unrighteousness"* (I Jn. 1:9).

As well, our Lord said in that which we refer to as the Lord's Prayer, *"and forgive us our debts, as we forgive our debtors"* (Mat. 6:12).

We must ever understand that sin is not a trifling matter. It is serious business, to say the least. While the believer does not have to confess and should not confess that he is a sinner, he most definitely must confess his particular sins to the Lord, for which we are instantly forgiven. In other words, the sinner coming to Christ must confess that he is a sinner, while the believer has only to confess his sins. There is a vast difference there.

Then there are some who teach that sin must never be mentioned by the preacher because if such is mentioned, this will cause a sin consciousness in the heart of the believer, which will cause the person to sin. So, the way to never sin, as they claim, is to never mention sin.

Now, that's strange when we consider that in Chapter 6 of Romans alone, Paul mentioned sin some 17 times.

No, sin must be spelled out by the preacher of the Gospel, but, as well, its only remedy must be spelled out, which is the shed blood of Jesus Christ.

THE UNCLEAN THING

"Or if a soul touch any unclean thing, whether it be a carcass of an unclean beast, or a carcass of unclean cattle, or the carcass of unclean creeping things, and if it be hidden from him; he also shall be unclean, and guilty.

"Or if he touched the uncleanness of man, whatsoever uncleanness it be that a man shall be defiled withal, and it be hid from him; when he knows of it, then he shall be guilty.

"Or if a soul swear, pronouncing with his lips to do evil, or to do good, whatsoever it be that a man shall pronounce with an oath, and it be hid from him; when he knows of it, then he shall be guilty in one of these.

"And it shall be, when he shall be guilty in one of these things, that he shall confess that he has sinned in that thing" (Lev. 5:2-5).

I hope the reader has noticed that the last phrase in these Scriptures, *"that he shall confess that he has sinned in that thing,"* once again completely refutes the erroneous teaching that sin is not to be mentioned, whether to God or anyone else.

Even though addressing dead animals and specifying that they were of the unclean type, which refers to animals other than the heifer, ox, bullock, goat, lamb, and ram, the emphasis seems to be on the fact of death itself.

Death in all its forms is a result of sin. It, as nothing else, portrays the horror of sin. In fact, concerning this, Paul said: **"Forasmuch then as the children are partakers of flesh and blood, He** (*Christ*) **also Himself likewise took part of the same; that through death** (*the crucifixion on the Cross*) **He might destroy him who had the power of death, that is, the Devil;**

"And delivered them who through fear of death were all their lifetime subject to bondage" (Heb. 2:14–15).

THE CROSS

The idea is, before the Cross, Satan had the power of death, and that was because of man's sin. When Jesus died on the Cross, thereby, atoning for all sin — past, present, and future — at least for all who will believe, this, in effect, destroyed Satan and his power. With sin being the legal right that gave Satan the power to hold man in bondage, it has now been conquered, and was conquered by what Christ did at the Cross (Col. 2:14–15).

The uncleanness of man, as described in Verse 3, among other things, had to do with one who had leprosy, had touched a leper, or had been defiled because he had touched a dead body and had not yet been purified. All of this, in a sense, was a type of sin, and the touching of such a person would defile the individual, which would be sin on his part as well! Consequently, he would need cleansing, forgiveness, and restoration.

As I'm certain that we can see here, sin, even in its simplest form, cannot be passed over by God. So, let us not think that certain little sins, which we might refer to as such, can be left in our lives. To be sure, the Holy Spirit, if allowed to have His way, will definitely convict us of all sin, irrespective as to what it might be (Jn. 16:8). In fact, there are many things which God constitutes as sin, but which we do not; however, irrespective as to what we might think, it's what God thinks that counts, as should be obvious.

The very attitude of some Christians is sin.

FAITH AND SIN

Paul said, *"Whatsoever is not of faith is sin"* (Rom. 14:23). Even though the definite article the is not used in front of the word *faith*, at least in this instance, still, the gist of the sentence is toward *the* faith, which is a synonym for the Christian experience.

What does it mean that a lack of faith constitutes sin?

Understanding that what Paul said was inspired by the Holy Spirit, which means that it's the Word of God, this means that we should pay careful attention.

The lack of faith addressed here has to do with one having faith in Christ and what Christ has done at the Cross. Everything should be hinged on the foundation of *"Jesus Christ, and Him crucified"* (I Cor. 2:2). Everything must stem from that particular aspect.

If, in fact, we as believers are attempting to guide our lives, to guide our walk, and to live as we ought to live by trusting in things other than the Cross, such a position insults God and constitutes sin. It is a rebellion against God's prescribed order, which, in effect, is the foundation sin of all sin. So, if one's faith is not in Christ and His finished work, automatically, that person is living in a state of sin. That may come as a shock to Christians, but it is the truth!

When we presently think of sin, we almost always think of acts of sin. That is labeled as *"works of the flesh"* (Gal. 5:19–21). The reason for the works of the flesh is that the believer, and Paul was addressing believers here, is operating from the premise of flesh (Rom. 8:8). That's the realm of the carnal mind (Rom. 8:6).

WHAT IS THE FLESH?

Even though we have addressed this subject already in this volume, considering that it is at least one of, if not the single most important aspect of the Christian experience, I think it would be difficult to overdiscuss the subject.

When Paul used the term *flesh*, he was speaking of one's own individual power, strength, and ability; in other words, what we can do from the human standpoint. In fact, these things aren't sin within themselves, but if we depend on them instead of Christ and what He has done for us at the Cross, we sin! Paul told us the reason we cannot live for God after this fashion.

He said, *"And if Christ be in you, the body is dead because of sin; but the Spirit is life because of righteousness"* (Rom. 8:10).

What did he mean by that?

At the Fall, man was so physically, mentally, and spiritually weakened that what God required of him, he simply could not do. Now, I don't mean that some of us can do it but most can't; I mean that *none* of us can, that is, if we try to live for God in any way except by Christ and the Cross.

Due to the Fall, man lives in a polluted atmosphere and is, as well, polluted himself. Even though believers fall into the category of new creations in Christ Jesus, still, we have not yet been glorified. Due to that fact, whatever is done in our lives to help us live for God must be instigated by the Holy Spirit (Rom. 8:11). He will function within our hearts and lives, helping us on a continuing basis, only on the premise of what Christ has done at the Cross and our faith in that finished work (Rom. 8:2). If we try to live for God in any other manner, and I speak of faith in Christ and the Cross, we automatically sin and, in fact, are in a state of sin because we have stepped outside of God's prescribed order. Thank the Lord that our Saviour makes intercession for us in such situations, but still, this defeated place and position takes a severe toll upon our Christian experience.

For any person who is trying to live for God by any means other than by faith, and we speak of faith in Christ and the Cross, such constitutes as one living in spiritual adultery (Rom. 7:1-4). This refers to an individual who is saved by the blood of Jesus, thereby married to Christ, but is being unfaithful to Christ, and is being unfaithful by trusting in things other than Christ and the Cross. I would trust by now that the reader has been made aware of the fact that everything hinges on the Cross, of which all of these sacrifices were types.

ATONEMENT

"And he shall bring his trespass offering unto the LORD *for his sin which he has sinned, a female from the flock, a lamb, or a kid of the goats, for a sin offering; and the priest shall make an atonement for him concerning his sin.*

"And if he be not able to bring a lamb, then he shall bring for his trespass, which he has committed, two turtledoves, or two young pigeons, unto the LORD: *one for a sin offering, and the other for a burnt offering"* (Lev. 5:6-7).

If sin was committed, sacrifice had to be offered. As is obvious here, if the person's financial status didn't allow him to bring a lamb or a goat, he could bring two turtledoves or two young pigeons. If he was so poor that he couldn't afford that, as Verse 11 tells us, he could bring a portion of fine flour. As is obvious, every strata of society was accommodated, but the fact is, and must not be overlooked, sacrifice must be offered for sin, irrespective as to whom the person might be.

As should be noted here, the type of sacrifices, especially in the first seven verses of this chapter, are somewhat intermingled. In fact, the trespass offering was but a sin offering of distinct types to make atonement for the trespasses named in the sins. Consequently, the first pigeon or turtledove was a sin offering, which required the shedding of blood, and the second was a burnt offering, symbolizing satisfaction to God by perfect obedience to Him in making atonement. Both symbolized the perfect obedience of Christ as man's substitute.

FORGIVENESS

"And he shall bring them unto the priest, who shall offer that which is for the sin offering first, and wring off his head from his neck, but shall not divide it asunder:

"And he shall sprinkle of the blood of the sin offering upon the side of the altar; and the rest of the blood shall be wrung out at the bottom of the altar: it is a sin offering.

"And he shall offer the second for a burnt offering, according to the manner: and the priest shall make an atonement for him for his sin which he has sinned, and it shall be forgiven him" (Lev. 5:8-10).

The priest made an atonement, and the sinner was forgiven. To forgive is to unbind. Forgiveness means the unbinding from off the soul of the death sentence bound upon it by the committed sin.

Life surrendered could alone unbind the sentence. In the slain lamb or the crushed wheat, this judgment appeared. The priest, the lamb, and the crushed wheat all symbolized Christ and His atoning work.

In Verse 1, the voice of swearing was the action of the Hebrew judge in adjuring by God a witness to utter the truth. To refuse to answer was to sin against Jehovah. We find an example of this in Jesus before Caiaphas, who at once replied, *"This is the divine method of swearing a witness."*

WHAT FORGIVENESS MEANS

As we have stated, the very word *forgive* means *"to unbind."* The person who is forgiven by God is loosed from the sentence of death, which was incurred because of the sin. Christ has taken the penalty which we should have taken, but if we had taken that penalty, we would have been lost forever.

Of course, such forgiveness is predicated solely upon the confession of the sin by the believer, which must be done to God (I Jn. 1:9). As bad as sin is, there is no limitation on the number of times that God will forgive. As long as the person confesses the sin — which, at the same time, means that he is sorry for the sin and is trying to rid himself of such — forgiveness will always be granted.

A believer can forgive another believer and, in fact, must do so if wrong has been committed against him. Unless the one who has committed the wrong admits the wrong, which is proper confession, the effect of forgiveness in such a case cannot actually be consummated. For forgiveness to be total and complete, it necessitates the action of two parties.

If we sin against the Lord, we must confess our sin to Him. He will then forgive and, in fact, has promised to do so (I Jn. 1:9). However, if the believer who has sinned will not confess the sin to the Lord, in other words, will not admit that he has sinned, forgiveness cannot be enjoined.

COMMANDED TO FORGIVE

While we believers are commanded to forgive those who trespass against us, irrespective as to whether they confess it or not, that is done for our good. As a believer, we cannot allow resentment or a grudge to build up in our hearts. So, we are commanded to forgive in order that such not be done; however, as stated, fellowship between the two parties cannot be enjoined unless both parties conduct themselves scripturally. That means that the person who has committed the wrong must confess it to the individual whom he has wronged, and the one who has been wronged must make certain that he forgives the wrong done to him. Fellowship can then be restored.

If a lamb or a goat was brought, it would be handled in the customary way. However, if two birds were brought (turtledoves or pigeons), one was to be offered as a sin offering, with the other offered as a burnt offering. Why were the birds treated differently than the lamb or the goat? In other words, concerning these two fowls, why was a burnt offering needed when it wasn't needed regarding the goat or the lamb?

The sin offering must make way for the burnt offering. After the sin offering, which made atonement, came the burnt offering, an acknowledgment of the great mercy of God in appointing and accepting the atonement. The burnt offering was required because not enough blood was shed, regarding the offering of the first bird as a sin offering.

THE BURNT OFFERING

The burnt offering, irrespective of the animal, presented a type of Christ offering Himself without spot to God. In other words, His sacrifice of Himself on the Cross was carried out in order that the righteousness of a thrice-holy God might be satisfied. In the burnt offering, the sinlessness of the victim (Christ) was transferred to the worshipper. In the sin offering, the sinfulness of the sinner was transferred to the victim.

As the Christian advances in this divine life, he becomes conscious that those sins he has committed are but branches from a root, streams from a fountain, and, moreover, that sin in his nature is that fountain — that root. This leads to far deeper exercise, which can only be met by a deeper insight into the work of the Cross. In a word, the Cross will need to be apprehended as that in which God Himself has *"condemned sin in the flesh"* (Rom. 8:3).

SIN IN THE FLESH

If one is to notice, it does not say, *"sin in the life,"* but the root from which these have sprung, namely, sin in the flesh. This is a truth of immense importance. Christ did not merely die for our sins, according to the Scriptures, but He was made sin for us (II Cor. 5:21). This latter is the doctrine of the sin offering.

In the burnt offering, we are conducted to a point beyond which it is impossible to go, and that is the work of the Cross as accomplished under the immediate eye of God, and as the expression of the unswerving devotion of the heart to Christ. In all cases, we begin with the Cross and end with the Cross.

If we begin with the burnt offering, we see Christ on the Cross doing the will of God — making atonement according to the measure of His perfect surrender of Himself to God. If we begin with the trespass offering, we see Christ on the Cross, bearing our sins and putting them away according to the perfection of His atoning sacrifice. In each and all, we behold the excellency, the beauty, and the perfection of His divine and adorable person.

THAT ALL MAY COME

"But if he be not able to bring two turtledoves, or two young pigeons, then he who sinned shall bring for his offering the tenth part of an ephah of fine flour for a sin offering; he shall put no oil upon it, neither shall he put any frankincense thereon: for it is a sin offering.

"Then shall he bring it to the priest, and the priest shall take his handful of it, even a memorial thereof, and burn it on the altar, according to the offerings made by fire unto the LORD: *it is a sin offering.*

"And the priest shall make an atonement for him as touching his sin that he has sinned in one of these, and it shall be forgiven him: and the remnant shall be the priest's, as a meat offering" (Lev. 5:11-13).

In this beautiful application, we find that provision is made for all of humanity. Whether the sinner was rich or poor, provision was made that a suitable offering could be rendered.

SIN MUST BE ADDRESSED

For the poorest of the poor, one who could not afford a lamb or a goat, or even two turtledoves or two young pigeons, they could bring the amount of flour required, which was small. So, we see here that sin had to be dealt with, irrespective as to whom the person might be. The Lord could not overlook the rich person, and neither could He overlook the poor person. So, provision was made, which, in effect, portrayed the Cross. The one sacrifice of Christ answered every need in every heart and life, irrespective of the need and irrespective of the person, at least for those who will believe (Jn. 3:16).

However, let it be understood, the non-bloody substitute, namely the flour, being permitted was only an exception for the benefit of the very poor, and only in the cases specified, which does not invalidate the general rule that without the shedding of blood, there is no remission of sin.

No oil was to be added to the flour, with oil being a type of the Holy Spirit. The reason is there was no shedding of blood in this particular offering. His work is accomplished only through the Cross, but which could not be carried out, except in some minor type, before the Cross. So, this offering of flour could be carried out without great harm being done.

THE THANK OFFERING

As well, as is stated in Verse 11, frankincense was not to be added either because it represented the perfect life of Christ, which would be given on the Cross in sacrifice.

Why was it prohibited with the sin offering and added to the thanksgiving offering? (Lev. 2:1).

The thanksgiving offering, or meat offering, to which it was biblically referred, was not a sacrifice offering that required the shedding of blood. It was a thanksgiving offering that was supposed to be rendered because the sin offering, or trespass offering, had been accepted by God, and the one who had failed had now been restored to fellowship. The meat offering was not an offering for sin; it was a thank offering in that sin had now been atoned.

THE FIFTH PART

"And the LORD spoke unto Moses, saying,

"If a soul commit a trespass, and sin through ignorance, in the holy things of the LORD; then he shall bring for his trespass unto the LORD a ram without blemish out of the flocks, with your estimation by shekels of silver, after the shekel of the sanctuary, for a trespass offering.

"And he shall make amends for the harm that he has done in the holy thing, and shall add the fifth part thereto, and give it unto the priest: and the priest shall make an atonement for him with the ram of the trespass offering, and it shall be forgiven him." (Lev. 5:14-16).

We find in the trespass offering, by the fifth part being added, that through the Cross, God has not merely received back what was lost, but has actually become a gainer. He has gained more by redemption than ever He lost by the Fall.

He reaps a richer harvest of glory, honor, and praise from the Cross of redemption than ever He could have reaped from those of creation.

The wrong has not only been perfectly atoned for, but an eternal advantage has been gained by the work of the Cross.

Actually, the Cross involved a mysterious wisdom, *"Which none of the princes of this world knew: for had they known it, they would not have crucified the Lord of Glory"* (I Cor. 2:8).

As well, as it regards the believer, faith evidenced in the Cross will give him back all that was lost, and more besides. As the Lord, He is a gainer also.

In no way is this meant to glorify sin. In other words, the idea of sinning that grace may abound is foolish indeed! Most sin, in fact, is committed by Christians, not because they want to do such, but simply because they do not know God's prescribed order of victory. In other words, through their ignorance, Satan has stolen much from them. The Cross gets it all back, and more!

THE MOST WONDERFUL PROMISE

We have here, in the Law of the trespass offering, one of the most wonderful promises found anywhere in the Word of God. It has to do with the fifth being added, the explanation of which, I think, will prove to be beautifully enlightening.

We find in the Law of the trespass offering, which is given in the next chapter, that this sin pertains to harm done to one's neighbor or fellow believer. In other words, we sin against another believer. Concerning this, Mackintosh said: *"There is a fine principle involved in the expression, 'against the Lord.' Although the matter in question was a wrong done to one's neighbor, yet the Lord looked upon it as a trespass against Himself. Everything must be viewed in reference to the Lord. It matters not who may be affected; Jehovah must get the first place. Thus, when David's conscience was pierced by the arrow of conviction, in reference to his treatment of Uriah, he* exclaims, 'I have sinned against the Lord' (II Sam. 12:13). This principle does not in the least interfere with the injured man's claim."

The Law of the trespass offering was that the person who had wronged his brother in the Lord must make amends for that wrong and then add a fifth, or 20 percent. To make it easy to understand, we suggest the following: If, through negligence, an Israelite was responsible for the loss of a lamb of another Israelite, he was required by law to pay for the lamb, plus add 20 percent to whatever the lamb was worth.

This seemed to apply only to property. It would be impossible to measure harm done to someone through lies, malicious gossip, etc.

TO RESTORE MORE THAN HAS BEEN LOST

We must look at the Law of this particular offering from both the standpoint of God the Father and, as well, the standpoint of the believer.

We should very well understand that God has been robbed of much, as it regards the revolution of Satan and fallen angels against Him and, as well, the terrible fall of man. He has been insulted and impugned in every capacity. His prized creation, man, has been all but destroyed.

So, it would be difficult for us to properly comprehend how in the world that He could be rightly compensated for His terrible loss! And yet, we will show you how that through the Cross, the Lord has not only been compensated for His loss, but due to the fifth required to be added, He will actually come out as a netgainer. However, it was only done through the Cross.

Let me give you an example. Man was originally created to live forever, but due to the Fall, death entered the picture and the results are obvious. However, due to the Cross, at the Resurrection, redeemed man will be given a glorified body, which will be far superior to that which was originally intended.

THE CROSS

As well, due to the Cross, the New Jerusalem will be brought down to this earth, with there actually being a new Heaven and a new earth, as stated, all made possible by the Cross. We find this in the last two chapters of Revelation. The reason we know that the Cross is responsible for this is because, in those last two chapters — with Satan, demon spirits, and fallen man locked away forever and forever, and with there being no hint of sin left on this earth or in the universe — Christ is still mentioned seven times as *the Lamb*. This tells us that all of these great things have come to pass all because of what Jesus did at the Cross.

So, in the work of the Cross, God has not merely received back what was lost, but, as well, He is an actual gainer. He has gained more by redemption than ever He lost by the Fall. He reaps a richer harvest of glory, honor, and praise in the work of redemption than ever He could have reaped from those of creation.

Let's say it another way: *"The sons of God"* could raise a loftier song of praise around the empty tomb of Jesus than ever they raised in view of the Creator's accomplished work. The wrong has not only been perfectly atoned for, but an eternal advantage has been gained by the work of the Cross. This is a stupendous truth. God is a gainer by the work of Calvary.

ALL BECAUSE OF WHAT JESUS DID AT THE CROSS

Concerning this, Mackintosh said: *"Who could have conceived this? When we behold man, and the creation of which he was lord, laid in ruins at the feet of the enemy, how could we conceive that, from amid those ruins, God should gather richer and nobler spoils than any which our unfallen world could have yielded? Blessed be the name of Jesus in all of this! It is to Him we owe it all. It is by His precious Cross that ever a truth so amazing, so divine, could be enunciated. Assuredly, the Cross involves a mysterious wisdom 'which none of the princes of this world knew; for had they known it, they would not have crucified the Lord of Glory'"* (I Cor. 2:8).

It is no wonder that the Holy Spirit gave forth the solemn decree: *"If any man love not the Lord Jesus Christ, let him be accursed"* (I Cor. 16:22).

Every knee shall bow at the feet of Jesus, whether in Heaven, earth, or under the earth, and every tongue shall confess that He is Lord to the glory of God the Father (Phil. 2:10–11), and all because of what He did at the Cross.

THROUGH THE CROSS

The first thing we must ever realize is that through the Cross, all victory has been won, all victory is being won, and all victory shall be won. I speak of the human race from the very beginning even into eternity future. As a believer, you must understand that, comprehend that, and believe that!

Secondly, you must act upon that tremendous premise; in other words, you must conduct yourself in the realm and respect of what Jesus did at the Cross. It must ever be the object of your faith. That is the only way, and I mean the only way, that you can live a victorious, overcoming, Christian life. It is the only way that you can enjoy the more abundant life, of which Jesus spoke in John 10:10. This is the only way that the powers of darkness can be defeated in your life, and you walk and live as a child of God should walk and live.

It's all in the Cross. That's the reason that Paul said, *"But God forbid that I should glory, save in the Cross of our Lord Jesus Christ, by whom the world is crucified unto me, and I unto the world"* (Gal. 6:14). If it is to be noticed, he didn't say that I should glory save in the Resurrection, or the throne, or anything else for that matter. No, by all means, we aren't denigrating the Resurrection, the throne of God, or anything that pertains to the Lord. We are saying that it was at the Cross and the Cross alone where all victory was won, and you as a believer must understand that.

THE BELIEVER

Considering all of this, and going back to the fifth that is added, we must, as well, come to the conclusion that man, as well as God, is a positive gainer by the Cross. By that, I'm not merely referring to the fact that salvation comes by the Cross. Of course, that is very, very important, in fact, all-important, but I am speaking rather of the following:

I am saying that due to the Cross, man will gain more than he lost by the Fall. No, by no means am I saying that it was good that Adam fell. In fact, it was the most horrible thing that one could ever begin to imagine, but where sin abounded, grace did much more abound (Rom. 5:20).

In other words, in essence, the Lord has said to Satan and all the cohorts of darkness, *Inasmuch as you have done this to My prized creation — man — through the Cross, I will give him back what he has lost, and even more besides* (Gen. 3:15).

Now let me look at the second part of this scenario. There are some of you holding this book in your hands who love the Lord supremely, but until you heard the Message of the Cross, Satan got the upper hand in your life time and time again. In other words, he robbed, plundered, and mutilated exactly as Jesus said he would do, i.e., he steals, kills, and destroys (Jn. 10:10).

However, now you have heard the Message of the Cross, you have believed the Message of the Cross, and you have started to act upon this foundation of the faith, for, in effect, the Cross is *the faith.* Now the Lord, through the Cross, is going to give you back all that Satan has plundered from you, plus he's going to give you even more than you lost. It's the Law of the trespass offering. Satan took from you that which was rightly yours, and now it will be restored — plus!

GRACE

Paul said, *"For sin shall not have dominion over you: for you are not under the Law, but under grace"* (Rom. 6:14).

What did Paul mean by that statement?

Let's look at the latter first.

The Law can tell a man what he ought to do, but it gives him no power to do it. Conversely, because of the Cross, grace — which is simply the goodness of God extended to undeserving saints — will give all the power that man needs to be what he ought to be. Jesus has fulfilled the Law in every respect, which means it's not incumbent upon us.

Does that mean that it's all right now to steal, to lie, etc.?

Of course, it does not! Those are moral laws of God, and they cannot change. So, how do we keep them?

Christ has already kept all of these laws for us. He lived His life of 33 and one-half years and never sinned one single time in word, thought, or deed. As stated, He did it all for us. The moment you were converted, you were changed over from lawbreaker to law-keeper.

I no longer live this life by trying to keep rules and regulations, but I live it by keeping my faith in Christ and what Christ has done for me at the Cross, which gives me the help of the Holy Spirit, who is God, and who can do anything. So, I don't worry about the Law inasmuch as it is automatically kept within my heart and within my life. At the moment the believer steps outside of grace over into law, he has tied the hands of the Holy Spirit, so to speak. This means that such a believer is once again going to have the sin nature rule him or her.

GRACE AND THE CROSS OF CHRIST

The believer must understand that it is the Cross of Christ which makes grace available to all of us. As we have just stated, grace is simply the goodness of God extended to undeserving people. God had just as much grace in Old Testament times as He does now, but it was the Cross that satisfied the legal requirements, making it possible for grace to extend to believers in copious amounts, in other words, all that we need.

God doesn't owe any man anything. Conversely, we owe God everything. Inasmuch as we are His children, He wants to give us good things, and He only requires one thing of us — that the Cross of Christ ever be the object of our faith.

Listen to what Jesus said: "**If any man will come after Me** *(the criterion for discipleship)*, **let him deny himself** *(not asceticism as many think, but rather that one denies one's own will power, self-will, strength, and ability, depending totally on Christ)*, **and take up his cross** *(the benefits of the Cross, looking exclusively to what Jesus did there to meet our every need)* **daily** *(this is so important, our looking to the Cross that we must renew our faith in what Christ has done for us, even on a daily basis, for Satan will ever try to move us away from the Cross as the object of our faith, which always spells disaster)*, **and follow Me** *(Christ can be followed only by the believer looking to the Cross, under-standing what it accomplished, and by that means alone [Rom. 6:3-5, 11, 14; 8:1-2, 11; I Cor. 1:17-18, 21, 23; 2:2; Gal. 6:14; Eph. 2:13-18; Col. 2:14-15])* **(Lk. 9:23).**

Furthermore, Jesus said that if we do not take up our Cross and follow Him, we cannot be His disciple (Lk. 14:27).

Without the Cross, there can be no grace. Even before the Cross, the sacrificial system was put in place, which actu-ally originated with Adam and Eve. There is evidence that Adam and Eve offered up sacrifices for a period of time but soon ceased. We see in Chapter 4 of Genesis man's problem and man's solution.

The Lord had told the first family that despite being driven from the Garden and despite their fallen condition, they could have forgiveness of sins and communion with Him. However, it would be by virtue of the slain lamb, which would epitomize and symbolize the Saviour who was to come.

Abel offered up a sacrifice as God demanded, and God honored it. His brother Cain offered up sacrifice, but it was of his own hands, in other words, it was not a lamb as had been demanded. In essence, Cain was saying that he was not a sinner and did not need a Saviour, so his sacrifice was rejected.

It must be understood that God already knows what we are, so He doesn't look at us nearly as much as He looks at the sacrifice. If the sacrifice is accepted, then the one offering the sacrifice is accepted. If the sacrifice is rejected, then the one offering the sacrifice is rejected. That's a solemn thought and must be understood without fail.

The believer must understand that the only thing standing between him and eternal Hell is the Cross of Christ, and that goes for every person who has ever lived — who is alive now, and who will be alive in the future.

While under the Law of Moses, the blood of bulls and goats could not take away sins (Heb. 10:4). This means that such limited God as to how much grace could be extended. When we read all of these rules and regulations, which every believer should read and study, it makes us realize how wonderful the Cross of Christ actually is. Thank God, Jesus satisfied it all. Now I don't have to bring a lamb, but only extend faith in Christ.

Many believers think of grace, but they don't actually realize how grace was and is made possible. It was and is made possible solely by the Cross of Christ. Our simple faith in Christ and what He has done for us at the Cross grants us an unlimited amount of grace, and so it does with every believer.

SATAN

Consequently, we might look at the law of the trespass offering in the following manner: Satan must give back to you all that he has stolen from you, which refers to the principle, and, as well, he must add the fifth.

However, I'm saying that in that manner only as a way of explanation. The truth is, Satan doesn't give anyone anything simply because he doesn't have anything to give, at least that's worth anything. The true meaning pertains to him being forced aside while God lavishes upon you all that Satan has taken from you — plus! The Evil One, despite your failures of the past, cannot do anything about the scenario. All he can do is stand helplessly by. It's the law of the trespass offering!

GUILT

"And if a soul sin, and commit any of these things which are forbidden to be done by the commandments of the Lord; *though he wist it not, yet he is guilty, and shall bear his iniquity.*

"And he shall bring a ram without blemish out of the flock, with your estimation, for a trespass offering, unto the priest: and the priest shall make an atonement for him concerning his ignorance wherein he erred and wist it not, and it shall be forgiven him.

"It is a trespass offering: he has certainly trespassed against the Lord*"* (Lev. 5:17-19).

The expressions, *through ignorance* and *wist it not* (knew it not), dispose of the popular fallacy that sincerity secures salvation.

As well, and as we have repeatedly stated, even though these transgressions were done in ignorance, the Lord still looked at it as sin, and to be sure, it would have negative results. The moment that true knowledge came to such an individual, he was to offer up the trespass offering. In other words, he couldn't (and neither can we) plead ignorance as it regards the Word of God.

Years ago, I was reading behind a particular English preacher, who has long since gone on to be with the Lord. He made a statement, which, at the time, I knew to be true, but I really did not quite understand exactly how it was true.

He stated, or words to this effect, *"The church must repent, not only of the bad things it has done and is doing but, as well, of the good things."*

When I read that, I knew instinctively that it was correct; but yet, I did not fully understand how it was correct. It is obvious that anyone must repent over things which we know to be bad, but good things?

PLACING TRUST IN GOOD THINGS

What he meant was this, which I have come to understand since the Cross has been opened up to me: it is sin for the believer, or the church as a whole, to place trust in the good things we do, thinking that it may earn us something with the Lord.

Now, almost everyone would read that and say, *"Well, I've always known that!"* Most of the time, those who say that are, even at that very moment, trusting in things other than the Cross.

Let me say it in a different way: It is impossible for a believer who doesn't understand the Cross — and I'm referring to the Cross as it regards sanctification — to properly live for the Lord. Every single time, that person will have his or her faith in something other than the Cross, which, in fact, is a given. In other words, as believers, we're going to make the object of our faith something. Even though we may load it up with Scriptures, and even though it may sound right, if it's not the Cross, it's not right, and, in fact, we are sinning. All of these things are good things in our sight and, in fact, may definitely be good things; however, our faith must ever rest in Christ and Him crucified (I Cor. 2:2). Anything else is sin.

Paul said: *"Examine yourselves, whether you be in the faith; prove your own selves. Know you not your own selves, how that Jesus Christ is in you, except you be reprobates?"* (II Cor. 13:5).

"God of eternity, Saviour and King,
"Help us to honor Thee, help while we sing;
"Now may the clouds of night break into splendor bright
"Jesus, our life and light, our Lord and King!"

"God of eternity, Ancient of Days,
"Glorious in majesty, Author of Praise;
"Hear Thou our earnest call, while at Your feet we fall,
"Jesus our all in all, our Lord and King!"

"God of eternity, Ruler divine,
"Strength of the mighty hills, all power is Thine;
"Boundless Thy reign shall be, wondrous Thy victory,
"Earth shall be filled with Thee, our Lord and King!"

"God of eternity, Love is Thy name,
"God of the earth and sea, Thee we proclaim;
"Love, thro' Thine only Son, Thy work of grace
      hath done;
"O blessed Three in One, our Lord and King!"

6

Sin Against a Fellow Believer

CHAPTER SIX

Sin Against a Fellow Believer

"*AND THE* **LORD** *spoke unto Moses, saying,*

"*If a soul sin, and commit a trespass against the* LORD, *and lie unto his neighbor in that which was delivered him to keep, or in fellowship, or in a thing taken away by violence, or has deceived his neighbor;*

"*Or have found that which was lost, and lies concerning it, and swears falsely; in any of all these that a man does, sinning therein:*

"*Then it shall be, because he has sinned, and is guilty, that he shall restore that which he took violently away, or the thing which he has deceitfully gotten, or that which was delivered him to keep, or the lost thing which he found*" (Lev. 6:1-4).

While all sin is ultimately against God, the greater thrust of the trespass offering, I think, pertains to one believer sinning against another believer in some way. Of course, under the old economy, it would have been one Israelite sinning against another Israelite. As should be obvious, this is a grievous sin as it regards the Lord, and it is not overlooked, even though it is between believers. In fact, I think it is obvious in these passages that God looks upon such a sin as worse than other sins. To sin against unbelievers is terrible to say the least, but to sin against a fellow believer is beyond abominable. Tragically, it happens, sad to say, everyday!

Believers must be very, very careful as to our conduct toward anyone, irrespective of whom that person might be. However, if we're dealing with other Christians, regardless of what they might do, we must ever understand that if they are true believers, Jesus died for them, and, in fact, they belong to Christ. Knowing and understanding that, our treatment of them and our attitude and conduct toward them must be according to whom they belong, namely the Lord!

In such a case, even though the believer in question may not own up to his perfidiousness, still, the Lord always and without exception, knows the truth of any and every matter. To the one who is in the wrong, irrespective of his claims, the Scripture concerning this plainly says, *"Avenge not yourselves, but rather give place unto wrath: for it is written, vengeance is Mine; I will repay, says the Lord"* (Rom. 12:19).

To be sure, nothing escapes the eye of God, and concerning everything, all must be accounted for, and all must give account!

NO ONE GETS BY

No one, but no one, gets by with wrongdoing. Jesus plainly said, *"Judge not, that you be not judged.*

"For with what judgment you judge, you shall be judged: and with what measure you mete, it shall be measured to you again" (Mat. 7:1–2).

So, whatever we maliciously say about others, ultimately and eventually, it will be said about us. Whatever we do to others, and I speak of that which is wrong, ultimately and eventually, it will be done to us.

Such judgment can be escaped if the one who has done the wrong will properly confess the wrong and seek forgiveness, both from the offended party and especially from God. Regrettably, most are loath to admit their wrongdoing, even when it is so very obvious!

THE FIFTH PART MORE

"Or all that about which he has sworn falsely; he shall even restore it in the principal, and shall add the fifth part more thereto, and give it unto him to whom it appertains, in the day of his trespass offering.

"And he shall bring his trespass offering unto the LORD, *a ram without blemish out of the flock, with your estimation, for a trespass offering, unto the priest:*

"And the priest shall make an atonement for him before the LORD: *and it shall be forgiven him for anything of all that he has done in trespassing therein"* (Lev. 6:5-7).

The Holy Spirit saw fit to address the fifth part the second time, with the first time being in Verse 16 of the previous chapter. As always, this is done with purpose. The Holy Spirit wants us to know the importance of what is being said. As well, He wants us to garner the truth that is being given, which, as it is with all Scripture, is of vital significance.

To be brief, and as we've already stated in Chapter 5, the great truth presented here is in conjunction with the sacrificial offering itself. This, of course, speaks of what Christ did on the Cross. We have the restitution demanded for wrong-doing, at least when the property of fellow believers has been harmed in some way, and, as well, we have the fifth part that is to be added.

RESTORATION

As it concerns you the reader, if you will believe the Lord and place your faith and trust totally in Christ — in His finished work on the Cross — then every single thing that Satan has stolen from you, and everything you've lost to the Evil One, will be restored, plus 20 percent more will be added. To be sure, those numbers I've given are not mine, but they belong to the Holy Spirit. As well, the Lord will definitely do that which He has promised, so you as a believer ought to understand this, believe this, and expect this!

As is seen in Exodus 22:1–9, when a person was guilty of any of the offenses specified there, the offender was condemned to make a fourfold restitution. The passage before us proclaims this amount as being reduced to the restitution of the principle with the addition of the fifth part. The reason for this difference is that the Law in Exodus deals with a culprit who is convicted of his crime in a court of justice by means of witnesses. However, the Law before us deals with an offender who, through compunction of mind, voluntarily confesses his offense, and to whom the offense could not be recognized and known without this voluntary confession. It is in this difference that a case for a trespass offering is made.

THE LAW OF THE BURNT OFFERING

"And the LORD spoke unto Moses, saying,
"Command Aaron and his sons, saying, This is the law
of the burnt offering: it is the burnt offering, because of the
burning upon the altar all night unto the morning, and the
fire of the altar shall be burning in it" (Lev. 6:8-9).

Beginning with Leviticus 6:8 through Leviticus, Chapter 7, we have the law of the burnt offering, the meal offering, the sin offering, the trespass offering, and the peace offering. We also have the law of the high priest's consecration offering.

The order in which the offerings are placed does not correspond here with that found in the opening chapters of the book. There, the sin offering comes last; here, the peace offering. This shows design. Only an absolutely perfect victim — the Lord Jesus Christ — could put away sin by the sacrifice of Himself; hence, the sin offering is placed last. However, only a fully accomplished atonement can give peace to the conscience, so, therefore, in the laws affecting the sacrifices, the peace offering is put last.

The burnt offering was to burn all night. In the morning, dressed in his clean linen garments, the priest was to gather its ashes and place them beside the altar, and then, in his garments of beauty, bring them with befitting glory unto a clean place. This represents the coming Kingdom Age, which, of course, speaks of a cleansed earth.

Through this night of mystery, the fragrance of Christ's offering up of Himself to God ascends continually. *In the morning*, He will appear to His people Israel in His double glory as the white-robed priest and the glory-crowned mediator.

The fire that consumed the burnt offering originally came from Heaven (Lev. 9:24), and was maintained perpetually burning by the unwearied ministry of the priests.

It was lacking in the second temple. It testified on the one hand to the unceasing delight of God in the sacrifice of Christ, and on the other hand, to His unceasing hatred of sin. False teachers today put this fire out by denying the doctrines of the atonement and of the wrath to come.

THE LORD SPOKE

Verse 9 could read: *"It, the burnt offering* (the evening sacrifice), *shall burn upon the hearth upon the altar all night unto the morning."*

Verse 8 records the fourth instance in which the formula, *"the LORD spoke unto Moses,"* is used in Leviticus (Lev. 4:1; 5:14; 6:1, 8), and as in the former passages, it introduces a further communication from the Lord to Moses.

Previously, the Law pointed out to the people under what circumstances and how they were to bring their sacred oblations. Now directions are given to the priests of how to conduct the sacrificial service of the people.

THE LINEN GARMENT

"And the priest shall put on his linen garment, and his linen breeches shall he put upon his flesh, and take up the ashes which the fire has consumed with the burnt offering on the altar, and he shall put them beside the altar" (Lev. 6:10).

Of course, the priest doing the officiating was a type of Christ, even as the whole burnt offering was a type of Christ.

As we have stated, the whole burnt offering typified Christ satisfying the demands of the thrice-holy God. Only a perfect sacrifice could do such, hence, the officiating priests dressed in the linen garment, which typified righteousness.

Christ was perfectly righteous, which means that His birth was perfect, and His life was perfect, which means that it was without sin of any shape, form, or fashion. This means that He satisfied the demands of the Law, which typified the righteousness of God, and which God demanded of all men. As our substitute, Christ kept the Law perfectly in every respect and did so as a man — *the* Man Christ Jesus, the second Man, as Paul referred to Him; and the last Adam (I Cor. 15:45–50).

Irrespective as to how many people died on crosses that day throughout the Roman Empire, and even if they had attempted to die as a sacrifice, the giving of themselves could not have been accepted by God simply because, due to original sin, all men were and are spiritually polluted. Christ alone could fit this description of perfect righteousness, and Christ alone did fit this description.

This blows to pieces the grossly erroneous doctrine of the Word of Faith people, which claims that the blood of any born-again man could redeem humanity. The difference in the born-again man and Christ is stupendous to say the least.

We have to be made the righteousness of God, while Christ is the righteousness of God (II Cor. 5:21). The difference there is vast! Imputed righteousness, which is actually what we have, is not the same as the perfection of righteousness, which is Christ.

The whole burnt offering transfers the righteousness of the victim to the sinner, while the sin offering transfers the guilt of the sinner to the innocent victim, namely Christ.

ASHES

After the fire had burned all night and had totally consumed the sacrifice, the priest was to take the ashes off the altar and deposit them on the ash heap to the east of the altar.

Considering that the sacrifice had been totally consumed, this refers to the fact that the sacrifice of Christ was total and complete. In other words, the ashes represented the fact that the totality of the sin problem, the root of sin, had been dealt with. This refers not only to man's condition, but what caused man's condition, which was the revolution of Satan in eternity past.

Preachers argue over whether certain things, such as healing, are in the atonement. To be sure, divine healing is in the atonement, as is every single thing that was lost in this terrible rebellion and revolution against God. Jesus left nothing unaddressed.

It is true that at the present time, we do not have all for which He has paid the price, that awaiting the coming Resurrection. However, according to the Scripture, we do have enough now to live a victorious, overcoming Christian life in regard to the settled fact that sin shall not have dominion over us (Rom. 6:14).

SIN

If sin is dominating the child of God in some way, this means that the believer is not properly availing himself of the great victory purchased by Christ at the Cross. Considering the price that He paid, it is a travesty of the highest sort for us not to avail ourselves of all that for which He has paid the price, at least that which we can have at present.

The phrase, *unto the morning,* found in Verse 9, proclaims the fact that the day or morning is coming when the long night of sin will be totally and completely finished. This speaks of the coming Kingdom Age when Jesus will come back to rule on this earth. However, its greater meaning pertains to the coming time of the new heavens and the new earth when former things will have passed away (Rev. 21:4), even as is described in the last two chapters of the book of Revelation. The Scripture then says, *"for there shall be no night there"* (Rev. 21:25).

OTHER GARMENTS

"And he shall put off his garments, and put on other garments, and carry forth the ashes without the camp unto a clean place" (Lev. 6:11).

To remove the ashes to a clean place, the priest was to change his sacred robes in which he had ministered at the altar. He was to put on other garments, though less holy, but not common, since the removing of the ashes was still a sacred function.

Great care was taken that the place to which the ashes were removed was well sheltered so that the wind should not blow them about. The priest was not allowed to scatter them but had to deposit them gently. No stranger was permitted to gather them or to make profit by the ashes.

The priest being required to change his garments when he removed the ashes each morning presented itself as a portrayal of the fact that Christ, of whom the priest was a type, had finished His work. This pertained to the satisfying of the righteousness of God, which was the holiest of all; hence, it required the linen garments. Now, Christ would embark upon another aspect of His ministry, which was to serve as our high priest, constantly making intercession for us (Heb. 7:25; 9:24).

This is the reason that the burnt offering was a sweet savour offering exactly as were the meal offering and the peace offering. The sacrifices for sin were not sweet savour offerings, which constituted the sin offerings and the trespass offerings.

The law of the burnt offering, which we are now studying, tells us that this was the holiest work of Christ. In other words, the Cross came up before God as the holiest work of the Saviour, eclipsing any and everything else that He had done. That's the reason that Paul said: **"But God forbid that I should glory** *(boast)***, save in the Cross of our Lord Jesus Christ, by whom the world is crucified unto me, and I unto the world"** (Gal. 6:14).

THE CROSS IS THE FOUNDATION OF ALL DOCTRINE

"And the fire upon the altar shall be burning in it; it shall not be put out: and the priest shall burn wood on it every morning, and lay the burnt offering in order upon it; and he shall burn thereon the fat of the peace offerings" (Lev. 6:12).

Concerning this, Charles Ellicott said: *"This is introduced here in this fashion, in order to caution the priest whose function it is to remove the ashes, that when engaged in this act, he is to take great care that in taking off the ashes from the altar, he does not knock away the pieces of fat of the burnt offering, which constitute the fuel, which could cause the fire to go out.*

"Each morning, the priest was to replenish the wood on the altar which had been consumed during the night."

It is said that there were three separate piles of wood by the altar, and it was kept that way at all times. The largest one was for the daily sacrifice to be burned, which was a whole burnt offering, and which was offered up twice a day, 9 a.m. and 3 p.m.

The second pile of wood was that which provided the coals of fire that could be put into the censers and, in fact, was done so twice a day at the time of the morning and the evening sacrifices. They were placed on the altar of incense, with incense poured over these coals of fire, which filled the Holy Place with a sacred fragrance and a sacred smoke. This was a type of the intercessory work of Christ, which is carried on in Heaven unto this very hour.

The third pile of wood was said to be the perpetual fire from which the other two portions were fed. It was not quenched, we are told, until the destruction of the temple by Nebuchadnezzar.

THE FIRE WAS NEVER TO GO OUT

The fact that the fire was to never go out proclaims the fact that the Cross alone is the answer to the sins of mankind and, furthermore, that it will ever be the answer. The fact that it was to never go out also proclaims the absolute necessity that we understand that the Cross is the foundation of our faith. It is not a mere doctrine, but rather the foundation of all doctrine.

While it can be spoken of as a doctrine, it must be understood that it is the foundational truth from which all supplemental doctrine springs. I'm sure that Jesus addressed what He had done on the Cross as more than a mere doctrine among doctrines.

If one properly understands the Cross, then one has a working knowledge of the Bible. To not understand the Cross means that in some way, the individual has a perverted view of the Word of God. In fact, the story of the Cross is, in effect, the story of the Bible. This is so closely intertwined that we might even turn it around and it would work accordingly, meaning that the story of the Bible is the story of the Cross. Once one begins to understand the Cross, then what I have just stated becomes overly obvious. The study of the tabernacle and of the sacrificial system, which we are studying now, all and in totality is a study of the Cross.

THE FAT OF THE PEACE OFFERINGS

With the burnt offering, the sin offering, and the trespass offering, a peace offering was to be presented and offered with each one of these offerings every time they were offered.

The peace offering, which we will study momentarily, presents the fact that the other offering, whatever it might have been, was accepted by God, and peace was thereby restored to the one who had sinned. It was the offering of a finished work and faith in that finished work.

THE PERPETUAL BURNING OF THE FIRE

"The fire shall ever be burning upon the altar; it shall never go out" (Lev. 6:13).

It is believed that when Moses dedicated the tabernacle, meaning that it had been constructed and now erected exactly as the Lord had demanded, the Lord sent fire down from Heaven and ignited the wood on the altar (Ex. 40:29–38; Lev. 9:24).

The fire on this altar, which was ignited originally by God, was to be kept perpetually by the priests. This means that it was to never go out because the need of the people was ever present, as it regarded cleansing from sin.

Presently, and I speak of the time of the New Covenant, even though it is a finished work, we are to ever look at the Cross as the answer, in fact, the only answer for the ills of man. This means that we are to preach the Cross continually, i.e., *"it shall never go out."*

The truth is, there is less preaching of the Cross presently than there has been at any time, I believe, since the Reformation. This means that the church presently is in worse condition than it has been at any time since the Reformation. The Holy Spirit is given less and less place because the preaching of the Cross has been given less and less place. The two — the Cross and the Holy Spirit — go hand in hand.

THE CROSS AND THE HOLY SPIRIT

Unfortunately, the denominational world attempted to preach the Cross without the Holy Spirit, and presently, they are basically left preaching much of nothing. The Pentecostals tried to preach the Holy Spirit without the Cross, which, incidentally, the Holy Spirit will not tolerate, and they are basically left now as little more than a hollow shell. In fact, they are chasing spirits thinking it's the Holy Spirit!

The Scripture is emphatic, this fire *"shall never go out!"* However, I'm afraid it is going out, making the altar, i.e., the Cross, totally ineffective. The Cross is Christianity, and to remove the Cross is to take the heart out of Christianity, leaving it no more, as stated, than a hollow shell.

THE LAW OF THE MEAT OFFERING

"And this is the law of the meat offering: the sons of Aaron shall offer it before the LORD, before the altar" (Lev. 6:14).

We are to now study the law of the meat offering, which, in effect, was a grain or cereal offering, which could be constituted as a thank offering.

The word *meat* then was used for all types of food, whereas meat at present refers to the flesh of animals. In fact, in this offering, there was no blood shed because it was a grain offering. It was offered along with the peace offering, the latter of which was a blood sacrifice, every time the other offerings were presented to God.

The meal offering, as the other offerings, was first for God and His glory and then for man and his need.

As the sin offering and the trespass offering, so was it most holy. Thus, the Holy Spirit testifies to the sinlessness of Christ as a man at the moment in which He was *made sin* upon the Cross.

In the first part of Chapter 2, the people were told of what this offering consisted and what portion belonged to the priests. Now we find that additional directions were given to the priests about the eating of the portions that belonged to them and about the treatment of the residue.

As we've already stated, this was not a bloody offering, which means it was not an animal sacrifice. In fact, it was the only sacrifice of the five that was not bloody. It was a thank offering, or as one might say, a thanksgiving offering, intended to be presented to the Lord in thanksgiving that the burnt, sin, or trespass offerings had been accepted.

While the sons of Aaron here did represent the actual sons of the high priest, the phrase is intended to comprise his lineal descendants who succeeded to the priestly office.

A SWEET SAVOUR

"And he shall take of it his handful, of the flour of the meat offering, and of the oil thereof, and all the frankincense which is upon the meat offering, and shall burn it upon the altar for a sweet savour, even the memorial of it, unto the LORD" (Lev. 6:15).

As is by now obvious, the meat offering was unlike the whole burnt offering in that it was not a bloody sacrifice. As the burnt offering taught the totality of the atonement as effected by Christ, so the meat offering taught the recognition of God's supremacy and submission to that supremacy. The burnt offering and meat offering taught these attitudes in two ways:

1. By requiring that a living creature, one substituting for the offerer himself, namely Christ, be surrendered up.
2. By calling for the offerer to also hand over to God, as a gift, a portion of some of the good things that he had originally received from God, in the form of thanksgiving.

The lesson taught to the Jew was that of the necessity of loyal service to God. By the meat offering, he was taught thanksgiving. Actually, the meat offering was such, as stated, that it could well have been referred to as a thanksgiving offering. The individual was also taught the need of purity and incorruption of spirit, with this quality being symbolized by the prohibitions against leaven and honey and the command to use salt (Lev. 2:11–13).

It is said that the relationship between the two sacrifices, that of the whole burnt offering and of the meat offering, was so close that the burnt offering was seldom offered without the accompaniment of the meat offering (Num. 15:2–4). This would hold true to a lesser extent for its accompaniment of the sin offering and the trespass offering.

THE GREATNESS OF CHRIST

The glory of the Lord Jesus Christ is so great that no one offering could symbolize His grandeur and greatness, regarding who He was and what He did, and we refer to the Cross. It, therefore, took some five separate offerings, those prescribed in this book of Leviticus, to encompass the Christ symbolism — and even then, the symbols pale into insignificance alongside the reality.

Likewise, man's oblation to God could not be symbolized by one offering. It would take several offerings to encompass man's worship of God. As we have just mentioned, the very heart of this particular offering is thanksgiving. Of course, it is obvious that thanksgiving must be done out of a free will (Lev. 2:1).

In fact, Israel's major problem was the sin of thanklessness or ingratitude. This is illustrated in their constant murmurings against Moses and against the Lord.

"And the people murmured against Moses, saying, What shall we drink?" (Ex. 15:24).

Understanding that, is it not possible that one of the most prevalent sins in the body of Christ today is that of thanklessness? Is it not true that we today are mostly unappreciative and ungrateful to God, despite all the good things that He does for us?

Paul said, *"Because that, when they knew God, they glorified Him not as God, neither were thankful"* (Rom. 1:21).

THE FLOUR

The phrase, *"And he shall take of it his handful, of the flour of the meat offering,"* pertains to Christ.

The flour of the meat offering was to be a fine flour. The grain had to be thoroughly ground to a powder consistency. There were to be no lumps in it anywhere and no foreign material of any kind. This powdery, pure white flour speaks of the perfection and purity of spirit which marked our Lord. He was perfect in everything that He did. He never had to apologize for a single statement in all of His life. He never lost His temper, nor did He ever speak crossly to anyone. He never had to say, *"I am sorry."* He was never gripped by jealousy, pettiness, vengefulness, stubbornness, or hatred in the way that we are. The fine flour truly symbolized His perfect character and His perfect humanity.

In essence, the fine flour represented the perfect humanity of our Lord, in fact, the only perfect humanity that has ever existed.

THE HANDFUL

This particular sacrifice called for only a small portion to be offered up at the brazen altar. The balance of the offering was to go to the priests for their own use. The meat offerings, therefore, must have gone far toward supplying the priests with food since for every handful of flour burned on the altar, nearly one gallon went to the priests. They were required to eat foods made with this flour within the precincts of the tabernacle, as was the case with the animal sacrifices that were considered most holy. So, what does this tell us?

The greater portion going to the priests proclaims to us the fact that all that Jesus did on the Cross, typified by the handful of flour there placed, was done for our benefit. Considering that almost all of the offering went to the priests, we learn from this that all that He did on the Cross was entirely for our benefit. In other words, He didn't die for Himself, for angels, or for God the Father, but altogether for us. While it is true that the whole burnt offering was, in effect, for God, that His righteousness be satisfied, still, this was necessary if man was to be redeemed. So, in essence, it was done for us!

THE OIL

The phrase, *and the oil thereof,* signifies the Holy Spirit.

The part that was to be burned on the brazen altar was to have a liberal portion of oil poured on it. The word *pour* in Leviticus 2:6 demands this. It was to be a liberal application.

This tells us three things:

1. Jesus was anointed with the Holy Spirit above anyone who has ever existed (Ps. 45:7).
2. The Holy Spirit not only superintended the life of the Saviour in every respect but, as well, superintended His death on the Cross, in effect, even telling Him when to die (Heb. 9:14).
3. The believer is to be literally baptized with the Holy Spirit, with the word *baptize* or *baptism* referring, as is obvious, to a total inundation (Acts 1:4–5).

FRANKINCENSE

Frankincense is a bitter, white substance, a resin that came from piercing a tree, which grew in the cracks of marble rock. There was very little fluid in this type of tree that produced this type of incense, so any fluid that was extracted from it, of necessity, would be precious.

The frankincense was not mixed with the oil and the flour, or with the salt, as a constituent element of the offering. It was, rather, scattered over all the components and was burned together with them in the *memorial.* This use of frankincense symbolized intercession — that of Christ on our behalf.

Frankincense was also used in the incense, which was placed on the altar of worship — the incense which routinely produced the cloud of beautiful fragrance in the Holy Place. This was done twice a day, at the time of the morning and evening sacrifices.

Just as the frankincense produced a sweet savour unto the Lord as it was offered on the altar of worship in the Holy Place, likewise, it would produce a sweet savour unto the

Lord when it was offered on the brazen altar as part of the offerer's sacrifice of thanksgiving (Lev. 2:2).

After the priest placed a handful of the mixture on the brazen altar and the flames burned through the flour, causing the oil to ignite, the sweet aroma of the frankincense would fill the air for a few moments. This would be a testimony to the glory and wonder of Christ and what He would do at the Cross, all on our behalf, which made His intercession possible.

THE MEMORIAL

The phrase, *"And shall burn it upon the altar for a sweet savour, even the memorial of it, unto the LORD,"* refers to something that must be remembered. This means that a memorial is something that keeps remembrance alive — but remembrance of what?

Jesus Himself told us,: *"And when He had given thanks, He broke it, and said, Take, eat: this is My body, which is broken for you: this do in remembrance of Me"* (I Cor. 11:24).

In a sense, the Lord's Supper is a form of the meat offering in a spiritual sense. It is done as a memorial *"till He come,"* and we must never forget what He has done for us.

I'm afraid that much of the modern church is forgetting the great sacrificial offering of Christ on the Cross. They are forgetting that this is the very foundation of *the* faith, in effect, the faith. They are forgetting that there is no salvation outside of faith in Christ and the Cross. They are forgetting that it's impossible for the saint to live a holy life without continued faith in the sacrifice of Christ. How do I know that?

I know it because the Cross is relegated more and more to a place of insignificance. This is proven by the foray of the modern church into humanistic psychology. There was a time that theology was the queen of the sciences in the universities of our land. Today, humanistic psychology has taken its place.

THE CROSS

There was a day when the Cross was held up as the answer to man's dilemma, but today, even as with the universities, the church instead holds up humanistic psychology as the answer. What a travesty! What an abomination!

Likewise, the Word of Faith people, who have made such inroads into the modern church, and all because false doctrine is always easily accepted, actually repudiate the Cross. They refer to it as *"the greatest defeat in human history."* Their teachers openly proclaim that the Cross should not be preached.

Kenneth Hagin, in the April 2002 issue of his monthly publication, plainly stated that if we preach the Cross, we are preaching death! He then encouraged preachers to preach the Resurrection or the throne, but don't preach the Cross. That seems strange considering that Paul said, *"I determined not to know anything among you, save Jesus Christ, and Him crucified"* (I Cor. 2:2).

Then, *"I am crucified with Christ"* (Gal. 2:20).

And then, *"For Christ sent me not to baptize, but to preach the Gospel: not with wisdom of words, lest the Cross of Christ should be made of none effect"* (I Cor. 1:17).

He then said, *"For the preaching of the Cross is to them that perish foolishness; but unto us which are saved it is the power of God"* (I Cor. 1:18).

And finally, *"But we preach Christ crucified"* (I Cor. 1:23).

He didn't say, *"we preach Christ on the throne,"* or *"we preach Christ resurrected."* He rather said, *"but we preach Christ crucified."*

Yes, the meat offering was to ever be a memorial of what Christ would do at the Cross. We must never forget that! It must be sung in our songs, proclaimed in our messages, explained in our teaching, and, in effect, the very center of all that we are in Christ and all that we believe.

It is the Cross! The Cross! The Cross!

MOST HOLY

"And the remainder thereof shall Aaron and his sons eat: with unleavened bread shall it be eaten in the holy place; in the court of the tabernacle of the congregation they shall eat it.

"It shall not be baked with leaven. I have given it unto them for their portion of My offerings made by fire: it is most holy, as is the sin offering, and as the trespass offering.

"All the males among the children of Aaron shall eat of it. It shall be a statute forever in your generations concerning the offerings of the LORD *made by fire: every one who touches them shall be holy"* (Lev. 6:16-18).

The meat offering contained no blood, as is obvious, but it was conjoined with an offering that was literally soaked in blood, and we speak of the burnt offering. So, too, our private offerings of thanksgiving contain no great sacrifice of our own; yet, even so, God looks upon our praise or thanksgiving offering as a sacrifice. The reason He does so is because of His Son, Jesus Christ. God willingly receives and accepts our display of thankfulness, even knowing that we have been given great blessings despite our basic unworthiness, because the ground around that Cross was literally soaked with the blood of His only Son.

THANKFULNESS TO THE LORD

So, when we thank God, we must always realize that He accepts our thanksgiving only because of His Son, the Lord Jesus Christ. Our thanksgiving in itself cannot please Him; our praises within themselves cannot please Him. If He is pleased, it is only because we do these things in remembrance of His only Son, who died and rose again from the dead. Even as the meat offering was attached totally and completely to the whole burnt offering, so must our worship, thanksgiving, and praises ever be attached to the Cross, or else it will not be accepted (Eph. 2:13–18).

The part eaten by Aaron and his sons, and all the priests who followed thereafter, was, in a sense, a symbolic picture of what Jesus was speaking about when He said to Israel, "-*Except you eat the flesh of the Son of Man, and drink His blood, you have no life in you.*

"Whoso eats My flesh, and drinks My blood, has eternal life; and I will raise him up at the last day.

"For My flesh is meat indeed, and My blood is drink indeed.

"He who eats My flesh, and drinks My blood, dwells in Me, and I in him" (Jn. 6:53–56).

Christ was not talking about literally eating His flesh and drinking His blood, for He then said, *"It is the Spirit who quickens; the flesh profits nothing: the words that I speak unto you, they are spirit, and they are life"* (Jn. 6:63).

IN CHRIST

Our Lord was speaking of His death on the Cross. By Him using the terminology that He did, He, in essence, was saying that His great work on the Cross must be accepted as more than a mere philosophical quest. Faith must be tendered completely in Christ and what He did for us in the sacrifice of Himself. When this is done, and I speak of such faith being registered, God literally places us *in Christ*. In other words, in the mind of God, we were literally in Christ when He died on the Cross, in effect, baptized into His death, then buried with Him by baptism into death, and then, raised with Him in newness of life (Rom. 6:3–5).

Untold millions accept Christ in a philosophical sense. By that I speak of Him being a great healer, a great miracle-worker, or even a great prophet. But that's not enough! That will save no one!

For Christ to be accepted, He must be accepted totally and completely, which was symbolized by the Passover lamb being eaten totally and completely, with none of it left remaining (Ex. 12:10).

To reject the Cross is to reject Christ. In effect, if the Cross is rejected or ignored in any way, the believer will find himself worshipping *another Jesus*, and doing so by *another spirit*, which produces *another gospel* (II Cor. 11:4).

NO LEAVEN

When the priests would prepare this particular offering of their own consumption, they must not add any leaven to it. Leaven is a type of yeast, which causes the corruption or fermentation of that in which it is placed; therefore, it was not to be used in this offering.

If leaven would have been blended into the flour along with the oil and the frankincense, the mixture would, no doubt, have swelled and frothed, thus creating the repulsive festering appearance that we find used throughout the Mosaic legislation as an image of moral evil.

In fact, when the Passover was to be observed, a detailed ritual was to be carried out, which referred to the cleaning of the house of any leaven. The family was to search and scrub the house so that no crumb of bread would be left in the house. Leaven, as stated, represents corruption; therefore, it should be readily understandable that no leaven would be included in this thanksgiving offering.

If there is unconfessed sin in our lives, which refers to leaven, God will not hear our prayers, and, therefore, our meat offering is made in vain. This flour was a type of Christ, and inasmuch as there was no sin in Him whatsoever, no leaven was to be put into this concoction, which, in effect, typified sin. His body was pure, perfect, and holy, which means that it was a perfect sacrifice.

We saw in the whole burnt offering what sin does to the individual. Its effect was symbolized perfectly in the required cutting up of the carcasses. The grizzly act of quartering and sectioning the slain animal symbolized the penetrating property of sin, which goes down into the very vitals of human beings. This helps to explain why Jesus had to pay the supreme sacrifice to rid man not only of the guilt of sin, but also the very root of sin.

MOST HOLY

Why was this offering most holy? It was most holy because it was an offering to the Lord made by fire. What does this mean?

Any offering that was placed on the fiery brazen altar and consumed by the altar's fire was considered most holy. Totally and completely, this refers to the Cross of Christ. That connection, and that alone, is what made the offering most holy.

The garments of the offerer did not make it holy. The detailed preparations did not make it holy. The style by which the offering was handed over to the priests did not make it holy.

The fire represented Calvary, and the offering's ingredients represented Christ and what He would do at the Cross; therefore, the holiness was in the Christ of Calvary and in nothing else!

How confused we get when we think our efforts somehow produce holiness! We wear our hair a certain length, and we think that the look we've achieved is holy. Our sleeves are a certain length, and we think that somehow this style is holy. We attend church so many times during the year, and in our minds, we think of this as being holy. We praise the Lord in a certain way, and this is supposed to denote some type of holiness.

THE WORKS OF MAN

We build our own little religion, in other words, and because we strictly adhere to it, we think of ourselves as holy. Conversely, we come to think of those who do not adhere to our own man-made standards as not being holy, unholy, or somehow unclean. We call ourselves people of holiness because we adhere to some set of rules.

When will we wake up and realize that our works and our own talents or abilities cannot produce any holiness? When will we see that all of our holiness, in totality, comes from the sacrifice of our Lord Jesus Christ at Calvary's Cross and our faith in that sacrifice, which, in effect, constitutes a holiness made by fire?

The point is, true holiness cannot be attained by works or even by religious observances; it can only be made by fire. Holiness cannot be created by man's efforts; it can only be made by fire. Satan will not bow before our man-made holiness, but he bows and trembles at that which is made by fire i.e., the Cross of Christ. We are holy simply and truly by having faith in Christ and what Christ has done for us at the Cross, and that alone! The fire represented the judgment of God poured out on Christ instead of us, at least those who trust Christ.

THE MALES

Only the males among the children of Aaron could eat this, symbolizing that it was through man, namely Adam, that sin was imposed upon the human race and, in effect, effected its destruction.

The Law of the meat offering closed with the words, *"every one who touches them shall be holy,"* which referred to the offerings made by fire. It is the same presently!

Christ alone and what He did at the Cross makes one holy, that is, if his faith is anchored in Christ and the Cross. Only the priests could touch it in those days. However, thank God, at this present time and, in fact, since the Cross, it is possible for anyone to touch that most holy sacrifice. When they do, a perfect righteousness is imputed to them, and they are holy.

THE MORNING AND EVENING SACRIFICES

"And the LORD *spoke unto Moses, saying,*
"This is the offering of Aaron and of his sons, which they shall offer unto the LORD *in the day when he is anointed; the tenth part of an ephah of fine flour for a meat offering perpetual, half of it in the morning, and half thereof at night"* (Lev. 6:19-20).

It seems that much was worked around the two sacrifices that were offered daily, namely the morning sacrifice, which was a whole burnt offering, and carried out at 9 a.m., and the evening sacrifice, which was another whole burnt offering, and carried out at 3 p.m. Along with the high priest preparing this on a daily basis, which he was required to do, the wicks on the golden lampstand would be cleaned twice a day, at this particular time, as well. Also, incense was offered on the golden altar at these two times each day.

Jesus was put on the Cross at the time of the morning sacrifice, and He died at the time of the evening sacrifice, meaning that He stayed on the Cross for six hours. Consequently, he fulfilled the type in totality.

While the high priest was to offer the meat offering everyday, the ordinary priests were to offer it only once, and that was on the day that he was consecrated to his office.

It seems that it was offered after the sacrifice of the whole burnt offering and before the drink offering.

It was to this practice that the apostle referred when he said, *"For such a high priest became us ... Who needs not daily, as those high priests, to offer up sacrifice first for His own sins,"* and I might quickly add, because Jesus had no sins (Heb. 7:26–27).

A SWEET SAVOUR

"In a pan it shall be made with oil; and when it is baked, you shall bring it in: and the baked pieces of the meat offering shall you offer for a sweet savour unto the LORD.

"And the priest of his sons that is anointed in his stead shall offer it: it is a statute forever unto the LORD; it shall be wholly burnt.

"For every meat offering for the priest shall be wholly burnt: It shall not be eaten" (Lev. 6:21-23).

This small amount of fine flour, which typified the perfect humanity of Christ, was to be sprinkled with oil and then baked. Along with the meat offering, it was to be placed on the brazen altar and then offered for a *"sweet savour unto the Lord."*

This was to be carried out by Aaron, who was high priest, and all who would follow in his stead, even down through the centuries. It was not to be eaten; it was to be wholly burnt.

As should be obvious, the high priest typified Christ, but more particularly, this ritual typified what Christ would do as it regarded the redemption of humanity. This offering being burned on the brazen altar signified the death that Christ would suffer, in essence, the price that He would pay.

There was one vast difference.

Whereas the earthly high priests, despite their office, were sinful men and, therefore, had to repeat this every day, Christ, being perfect in every respect, would have to offer up this sacrifice — the sacrifice of Himself — only once. That would forever suffice (Heb. 10:12).

As we have previously stated, while the Cross of Christ took place nearly 2,000 years ago, still, it has continuing positive results, in fact, positive results which will never be discontinued.

THE LAW OF THE SIN OFFERING

"And the Lord spoke unto Moses, saying,

"Speak unto Aaron and to his sons, saying, This is the law of the sin offering: In the place where the burnt offering is killed shall the sin offering be killed before the Lord: it is most holy" (Lev. 6:24-25).

The sin offering was killed in the place where the burnt offering was slain and its body (the sin offering) burned outside the camp.

So desperate a malady is sin that anything that came in contact with the sin offering had to be washed, broken, or scoured.

The sin offering, whose blood was brought into the sanctuary, symbolizes Christ bearing before God the sin of the whole world.

The sin offering, whose blood was not so brought in, but whose flesh was eaten by the priest, presented Christ as making His own the sins of the individual sinner who believes upon Him.

The burnt offering and the sin offering being slain upon the one spot sets out the unity of the death of Christ in its two aspects: at Golgotha, He was at once — in the same moment — accursed of God as the sin offering, and beloved of the Father as the burnt offering.

THE PERSONAL HOLINESS OF CHRIST

The personal holiness of Christ was more strikingly presented in the sin offering than in any of the other sacrifices. The Holy Spirit through Moses said, *"It is most holy."* He even went so far as to say, *"Whatsoever shall touch the flesh thereof shall be holy ... All the males among the priests shall eat thereof: it is most holy"* (Lev. 6:27, 29).

This was said of the meat offering, sin offering, and the trespass offering.

Concerning this, Mackintosh said: *"This is most marked and striking. The Holy Spirit did not need to guard with such jealousy the personal holiness of Christ in the burnt offering; but lest the soul should, by any means, lose sight of that holiness while contemplating the place which the Blessed One became the sin offering, we are again and again reminded of it by the words, 'It is most holy.'"*

Mackintosh went on to say: *"The same point is observable 'in the Law of the trespass offering' (Lev. 7:1–6). Never was the Lord Jesus more fully seen to be 'the Holy One of God' than when He was 'made sin' upon the cursed tree. The vileness and blackness of that with which He stood identified on the Cross, only served to show out more clearly that He was 'most holy.' Though a sin-bearer, He was sinless; though enduring the wrath of God, He was the Father's delight; though deprived of the light of God's countenance, He dwelt in the Father's bosom."*

As should be obvious, this completely shoots down the erroneous theory of the Jesus Died Spiritually doctrine. This is taught by those of the Word of Faith group, which, in effect, states that Jesus became one with Satan on the Cross, died as a sinner, and went to the burning side of Hell, where He was tortured for three days and nights, until God said, *"It is enough."* At that time, they continue to say, Jesus was born again, as any sinner must be born again in order to be saved. He was then resurrected from the dead.

Consequently, their faith is not in what He did at the Cross, but rather of what He did, they claim, in the burning side of Hell.

There is not one shred of this in the Bible. It is pure fiction from beginning to end. Also, the Law of the sin offering, and that it was most holy in the eyes of the Lord, completely debunks the idea of Jesus dying spiritually on the Cross.

THE OLD TESTAMENT

Once again, we go back to the fact that many of these erroneous doctrines are perpetrated on false ideas simply because the person doing the perpetrating doesn't know and understand the Old Testament or the veracity of the Cross of Christ. This is at least one of the many reasons that the book of Leviticus is of such significance. In the five sacrifices presented, it beautifully portrays the one sacrifice of Christ, thereby, giving us its vast significance, at least as far as we can understand such. The truth is, as human beings, we will never be able to fully comprehend and understand all that Christ did for us at the Cross. He not only addressed the human need, but, as well, He addressed what Satan did in his revolution against God, which originated sin (Eph. 1:10).

The Scripture is emphatic that, *"In the place where the burnt offering is killed shall the sin offering be killed before the LORD: it is most holy."*

As we have stated, the burnt offering stipulated Jesus Christ offering to God His total perfection, and doing so in sacrifice that the righteousness of God might be satisfied. There had to be a perfect victim who would give up his life, and that perfect victim was Christ because that perfect victim could only be Christ. No one else could fit the bill, so to speak!

In the sin offering, Christ would be the sin-bearer of the whole world, but in this, He would be looked at by God as even holier than in the representation of the burnt offering.

HOLY

"The priest who offers it for sin shall eat it: in the holy place shall it be eaten, in the court of the tabernacle of the congregation.

"Whatsoever shall touch the flesh thereof shall be holy: and when there is sprinkled of the blood thereof upon any garment, you shall wash that whereon it was sprinkled in the holy place" (Lev. 6:26-27).

God gave the sin offering as food for the priests to bear the iniquity of the congregation and to make atonement for them (Lev. 10:17). Once again, we go back to John, Chapter 6, in the eating of the flesh and the drinking of the blood regarding Christ.

The flesh provided by the sin offering constituted a part of the livelihood of the priests as it constitutes our spiritual livelihood presently (Ezek. 44:28–29). The officiating priest to whom fell this obligation could invite not only his family but other priests and their sons to partake of it. Covetous priests abused this gift (Hos. 4:8).

It was to be eaten in the Holy Place of the sanctuary. In fact, eight of the offerings (there were others besides the blood sacrifices) had to be eaten in the precincts of the sanctuary:

1. The flesh of the sin offering (Lev. 4:26).
2. The flesh of the trespass offering (Lev. 7:6).
3. The peace offering of the congregation (Lev. 23:19–20).
4. The remainder of the omer (Lev. 23:10–11).
5. The meat offering of the Israelites (Lev. 2:3–10).
6. The two loaves (Lev. 23:20).
7. The shewbread (Lev. 24:9).
8. The leper's log of oil (Lev. 14:10–13).

THE BLOOD

So peculiarly sacred was the sin offering that when any of its blood chanced to spurt upon the garment of the officiating priest or the one who brought the sacrifice, the spot that received the stain had to be washed in the room of the court provided for this purpose. Therein was a well that supplied the water for the sanctuary, thus preventing the blood from being profaned outside the Holy Place.

This proclaims to us the preciousness of the blood.

It was to be handled in two ways:

1. If it pertained to the priest who had sinned or the nation as a whole, some of the blood of the sacrifice was to be sprinkled seven times on the golden altar, with blood then applied to the four horns of that altar. The balance of the blood was to be poured out at the base of the brazen altar.

2. If it was a ruler who sinned, or the common people, the blood was not to be sprinkled on the golden altar or applied to its horns, but was rather to be applied to the horns of the brazen altar and then poured out at its base.

All of this means that extra care had to be taken that none of the blood was spilled any other place. If even one drop was spilled upon the garment of the priest who was doing the officiating, as stated, his garment had to be washed immediately, and done so in a particular place, i.e., the Holy Place.

As stated, this proclaims the preciousness of the blood and, as well, that it was the shed blood of Christ that brought about our salvation because it represented the poured out life of Christ on the Cross (Eph. 2:13–18).

THE AWFULNESS OF SIN

"But the earthen vessel wherein it is sodden shall be broken: and if it be sodden in a brazen pot, it shall be both scoured, and rinsed in water.

"All the males among the priests shall eat thereof: it is most holy.

"And no sin offering, whereof any of the blood is brought into the tabernacle of the congregation to reconcile withal in the holy place, shall be eaten: it shall be burnt in the fire" (Lev. 6:28-30).

We learn from this of the awfulness of sin. So desperate a malady is sin that anything that came in contact with the sin offering had to be washed, broken, or scoured.

All these regulations were calculated to express the polluting nature of sin and the translation of guilt from the sinner to the sacrifice. We learn from this, as well, that there are no such things as venial sins (small sins); the least sin deserves death.

THE BELIEVER AND SIN

This means that if we properly understand sin as we ought to, at the same time, in order to have peace, we, as well, must understand the Cross. Many believers, because of the guilt of condemnation, have been led to a mental and emotional anguish that has robbed them of all peace. In fact, some have even committed suicide under such stress.

If a believer walks after the flesh (Rom. 8:1), such a believer will have a miserable lifestyle because of condemnation. He may confess the opposite and may deny such, but trying to ignore a 3,000-pound elephant in one's living room takes a stretch of the imagination. In other words, it cannot be done!

The more consecrated a believer is, the more this problem presents itself. Such a believer wants to live right, wants to walk right, and wants to be right, but despite all of his efforts otherwise, finds himself doing wrong, with the wrong continually getting worse. In fact, Chapter 7 of Romans bears this out. It concludes with Paul saying, *"O wretched man that I am! Who shall deliver me from the body of this death?"* (Rom. 7:24). Regrettably, that's the exact state in which most of Christendom presently finds itself.

They do not know how to address sin, at least according to the Word of God, which means they don't know how to have victory over sin.

THE BELIEVER AND THE CROSS

The only answer for sin, which is the problem, is the Cross. While many in the church may allude to other things and may claim other things, the truth is, sin is the problem. This is abundantly clear in the teaching given us in the Law of the various offerings. Some may claim the problem to be physical, while others claim it to be emotional. Others may claim that it is domestic or material; however, irrespective as to what the problem might be, the root cause in some way is sin. It may be the sin of someone else, or it may be the sin of the individual in question, but the cause — indirect or direct — is sin, and is always sin! That's the reason it is hopeless and helpless to try to address the problem any other way. That's the reason that humanistic psychology is such a crock; as well, the same can be said for those who promote this wisdom of the world.

Neither humanistic psychology nor any other effort by man can address itself to the sin question. It is the Cross and the Cross alone that answers this horrible malady of the human race.

Let us say it again: There is no answer for sin but the Cross. If we try something else, we try in vain! If we look to anything else, we look in vain! If we claim anything else, we claim such in vain!

WHAT IS THE CHURCH DOING ABOUT THE CROSS?

Now let me ask this question: How is the modern church addressing its problems? The answer to that is obvious. It is looking to anything and everything except the Cross.

Let me give you an example: concerning the Assemblies of God, the largest Pentecostal denomination, if a preacher has a problem, he can never be accepted in good standing unless he is signed off by a psychologist. This means that there is no faith in the Cross, but rather the frail efforts of pitiful man. To be sure, most every other Pentecostal denomination falls into the same category, at least those of which I am aware.

However, the Holy Spirit is bringing the Message of the Cross into full view of the church to where it has absolutely no choice but to either publicly reject it or accept it. As we've said repeatedly, the Cross of Christ is the dividing line between the true church and the apostate church. In fact, it has always been that way; however, the Holy Spirit is making the Cross of Christ, and all for which it stands, so prominent that it can no longer be ignored (I Cor. 1:17–18, 21, 23; 2:2; Eph. 2:13–18; Col. 2:14–15; Gal. 6:14).

CHRIST AND HIS SACRIFICE

The sin offering, whose blood was brought into the sanctuary, symbolized Christ bearing before God the sin of the whole word. The sin offering, the blood of which was not so brought in, but its flesh was eaten by the priests, presents Christ as making His own the sins of the individual sinner who believes upon Him.

The meaning of Verse 30 in Leviticus, Chapter 6, is this: Regarding the sins of priests and of the nation of Israel as a whole, the blood was to be brought into the tabernacle, sprinkled seven times on the golden altar, and, as well, the blood was applied to the four horns. The flesh of this animal, which served as the sin offering, was not to be eaten by the priests, but was to be taken out to a clean place, in fact, where the ashes were taken, and there, burnt in the fire.

If it was a sin offering, which referred to rulers and the common people, the blood then was not taken into the Holy Place, but was rather applied to the four horns of the brazen altar and then poured out at the base. Of the flesh of this particular animal, the priests could partake.

It all had to do with where the blood was applied.

SINS OF IGNORANCE

This tells us, as should be obvious, that the sins of priests, and of the nation as a whole, constituted that which was more serious. The sins of the nation as a whole were probably carried out because of the sins of the priests, and we speak of sins of ignorance. So, the flesh of such an offering could not be eaten but had to be burned.

As previously stated, it is the same presently with the thousands of preachers who sin ignorantly, thereby, causing the church to sin when they tell people how to live for God but in all the wrong ways. In other words, they are telling them to live for the Lord outside of the boundaries of the Cross, which is sin!

With many of these preachers, it is done through ignorance, but it is still sin, and it will still cause great problems in the body of Christ. The only answer to the dilemma is for the preacher to understand the Cross and then to preach the Cross to his people. This is why Paul said, *"We preach Christ crucified"* (I Cor. 1:23).

"Five bleeding wounds He bears,
"Received on Calvary;
"They pour effectual prayers,
"They strongly plead for me:
"'Forgive him, O forgive,' they cry,
"Nor let the ransomed sinner die."

"The Father hears Him pray,
"His dear Anointed One;
"He cannot turn away,
"The presence of His Son;
"His Spirit answers to the blood,
"And tells me I am born of God."

7

The Law of the
Trespass Offering

.

CHAPTER SEVEN

The Law of the Trespass Offering

"LIKEWISE THIS IS the law of the trespass offering: it is most holy.

"In the place where they kill the burnt offering shall they kill the trespass offering: And the blood thereof shall he sprinkle round about upon the altar.

"And he shall offer of it all the fat thereof; the rump, and the fat that covers the inwards,

"And the two kidneys, and the fat that is on them, which is by the flanks, and the caul that is above the liver, with the kidneys, it shall he take away:

"And the priest shall burn them upon the altar for an offering made by fire unto the LORD: *it is a trespass offering"* (Lev. 7:1-5).

The trespass offering was most holy as well.

The requirements for the trespass offering were very similar to the sin offering. Both were intended as remedies for the sins of spiritual weakness; intended upon life still subject to the trials and temptations of this world.

One point of difference between them was in the mode of disposing of the blood. Both were bloody offerings, but the blood in the case of the sin offering was to be put on the four horns of the altar. In the trespass offering, it was to be sprinkled *"round about upon the altar."*

As stated, the meat offering, the sin offering, and the trespass offering were labeled *most holy*. The whole burnt offering and the peace offering were holy, but they were not labeled as most holy.

WHY WERE SOME HOLY AND SOME MOST HOLY?

Without what Christ did at the Cross, sinful man couldn't be saved. That's the reason the sin offering and the trespass offering are labeled *most holy*. The meat offering falls into the same category simply because, in essence, it refers to thankfulness on our part for what He has done to deliver us from sin.

All of the instructions given here, by and large, pertain to the priests. This means that the far greater responsibility lay with the priests. As well, the glory of our salvation does not lie with us, the sinner; it lies with the Lord Jesus Christ. About all the person could do under the old economy was to bring his offering and to believe the instructions he was given concerning the atonement. Likewise, at this particular time, under the New Covenant, all the failing believer can do is present himself before the Lord and believe. All the work is done by our Great High Priest.

According to Verses 2 through 5, the priests were given careful instructions regarding the kidney, the caul, and the fat. This represented the prosperity, the life, and the living of the individual, and that the Lord is the author of such.

If it is to be noticed, the blood of the trespass offering was not to be placed on the horns of the altar, as was the rule in the ordinary sin offering, but cast against the inner side of the altar, as with the burnt offering and peace offering.

In all of these sacrifices, with the exception of the meat offering, there was an ample display of blood.

THE BLOOD

The psalmist sang, *"How amiable are Your tabernacles, O LORD of Hosts!"* (Ps. 84:1).

Concerning this, Seiss said: *"Approaching those admirable courts, our attention would have been attracted on all sides with marks of blood. Before the altar, 'blood'; on the horns of the altar, 'blood'; in the midst of the altar, 'blood'; on its top, at its base, on its sides, 'blood'; and tracked along into the deepest interior of the tabernacle, 'blood'!"*

Most of humanity would think of such as disgusting, but he who has learned to look at things from a spiritual sense — to see the blood in the realm of forgiveness and the grace of God to lost sinners — will know how precious the blood is and will know very well how to appreciate it.

Paul said that the preaching of Christ crucified was to the Jews a stumbling block and to the Greeks foolishness; but to those of us who know what sin actually is, and what is implied in redemption from it, will ever hail the announcement of the Cross as the most glad tidings that ever fell upon the ear of earth.

MOST HOLY

"Every male among the priests shall eat thereof: it shall be eaten in the holy place: it is most holy.

"As the sin offering is, so is the trespass offering: there is one law for them: the priest who makes atonement therewith shall have it.

"And the priest that offers any man's burnt offering, even the priest shall have to himself the skin of the burnt offering which he has offered.

"And all the meat offering that is baked in the oven, and all that is dressed in the frying pan, and in the pan, shall be the priest's that offers it.

"And every meat offering, mingled with oil, and dry, shall all the sons of Aaron have, one as much as another" (Lev. 7:6-10).

We may grow weary at all of these tedious instructions, which is the reason the book of Leviticus is seldom read. However, if we fully understand the sin question and what it took to redeem humanity from its awful clutches, then we would linger long over every word, asking the Holy Spirit to reveal more and more the meaning to our hearts. Of course, we are speaking of the Cross, to which all of these instructions pointed.

Understanding the meat offering, the sin offering, and the trespass offering as most holy proclaims to us in no uncertain terms the absolute holiness, the *most holiness*, of the Cross of Calvary.

The sin offering and the trespass offering were so very similar that there was actually one law for the both of them. The same rule, as stated in Leviticus 6:27–28, applied to both offerings; hence, what was omitted in the regulation of the one must be supplied from the directions given in the other.

THE BURNT OFFERING

Attached to the instructions given regarding the trespass offering, there are various instructions again given as it regards the burnt offering and the meat offering.

For instance, the burnt offering was consumed totally on the altar, with the exception of the skin. This was to be stripped from the carcass and given to the officiating priests.

As well, as it regarded the meat offering, with the exception of the memorial part, which was burnt upon the altar, it was to go to the particular priest who offered it.

All the priests were to share equally according to the instructions given by the Lord.

THE LAW OF THE SACRIFICE OF PEACE OFFERINGS

"And this is the law of the sacrifice of peace offerings, which he shall offer unto the LORD.

"If he offer it for a thanksgiving, then he shall offer with the sacrifice of thanksgiving unleavened cakes mingled with oil, and unleavened wafers anointed with oil, and cakes mingled with oil, of fine flour, fried.

"Besides the cakes, he shall offer for his offering leavened bread with the sacrifice of thanksgiving of his peace offerings.

"And of it he shall offer one out of the whole oblation for an heave offering unto the LORD, and it shall be the priest's that sprinkles the blood of the peace offerings.

"And the flesh of the sacrifice of his peace offerings for thanksgiving shall be eaten the same day that it is offered; he shall not leave any of it until the morning" (Lev. 7:11-15).

Verses 11 through 21 portray the law of the sacrifice of peace offerings.

Verse 12 tells us that the peace offerings were at times offered as a *thanksgiving*.

In Verse 13, the offerer is instructed to use *"leavened bread with the sacrifice."* This was permitted in the thank offering, even though it was a form of corruption and, thereby, a type of sin, because this was the spontaneous expression of devotion from lives that were not entirely rid of sin and evil in every case.

The eating of the leavened bread was a constant reminder that the offerer was a poor, weak sinner, and that all of the grace was in the Lord Jesus Christ.

There were some offerings of thanksgiving that were given with unleavened cakes, which signified the perfect, unblemished, sinless body of the Lord Jesus Christ.

Verse 15 indicates that the offerer of the peace offering could have a feast with his friends, which would symbolize the blessings of the Lord.

Verse 19 speaks of *"touching any unclean thing."* This principal, which made one unclean, also applied to touching any holy thing which made one clean or holy. It typifies two things:

1. The touching of Satan (his works) makes one unholy.
2. Touching Christ makes one holy.

LEAVENED BREAD

The law of the peace offering commanded unleavened cakes (Lev. 7:12) and leavened bread (Lev. 7:13). The first symbolized the sinless humanity of Christ; the other, the sinful humanity of the worshipper. The one had sin on Him (actually our sin), but not in Him; the latter, the sinful worshipper, had sin in him and on him.

The peace offerings could be offered as a thanksgiving offering, even as the meat offering. This would be an acknowledgment of special mercies received from God for whatever! It was to this sacrifice that Paul alluded when he said, *"By Him therefore let us offer the sacrifice of praise to God continually"* (Heb. 13:15).

In Verses 12 through 14, no mention is made of the number of cakes or the quantity of oil. Consequently, this must have been left up to the decision of the administrators of the laws.

These cakes were to be eaten with the flesh of the peace offering and had to be baked before the victim was slaughtered.

These particular cakes were to be unleavened because they represented the sinless humanity of Christ.

THE PEACE OFFERING

However, along with these cakes, he was to also offer leavened bread, which he would also eat. It was leavened simply because it represented the life of the offerer, which was not completely free from sin, as no human being is completely free from sin.

The peace offering was offered at times after the other offerings. It was the only offering of which the offerer could partake. A small portion was to be burnt on the brazen altar, a portion given to the priests, which we will address momentarily, with the offerer taking the remainder. With this, he could have a feast with his friends and family, signifying that peace with God had been restored. Sin, in whatever form, destroys that peace; consequently, the proper sacrifices had to be offered in order to atone for the sin. Then the peace offering could be offered.

THE CAKES

There were four different kinds of cakes — unleavened cakes mingled with oil, unleavened wafers anointed with oil, cakes mingled with oil, of fine flour, fried; and lastly, there was the leavened bread.

Of these four different types of cakes or bread, the officiating priest was to wave one of each of the four kinds before the Lord as a heave offering (Ex. 29:24, 28). After he waved them before the Lord in thanksgiving to the Lord, he could have these four loaves as his portion, with the rest or the remaining cakes belonging to the owner of the sacrifice, which he could partake of with the roasted flesh of the sacrifice.

To the priest was given the breast and the shoulder of the animal. The one bringing the sacrifice would be given that which remained, with the exception of the fat, which was burned on the altar (Lev. 7:4–5). However, there was one stipulation: all of the flesh of the peace offering had to be eaten the same day it was offered. None was to be left until the morning.

This typified that we must partake of all of Christ and not merely a part of Christ. Many desire Him as Saviour but reject Him as the baptizer with the Holy Spirit. In fact, this list is long, with many picking and choosing. Sorry! According to the Scriptures, such cannot be done. It is all of Christ or none of Christ!

BLESSINGS AND THE CROSS

"But if the sacrifice of his offering be a vow, or a voluntary offering, it shall be eaten the same day that he offers his sacrifice: and on the morrow also the remainder of it shall be eaten:

"But the remainder of the flesh of the sacrifice on the third day shall be burnt with fire.

"And if any of the flesh of the sacrifice of his peace offerings be eaten at all on the third day, it shall not be accepted, neither shall it be imputed unto him who offers it: it shall be an abomination, and the soul that eats of it shall bear his iniquity" (Lev. 7:16-18).

The peace offering for thanksgiving was eaten the same day that it was offered. The peace offering for a vow was eaten the same day or the next day because a vow, or a voluntary offering, necessarily affected the heart more than an ordinary thanksgiving.

Concerning this, Williams said: *"This law taught the offerer to closely associate the death and sufferings of the slain lamb with the blessings for which he gave thanks. It teaches men today the same lesson. To disassociate worship and thanksgiving from the anguish and blood-shedding of the Lord Jesus, in other words, to separate all of this from the Cross, is to offer to God an abomination, and to bring death into the soul and into the church."*

UNCLEANNESS

"And the flesh that touches any unclean thing shall not be eaten; it shall be burnt with fire: and as for the flesh, all that be clean shall eat thereof.

"But the soul that eats of the flesh of the sacrifice of peace offerings, that pertain unto the LORD, having his uncleanness upon him, even that soul shall be cut off from his people.

"Moreover the soul that shall touch any unclean thing, as the uncleanness of man, or any unclean beast, or any abominable unclean thing, and eat of the flesh of the sacrifice of peace offerings, which pertain unto the LORD, even that soul shall be cut off from his people" (Lev. 7:19-21).

Ceremonial cleanliness was obligatory before eating the peace offering. Disobedience in this matter entailed death. To profess faith in the person and atonement of Christ and claim fellowship with Him but be secretly unclean ensures the wrath of God. This vividly proclaims the following truth: Jesus Christ saves us *from* sin, not *in* sin. The idea that the believer is no different from the unbeliever, with the exception of faith in Christ, could not be more wrong. The idea that we can claim faith in Christ, while at the same time continuing in the sin business, as well, could not be more wrong. These Old Testament types completely repudiate such erroneous thinking.

THE WAY OUT OF SIN

The Lord has a way that the believer can overcome the law of sin and death. It is by the *"law of the Spirit of life in*

Christ Jesus" (Rom. 8:2). By the word law being used, this means that the Holy Spirit works within the confines of that formulated by the Godhead. What are those confines?

The phrase, *in Christ Jesus*, explains what it is, which refers to what Christ did at the Cross, and exclusively as to what Christ did at the Cross.

The believer is to express faith in Christ and His finished work and is to do so at all times. The Holy Spirit, who works within the boundaries of the finished work of Christ, will then work mightily on behalf of the child of God who expresses such faith, giving such a believer total and complete victory over the law of sin and death. However, let it be understood that the law of the Spirit of life in Christ Jesus is the only law in the world that is more powerful than the law of sin and death. If the law of sin and death is approached in any other manner, there will be nothing but failure and wreckage. The Cross is the answer for sin, and the Cross alone is the answer for sin!

THE FAT

"And the LORD spoke unto Moses, saying,

"Speak unto the children of Israel, saying, You shall eat no manner of fat, of ox, or of sheep, or of goat.

"And the fat of the beast that dies of itself, and the fat of that which is torn with beasts, may be used in any other use: but you shall in no wise eat of it.

"For whosoever eats the fat of the beast, of which men offer an offering made by fire unto the LORD, even the soul that eats it shall be cut off from his people" (Lev. 7:22-25).

Fat is first mentioned in the Bible in Genesis 4:4, where it is said that Abel offered the fat of the firstlings of his flock to the Lord. Evidently, in giving instructions to the first family, the Lord had instructed them that the fat of sacrificed animals belonged exclusively to Him.

The fat of sacrificial animals, such as heifers, sheep, or goats, could not be eaten, irrespective as to whether the animal was to be offered in sacrifice or not. However, the fat of other tame or wild animals that are clean, such as deer, etc., was lawful to be eaten.

Why this prohibition of fat and, as well, that it had to be burned on the altar as belonging to Jehovah, and must be burned the same day the sacrificial animal was slain?

The best animals were to be offered in sacrifice, as would be obvious, and the fat of the animal signified its health and prosperity. Consequently, it served as a type of God giving His very best as it regards the Lord Jesus Christ, from whom we receive all things from the Lord.

As well, the fat being burned on the altar symbolized the means by which all of these good things come to us, and that is through the Cross.

THE BLOOD

"Moreover you shall eat no manner of blood, whether it be of fowl or of beast, in any of your dwellings.

"Whatsoever soul it be that eats any manner of blood, even that soul shall be cut off from his people" (Lev. 7:26-27).

The prohibition against the eating of blood was brought over into the New Covenant (Acts 15:19–20).

Concerning this, Williams said: *"The reverence due to the person and to the work of the Messiah was enjoined by the two laws respecting the 'fat' and the 'blood.' They*

express excellency and efficiency. 'This is My Beloved Son'
declared the one; and 'peace through the blood of His Cross,'
proclaimed the other" (Col. 1:20).

THE LAW OF THE SACRIFICE
OF THE PEACE OFFERINGS

"And the LORD spoke unto Moses, saying,
"Speak unto the children of Israel, saying, He who offers
the sacrifice of his peace offerings unto the LORD shall bring
his oblation unto the LORD of the sacrifice of his peace offer-
ings" (Lev. 7:28-29).

The following is the law of the sacrifice of peace offerings.

The wave breast and the heave shoulder were to be eaten by the priests.

Before it was eaten, the breast was to be lifted up on high by the priest and then waved before the Lord. Before it was eaten, the shoulder was to be heaved, which means to be lifted up before God as expressive of its preciousness and acceptability to Him.

The breast that was waved was to be waved to the four corners of the earth as setting forth the sufficiency of this offering to give life to the world, namely Christ.

Further, Christ's shoulder upholds, and His breast consoles all those who trust in Him.

The peace offerings, as stated, were actually what their name specified. The peace offering being offered to God signified that peace had been interrupted by sin and now had been restored. The offering of their sacrifice generally followed the sacrifices of the burnt offering, and even the sin offering and trespass offering.

WHOLE BURNT OFFERINGS

In the burnt offering, sin was not directly involved. This sacrifice represented Christ giving His life and satisfying the demands of a thrice-holy God. Only a perfect sacrifice could serve, and only Christ, God's only Son, could fit that particular bill. Of course, irrespective as to the reason Christ was on the Cross, the necessity of such was all because of sin. Until the Law of Moses was given, all the offerings from the time of Abel were, in fact, whole burnt offerings.

In that peace was restored, the one who offered the sacrifice would be given a portion that he might have a feast with his family and friends, signifying the restoration. It was to be a festive occasion of joy! The priests were to receive a portion, as well, which we will address momentarily. In the realm of the fat, which was to be burned on the altar, as it always was to be burned, God, as well, would receive His portion. This signified that He had accepted the sacrifice.

In a sense, He always accepted the sacrifices, irrespective as to the condition of the offerer. In fact, it was the sacrifice that was minutely inspected and never the offerer of the sacrifice. If the sacrifice was accepted, the offerer was accepted as well. It is the same presently!

We are accepted by God not at all because of who we are, but rather because of who and what Christ is. He has been inspected minutely by God the Father and accepted on all points, thereby, faith in Him guarantees our acceptance (Jn. 3:16; Eph. 2:8–9, 13–18; Col. 2:14–15).

THE WAVE OFFERING AND THE HEAVE OFFERING

"His own hands shall bring the offerings of the LORD made by fire, the fat with the breast, it shall he bring, that the breast may be waved for a wave offering before the LORD.

"And the priest shall burn the fat upon the altar: but the breast shall be Aaron's and his sons'.

"And the right shoulder shall you give unto the priest for an heave offering of the sacrifices of your peace offerings.

"He among the sons of Aaron, who offers the blood of the peace offerings, and the fat, shall have the right shoulder for his part.

"For the wave breast and the heave shoulder have I taken of the children of Israel from off the sacrifices of their peace offerings, and have given them unto Aaron the priest and unto his sons by a statute forever from among the children of Israel" (Lev. 7:30-34).

THE FOUR REGULATIONS

1. The one who offered a peace offering was to give a portion of it to the priest. The priest was a type of Christ, and, as such, the part being given to Him showed that He alone could effect peace. As stated, the fat burned on the altar from the sacrifice signified the manner in which Christ has made it possible for believers to have peace. It is by faith and trust solely in the Cross of Christ.

2. The right shoulder was to be given to the priest offering the blood of atonement and who burned the fat. The shoulder and the breast signified the strength and the love of the Lord Jesus Christ given unto His people.

3. The wave offering derived its name from the fact that whatever was offered was waved first of all toward the brazen altar, symbolizing the price that Christ would pay, and thanking Him for paying it. Then the priest would turn, continuing to lift the offering high, and wave the breast toward the four corners of the universe, in effect, saying that what Christ would do at the Cross would suffice for all.

4. The heave offering was a little bit different than the wave offering in that the heave offering was lifted up and down several times — up as a symbol of offering it to God who is above, and down again as a symbol of God coming to this earth and becoming man in the form of the Lord Jesus Christ.

A STATUTE FOREVER

"This is the portion of the anointing of Aaron, and of the anointing of his sons, out of the offerings of the LORD made by fire, in the day when he presented them to minister unto the LORD in the priest's office;

"Which the LORD commanded to be given them of the children of Israel, in the day that He anointed them, by a statute forever throughout their generations.

"This is the law of the burnt offering, of the meat offering, and of the sin offering, and of the trespass offering, and of the consecrations, and of the sacrifice of the peace offerings;

"Which the LORD commanded Moses in Mount Sinai, in the day that He commanded the children of Israel to offer their oblations unto the LORD, in the wilderness of Sinai" (Lev. 7:35-38).

The portion mentioned here speaks of the wave offering and the heave offering, which belonged to the priests, which they could eat on the day of the offering of the sacrifice.

The statute that these two parts of the peace offering were to be given to Aaron and his descendants who may officiate at the sacrifice was binding upon the Israelites as long as the priesthood lasted.

THE GREATEST LEGISLATION
THE WORLD HAD EVER KNOWN

All of this was given to Moses on Mount Sinai. It was the greatest legislation by far that the world had ever known. It was in totality instituted by God. Man had no part whatsoever in this which was given, all originating with the Lord.

However, all of this given was totally and completely formulated for man. The Lord, as should be obvious, didn't need such. This tells us several things:

It tells us of the awfulness of sin. I'm afraid that we do not quite realize the deadliness of this horror. We may chafe at the minute instructions given, meaning little to us presently; however, if we understand all of these laws and statutes as referring to the Lord Jesus Christ and what He would do at the Cross, then they take on a brand-new meaning.

In fact, it is impossible for one to properly understand the New Testament unless one properly understands the Old Testament. When we are made to realize that Jesus has paid it all, in other words, satisfied every single rule and regulation, and did so by the sacrificial offering of Himself on the Cross, then we are made to realize the greatness of Christ, at least as much as a poor human being can know.

"Marvelous message we bring,
"Glorious carol we sing,
"Wonderful word of the King:
"Jesus is coming again!"

"Forest and flower exclaim,
"Mountain and meadow the same,
"All earth and heaven proclaim:
"Jesus is coming again!"

"Standing before Him at last,
"Trial, and trouble all past,
"Crowns at His feet we will cast:
"Jesus is coming again!"

8

The Consecration
of the Priests

CHAPTER EIGHT

The Consecration of the Priests

"AND THE LORD spoke unto Moses, saying,
"Take Aaron and his sons with him, and the garments,
and the anointing oil, and a bullock for the sin offering, and
two rams, and a basket of unleavened bread" (Lev. 8:1-2).

This chapter pertains to the consecration of the priests.

Even though Aaron had been chosen by the Lord as the great high priest, he and his sons, who were priests, as well, had to undergo the same sacrificial offerings as the worst sinner in Israel.

All of this was a reminder that even though Aaron was called, anointed, and directed by God, still, he was flawed flesh and needed a redeemer.

The anointing oil was a type of the Holy Spirit.

The bullock for the sin offering and two rams, as well as the unleavened bread, stood for sacrifice and cleansing, with the unleavened bread standing for the perfection demanded by God that could never be obtained except by sacrifice.

All of the congregation of Israel was commanded to observe these rituals that they may know and understand that Aaron, even though the great high priest, was still a poor mortal exactly as they were.

Verse 4 speaks of commands. Note that these were not suggestions; they were commands. Moses had to carry them out to the letter.

The washing with water spoke of cleansing and was a type of that accomplished by the blood and the Word.

The coat spoke of Christ's deity.

The girdle spoke of the service of Christ to humanity.

The robe spoke of His righteousness.

The ephod was that which had the names of the children of Israel on each shoulder—six to a side. The Lord would carry His people on His shoulders.

The breastplate of Verse 8 contained the 12 precious stones listing the names of the Twelve Tribes of Israel. It was over the heart of the great high priest, referring to the fact that the Lord carries His people on His heart as well as His shoulders.

In a pouch under the breastplate were the Urim and the Thummim. The two words mean *"lights"* and *"perfection."* They concerned the leading of the Holy Spirit.

The mitre of Verse 9 spoke of authority. Jesus is the Head of the church.

A SACRIFICE, A PRIEST, AND A PLACE OF WORSHIP

As we study this part of Leviticus, we will find that its major subject includes a sacrifice, a priest, and a place of worship. Chapters 8, 9, and 10 pertain to priesthood, but sacrifice is the foundation of it all. This speaks of the Cross of Christ. The sinner needs a sacrifice; the worshipper needs a priest. Christ is both. The place of worship consummates in the heavens, even as it originates in the heavens.

According to Williams, these three chapters make prominent the following:

- The authority of the Bible.
- The preciousness of the blood.
- The power of the Holy Spirit.

Even though all of this is very intricate, very detailed, and very complicated, yet, all of it in every detail points to Christ and what He would do to redeem humanity, which refers to the Cross. There is no way that any serious Bible student could study Leviticus and not see this of which we speak. The book drips with blood, with it all speaking of the blood that Christ would shed at the Cross. In some way, every single thing points to His perfection, His sacrifice of Himself, and His high priestly ministry, which continues unto this hour.

Mackintosh said: *"As a sacrifice, and only as a sacrifice, He introduces His people into a settled relationship with God; and as a priest, our Great High Priest, He maintains us therein, according to the perfection of what He is."*

He continued, *"As sinners, by nature and by practice, we are 'brought near to God by the blood of the Cross'; we are brought into an established relationship with Him; we stand before Him as the fruit of His own work. He has put away our sins in such a manner as suits Himself, so that we might be before Him to the praise of His name, as the exhibition of what He can accomplish through the power of death and resurrection."*

OUR GREAT HIGH PRIEST

As this chapter portrays the anointing of Aaron as the great high priest — the type of Christ — we are made to know and realize our need for the services and, in fact, the continued services of our Great High Priest, the Lord Jesus Christ.

We have been totally and completely delivered from all sin by our faith in Christ and what He has done for us at the Cross, thereby, perfectly accepted in the beloved. Though complete in Christ and highly exalted (Eph. 2:6), yet, within ourselves, we are still poor, feeble creatures — ever prone to wander, ready to stumble, and exposed to manifold temptations, trials, and snares.

As such, as any honest believer will have to admit, we need — in fact, we must have — the ceaseless ministry of our Great High Priest. His very presence in the sanctuary above maintains us in the full integrity of that place and relationship in which, through grace, we stand. Paul beautifully, but even bluntly, wrote, *"He ever lives to make intercession for them"* (Heb. 7:25).

The truth is, we could not stand for a moment down here if He were not living for us up there. *"Because I live, you shall live also"* (Jn. 14:19).

WHAT IS INTERCESSION?

As it pertains to Christ, it is simply His presence at the throne of God, all on our behalf (Heb. 1:3). This means that God has accepted Him — has accepted His sacrifice of Himself, has accepted its finished work — and His very presence before God guarantees intercession on our behalf. If He had to do anything else, that would mean that the work at Calvary was incomplete, which we know is not the case (Heb. 1:3).

Some Christians have the erroneous idea that Jesus has to pray for us; plead our case before the Father. While the spirit of that is definitely present because He most surely is our Advocate (I Jn. 2:1–2), still, He is that by His presence and His presence alone. The Scripture says: **"For Christ is not entered into the holy places made with hands, which are the figures of the true** *(referring to the Old Testament tabernacle and temple)*; **but into Heaven itself, now to appear in the presence of God for us"** **(Heb. 9:24).**

If it is to be noticed, the word *appear* is used here, meaning that His presence before God guarantees intercession.

CALVARY PAID IT ALL

In our understanding of the Scriptures, we must always comprehend the fact that Calvary paid it all. There is nothing left owing and nothing left to be done; it has all been done. In fact, religion says, *"Do,"* while the true Gospel says, *"Done!"*

As well, it's Heaven and not earth that is the sphere of Christ's priestly ministry, although the effects of that ministry are definitely felt and experienced by all believers. Christ is our Great High Priest.

In fact, there is no such thing now, and I speak of time since the Cross, that God recognizes any priest upon this earth. To be a priest, one would have to show his descent from Aaron, and unless he can trace his pedigree to that ancient source, he has no right to exercise the priestly office. Even the sons of Aaron have no right since Jesus has fulfilled all of the Old Testament types and shadows which were designed to point to Him anyway, and which He settled by His work at the Cross. Christ is our Mediator and our Mediator alone.

CHRIST IS OUR MEDIATOR

Let us say it again: Christ is our Mediator and our Mediator alone, and there is no need for another. So, whether he realizes it or not, for a man to say that he is a priest, he is, in effect, saying that Christ didn't finish His work and that He still needs the help of poor mortals because a priest actually served as a mediator. As well, the only ones who were ever recognized as priests were those under the Mosaic Covenant. This refers to a go-between between God and man. Since Jesus went to the Cross, He forever did away with the need for earthly priests. The Scripture plainly says, *"For there is one God, and one mediator between God and men, the man Christ Jesus"* (I Tim. 2:5). Notice that the Scripture says one — not 1,000, not 500, not 10, not even two, just one — and that One is the Lord Jesus Christ. So, the priesthood of the Catholic Church, or any other religion for that matter, is an abomination in the eyes of God. It is the highest insult that can be tendered toward Christ and His finished work.

Incidentally, Chapter 8 of Leviticus goes back to Chapter 29 of Exodus, which provides far more detail.

THE ANOINTING OIL

The oil was a type of the Holy Spirit, which was on Christ as it had never been on another man. However, while Aaron, even though a type of Christ, had the Holy Spirit to help him regarding his office, still, he only had His help in a very limited way.

Before the Cross, while the Holy Spirit was definitely present in the world and has been from the very beginning, His activities were very limited because the blood of bulls and goats could not take away sins (Heb. 10:4). This means that the terrible sin debt, and we speak of original sin, still hung over the head of every believer, so to speak, even the greatest ones of the Old Testament. In fact, this is the very reason that Jesus said of John the Baptist, who was the last great prophet before Christ: *"Verily I say unto you, among them who are born of women there has not risen a greater than John the Baptist: notwithstanding he who is least in the kingdom of Heaven is greater than he"* (Mat. 11:11).

What did Jesus mean by that statement?

He wasn't meaning that we are better morally or character-wise than John the Baptist, but rather, since the Cross, we have far better privileges than those under the Old Covenant. The Cross, incidentally, paid the total sin debt — past, present, and future — at least for those who will believe. Since the Cross, the Holy Spirit can now come into the heart and life of the believer, which He does at conversion, to abide forever (Jn. 14:16). The Cross, and the Cross alone, has made everything possible.

THE BULLOCK, THE TWO RAMS, AND THE BASKET OF UNLEAVENED BREAD

As we enter into the consecration of the priesthood, we find that even though Aaron was to be the great high priest — the closest type to Christ of any human being under the old economy — he and his sons, who were also priests, had to undergo the same sacrificial offerings as the worst sinner in Israel.

As we look at these sacrifices, we must be made to realize that even though a righteous Sovereign may feel for and pity those whom He has created, still, He dare not have fellowship with them except on the basis of judgment satisfied, hence, the necessity of the sacrifices. The sacrifices would point to the One who was to come, who would be the sacrifice, namely, the Lord Jesus Christ.

THE GREAT CHASM

There is a great chasm between man and his God. The fallen one goes on sinning, and the wronged Sovereign must go on maintaining His righteous administration. Man cannot of himself come to God and is terrified when he thinks of His presence. God cannot sacrifice His sovereignty or tarnish His throne by advancing favors to those who continue to trample everything sacred under their feet. In fact, the whole bent and drift of man's natural affections are against God. It is not in man to turn or change himself, and God cannot reverse His own immutability, or retire from His eternal constitution of righteousness and holiness. The simple fact is, *"They that are in the flesh cannot please God"* (Rom. 8:8). Then Jesus said, *"No man comes unto the Father, but by Me"* (Jn. 14:6).

Nothing can recover a man from sin — not the powers and workings of nature, not good works, not money, and not education — nothing but Christ. In fact, faith in Christ and what Christ has done for us at the Cross is the only thing that will recover a man from sin. Christ without the Cross could not have saved anyone!

KNOWLEDGE OF GOD

Even when men had a right knowledge of God, all of these things we have mentioned were not competent within themselves to keep that knowledge alive in them.

The Scripture plainly says: *"Because that, when they knew God, they glorified Him not as God, neither were thankful; but became vain in their imaginations, and their foolish heart was darkened.*

"Professing themselves to be wise, they became fools,

"And changed the glory of the uncorruptible God into an image made like to corruptible man, and to birds, and four-footed beasts, and creeping things.

"Wherefore God also gave them up to uncleanness through the lusts of their own hearts, to dishonour their own bodies between themselves:

"Who changed the truth of God into a lie, and worshipped and served the creature more than the Creator, who is blessed forever. Amen" (Rom. 1:21-25).

This is Scripture, and it is also history. Seiss said: *"Nor is it difficult to trace the philosophy of it. It requires only a little attention and analysis of our most common and most inward impressions and experiences under the workings of nature."*

So, we see from Aaron and his sons that all men must have a sacrifice. Incidentally, Aaron and his sons were chosen by God, anointed by God, and directed by God.

They were to offer up a bullock for the sin offering because they were sinful men, as are all men. They were then to offer two rams — one for a whole burnt offering and the other for a consecration offering. The latter was to be done with unleavened bread. In effect, four great offerings were sacrificed, but in this order: the sin offering first, followed by the burnt offering, the meal offering, and the peace offering.

THE HOLY SPIRIT

That which the Holy Spirit is impressing upon us in these instructions is man's internal need for a Saviour, and that the Saviour is obtainable only on the premise of justice satisfied. That justice, and we speak of the justice of God, was satisfied, and, in fact, could only be satisfied, by the sacrificial, atoning death of Christ on the Cross.

When we look closely at false doctrine, in some way, it will always be found that the error begins with a wrong inter-pretation of the Atonement. In other words, if one perverts the Cross, one will pervert the entirety of the Word of God. If one properly understands the Cross, which serves as a proper foundation, then one will understand the Bible, which serves as the story of the Cross, and that alone! While the story, as the Bible presents it, may have broad aspects (and, in fact, does), still, all of those aspects, whatever they might be, always center up on the Cross. I speak of all the great doctrines of the Bible!

ALL OF ISRAEL

"And gather you all the congregation together unto the door of the tabernacle of the congregation" (Lev. 8:3).

There were upwards of 3 million people in the wilderness at this time. This was only about one year since they had been delivered from Egyptian bondage.

Even though all were commanded together (considering the great number of people), the far greater majority could not have witnessed the proceedings as far as firsthand information was concerned. Still, they were commanded to be there.

No doubt, when Moses began to carry out the consecration rituals, those who, in fact, did see what was happening would have told all who stood nearby, until the entirety of the congregation would have had some knowledge as to what was taking place.

At least one of the reasons for the Lord telling Moses that they must gather close was that they might understand that even the highest among them, namely Aaron in this case, was still dependent on the sacrifice. That was true for the highest as much as it was for the worst sinner among them. I am positive this lesson was not lost on those who were gathered.

THE CROSS AT PRESENT

From this example, we must understand that just as much as the sacrifice was applicable to all in Moses' time, it is still applicable to all presently and, in fact, always has been. The Cross of Christ was the answer at the very beginning for man's dilemma (Gen. 3:15; Chpt. 4), and it is the answer now. The only way to God is through Jesus Christ (Jn. 14:6), and the only way to Christ is through the Cross (Jn. 1:1-2, 14, 29).

The problem with the church presently is that it has substituted Jesus Christ and Him crucified for a Crossless Christ! Paul said to do such only brings about *"another Jesus"* (II Cor. 11:4).

Whenever the church promotes humanistic psychology in any shape, form, or fashion as the answer to man's dilemma, they are presenting to the world a Crossless Christ. Whenever the Word of Faith people make faith the object of faith instead of Christ and Him crucified, they, too, present a Crossless Christ.

THE COMMANDS OF THE LORD

"And Moses did as the LORD *commanded him; and the assembly was gathered together unto the door of the tabernacle of the congregation.*

"And Moses said unto the congregation, This is the thing which the LORD *commanded to be done"* (Lev. 8:4-5).

This is a repeat of the instructions given in Exodus 29:1–37. According to tradition, this ceremony took place on February 23.

I want the reader to pay careful and strict attention to the phrase, *"This is the thing which the Lord commanded to be done."* These are priceless words.

He did not say, *"This is the thing which is expedient, agreeable, or suitable."* Neither did He say, *"This is the thing which has been arranged by the fathers, the decree of the elders, or the opinion of the doctors."* In fact, Moses knew nothing of such so-called authority. He knew only the voice of the Lord, and that voice alone he followed.

Furthermore, he would bring every member of the congregation of Israel under the sound of that voice, so to speak. In fact, there was no room left for tradition, for the opinions of men, or for the ideas of man in any capacity.

Concerning this, Mackintosh said: *"Had the Word been disregarded, the glory would not have appeared. The two things were intimately connected. The slightest deviation from 'thus saith Jehovah' would have prevented the beams of the divine glory from appearing to the congregation of Israel. Had there been the introduction of a single rite or ceremony not enjoined by the Word, or had there been the omission of ought which that Word commanded, the Lord would not have manifested His glory. He could not sanction, by the glory of His presence, the neglect or rejection of His Word. He can bear with ignorance and infirmity (spiritual weakness), but He cannot sanction neglect or disobedience."*

THE GREAT SIN OF THE MODERN CHURCH

Ignoring the Word, changing the Word, adding to the Word, or taking from the Word is the great sin of the modern church. How long will it take us to learn that God means what He says and says what He means?

For instance, the modern church promotes humanistic psychology as the answer to the aberrations and perversions of man. It does this despite the fact that the Holy Spirit through Peter said: *"According as His divine power has given unto us all things that pertain unto life and godliness, through the knowledge of Him who has called us to glory and virtue:*

"Whereby are given unto us exceeding great and precious promises, that by these you might be partakers of the divine nature, having escaped the corruption that is in the world through lust" (II Pet. 1:3–4).

Due to the Word presently being handled so loosely, many take exception to our insistence that the attack on the Atonement is basely wrong, as it is carried out by the Word of Faith people when they claim that the Cross is of little consequence. The truth is, their erroneous doctrine — as it concerns the Atonement and almost everything else — will cause Christians to be wrecked and souls to be eternally lost. So, there could be nothing worse than that!

THE MESSAGE OF THE CROSS

As few people in the world, I think, I have been made to realize how necessary it is that we adhere strictly to the Word. Even when we stray from the Word through ignorance, or we do not know how to apply the Word because of ignorance, such ignorance cannot be overlooked by God and, to be sure, will reap its bitter fruit.

As it regards the great Message of the Cross, which is actually the foundation of all doctrine as it regards the Word of God, I understood that message as it regarded salvation and strongly preached it all over the world. The result was that hundreds of thousands were brought to a saving knowledge of Jesus Christ, and I exaggerate not! However, as far as the Message of the Cross regarding sanctification, this I understood not at all.

As a result — despite my sincerity, my zealousness, and the fact that I tried so very, very hard — I lived Chapter 7 of Romans all over again. This was because of not understanding God's prescribed order of victory as it regarded the Cross respecting sanctification, even as virtually all modern Christians are doing presently. To be sure, if we do not understand the Message of the Cross as it refers to sanctification, we definitely will relive Chapter 7 of Romans, even as Paul lived it. To be sure, it will not be a pretty picture.

STRICT ADHERENCE TO THE WORD

We sometimes think that sincerity or zealousness will suffice. It won't! There must be a strict adherence to the Word, and for that adherence to be strict, it must be properly taught and preached behind the pulpit. That's why Paul emphatically stated, *"We preach Christ crucified"* (I Cor. 1:23).

That's why he also said, *"For Christ sent me not to baptize, but to preach the Gospel: not with wisdom of words, lest the Cross of Christ should be made of none effect"* (I Cor. 1:17).

As we've already said repeatedly in this volume, the church has been pushed away from its true foundation of the Cross to such an extent that it hardly knows where it's been, where it is, or where it's going. In fact, and I say this with great sadness of heart, the church is in worse condition presently, I believe, than it has been since the Reformation.

DESPERATION PRECEDES REVELATION

I don't know if my heading is true with everyone, but I do know it was true with Paul, and I definitely know that it was true with me.

In the late fall of 1991, I laid my Bible on the table in front of me and said to a group of friends who were there, *"I don't know the answer, but I know the answer is found in the Word of God, and by the grace of God, I intend to find that answer."*

To be sure, those words were not stated matter-of-factly. They were stated from the hurt of a broken heart and through bitter tears. I meant what I said!

For some six years, day and night, I sought the Lord with tears, asking Him to show me the answer to my dilemma and, in fact, the dilemma of the entirety of the church world. In the summer of 1997, He began to answer that prayer. He first took me to Romans, Chapter 6. He began to unfold to me that which He had given to Paul so long, long ago. That's the reason I constantly say that what we are teaching isn't new, but actually that which was taught by Paul.

NO CONDEMNATION

I will never forget that morning when the Lord began to move upon me as it regarded the answer to my petition. I was studying, as stated, Chapter 6 of Romans. From that great chapter, the Holy Spirit began to move upon my heart, opening it up to me, and instantly I knew that this was the answer. I will never forget that day, and I will never forget what the Lord has done and, in fact, continues to do even unto this hour. I trust He will ever continue because it is impossible to exhaust the potential of the Cross.

As the Lord began to give me this revelation, I don't think it would be possible to reveal the joy that flooded my soul and continues unto this moment.

I know what it is to say as Paul, *"O wretched man that I am! Who shall deliver me from the body of this death?"* (Rom. 7:24).

I also now know what it is to say: *"There is therefore now no condemnation to them which are in Christ Jesus, who walk not after the flesh, but after the Spirit.*

"For the law of the Spirit of life in Christ Jesus has made me free from the law of sin and death" (Rom. 8:1–2).

If we adhere to the Word, we will reap the benefits of the Word! If we stray from the Word, we will reap that direction, as well, but it definitely won't be benefits.

THE CROSS AND THE MODERN CHURCH

It is my belief that the church is in such terrible condition, actually epitomizing the Laodicean church of Revelation 3:14–22, because it has strayed from the foundation of the Cross of Christ. To put it bluntly, the church no longer preaches the Cross. It preaches psychology; it preaches various fads; it preaches intellectualism; and it preaches a plethora of works, but it is no longer preaching the Cross.

As a result, the churches are full of people who aren't saved, and the few who are saved, for the most part, are, as one of my associates said, *"miserably saved!"* In other words, modern believers, and I speak of true believers, simply do not know how to live for God. They don't know how to live for God simply because they do not know and understand the Message of the Cross as it refers to sanctification. The laity in the pew is in this condition because the preachers behind the pulpits do not know the Message of the Cross.

THEOLOGICAL OR MORAL

The Message of the Cross is not a difficult message. In fact, it is very simple. Paul told the Corinthians: *"But I fear, lest by any means, as the serpent beguiled Eve through his subtilty, so your minds should be corrupted from the simplicity that is in Christ."* He then went on to say: *"For if he who comes preaches another Jesus, whom we have not preached, or if you receive another spirit, which you have not received, or another gospel, which you have not accepted, you might well bear with him"* (II Cor. 11:3–4).

The Message of the Cross, regarding both salvation and sanctification, is not difficult to understand. In effect, the Holy Spirit through Paul referred to this message as the *simplicity of Christ*. So, this means that if preachers or anyone rejects the Cross, it is definitely not from theological reasons. In other words, it is not because it is too difficult to understand. This means that the reason for rejecting the Cross is definitely not theological, but rather moral.

WHAT DO WE MEAN BY MORAL?

It means that men reject the Cross simply because of pride and self-will. Like Cain of old, they do not refuse to offer up sacrifice; in fact, they offer up beautiful sacrifices. However, it's a sacrifice of their own hands and not that of Christ, i.e., Christ and Him crucified. As I've already said several times in this volume, the Holy Spirit is drawing the line. On one side is the true church, and on the other side is the apostate church. That line is the Cross of Christ. As Martin Luther said so long ago, *"As men view the Cross, so they view the Reformation."* I'll say the same thing presently: as men view the Cross, so they view Christ!

In fact, the Cross has always been the dividing line, but the Holy Spirit is making it more prominent now than ever before, and for all the obvious, scriptural reasons.

Concerning the Cross, may we, in effect, say as Moses of old, *"This is the thing which the* LORD *commanded to be done"*?

THE WASHING

"And Moses brought Aaron and his sons, and washed them with water" (Lev. 8:6).

As it concerned the rite of consecration, the very first initiation as directed by the Lord was the bathing of Aaron and his sons, which symbolized their purification from sin. This denoted the washing or bathing of the entirety of the body. This was not done in the presence of the people, as would be obvious, but in a baptistery, so to speak, behind a curtain.

All of this represented Christ, both in the person of Aaron and his sons, and, as well, in the ritual of washing. This was meant to portray the sublime purity of Jesus, who was *"holy, harmless, undefiled, separate from sinners."*

Concerning this, Seiss said: *"It was partly in token of this pureness and separation that John, as another Moses, so to speak, baptized Christ in the River Jordan. In fact, Christ needed no cleansing. He always was pure. But, to indicate this purity, and to enter upon His priesthood in the regular way, He consented to be washed, as was Aaron. In fact, His baptism was part of his priestly installation. It is one of the items of proof that He meant to be, and is, a priest."*

THE LEVITICAL LAW

As we look at the Levitical Law, whether it pertained to the tabernacle, its sacred vessels, the sacrificial system, or the priesthood, we must always understand that the object of all of this was Christ. More particularly, it was Christ and what He would do for humanity by dying on the Cross. It pointed to Him in this respect in every capacity.

If our eyes and our attention fasten merely onto the individuals here involved, we will miss the entirety of the picture. To get the full import of what all of this meant, we must ever look away to Christ, realizing that all of this in every detail represented Him in His atoning, mediatorial (high priestly), and intercessory work. Failure to see that will bring back a failure of understanding. Christ atoned through the Cross; Christ mediates through the Cross; Christ intercedes because of the Cross!

THE SACRED VESTMENTS OF AARON

"And he put upon him the coat, and girded him with the girdle, and clothed him with the robe, and put the ephod upon him, and he girded him with the curious girdle of the ephod, and bound it unto him therewith.

"And he put the breastplate upon him: also he put in the breastplate the Urim and the Thummim.

"And he put the mitre upon his head; also upon the mitre, even upon his forefront, did he put the golden plate, the holy crown; as the LORD commanded Moses" (Lev. 8:7-9).

Regarding this part of the installation and the consecration, the whole of the congregation of Israel had to be gathered together to witness this solemn occasion. To be sure, this scene must have presented an imposing spectacle.

In the background stood Mount Sinai in solemn silence, terrible in the imaginations of the people, for the fires had so lately enveloped it, and the Holy Law had thundered down from its summit.

In the valley beneath the mount stood the thousands of Israel. In fact, there were probably nearly 3 million people present that day. The princes of Jacob would have stood about the door of the sanctuary in devout expectancy. They would have conveyed all that was happening to the many thousands of Israel who awaited all of this with bated breath. Of course, it would not have been possible for all of these people to have personally observed these proceedings because, due to the large number, many would have had to stand far back from the actual site of the consecration. However, it is certain that they were informed as to what was taking place even as it took place.

THE SHADOW OF THINGS TO COME

In the center of all this hung the cloudy pillar, stretching high into the heavens, its shadow resting upon the holy tabernacle. As stated, all of this had to have been an imposing sight.

As imposing as it was, I'm sure that the far greater majority of the congregation of Israel little understood the full import of what was taking place. In fact, I don't think it was possible at that time for them to properly understand. It was then veiled in type and symbol. Paul referred to it as a *"shadow of things to come"* (Col. 2:17).

So, one might well ask, *"How were they saved in those days by comparison to the present?"*

In fact, they were saved then exactly as we are now. The sacrifices were a symbol of the One who was to come. They were to have faith in the One who was to come, whom the sacrifices represented. Faith in that coming One guaranteed salvation, even as faith in the One who has come now guarantees salvation (Rom. 10:9–10; Eph. 2:8–9).

As someone has well said, *"The Old Testament saints were saved by looking forward to the Cross, while we are saved by looking backward to the Cross."*

All of Israel was to witness this occasion because it affected all of Israel. The Gospel of Jesus Christ is not for a select few; it is for all!

SYMBOLIC OF CHRIST

We will find that the following things mentioned symbolize Christ in some way, which, of course, speaks to us presently.

THE COAT

This item was worn next to the skin. It typified the deity of Christ.

At the Fall in the Garden of Eden, the Scripture says, *"Unto Adam also and to his wife did the Lord God make coats of skins, and clothed them"* (Gen. 3:21).

In effect, these coats made by the Lord God for Adam and Eve proclaim the fact that God would become man, and would die on a Cross in order to provide a covering for lost humanity. That covering, and that covering alone, will do!

While the humanity of Christ was portrayed outwardly, the deity was always within. While He willingly laid aside the expression of His deity, He never for a moment lost possession of His deity.

THE GIRDLE

This spoke of His humanity and, more particularly, His humanity as it regarded service. John said Jesus, *"took a towel, and girded Himself"* (Jn. 13:4).

The girdle was a narrow, long band or belt of linen tied around the waist to confine the ephod close to the body.

THE ROBE

This was sometimes referred to as the *robe of the ephod*, and was a seamless garment, curiously embroidered with blue, purple, scarlet, and gold. Its lower border was ornamented with a roll of red pomegranates (denoting fruit) and little golden bells encircling the entire robe in alternate succession. It was a garment which extended from the shoulders to a little below the knees. It portrayed the righteousness of Christ.

THE EPHOD

This was the distinctive vestment of the high priest. It was a sleeveless garment and was worn over the shoulders. It was made of blue, purple, scarlet, and fine twined linen, interwoven with golden threads. It signified the working, moving, and operation of the Holy Spirit within and upon Christ (Jn. 3:34).

THE CURIOUS GIRDLE

This could be referred to as a *band*, which was attached to the ephod, which wrapped around the waist of the high priest and tied at the front. As the ephod typified the Holy Spirit upon Christ, the curious girdle typified the work of the Spirit within the life of Christ (Lk. 4:18–19).

THE BREASTPLATE

This is called more fully, *the breastplate of judgment.*

This was a fabric about nine inches square, set with 12 different jewels, large, and well arranged. Its two upper corners had gold rings, by which it was connected with jeweled shoulder pieces with wreathed chains of gold. At its lower corners, it was fastened to the girdle with blue ribbons.

The 12 jewels stood for the Twelve Tribes of Israel, and each jewel had upon it the name of its tribe. They were the most precious things belonging to the priest's attire.

In its total compilation, it signified not only Israel of old but, as well, spiritual Israel, which speaks of the church. It is that for which Christ died, therefore, it was worn over the heart of the high priest.

THE URIM AND THE THUMMIM

These were inserted in a pouch, which was made into the back of the breastplate. The two words, *Urim* and *Thummim,* mean *"lights"* and *"perfection."* The Scripture doesn't say exactly what they were. Many believe they could have been two precious stones, with the word *yes,* inscribed on one, and the word *no* inscribed on the other. They were used by the high priest for spiritual direction. An example is David enquiring of the high priest, as found in I Samuel 30:7–8.

THE MITRE

This was a hat or a turban of sorts, made of fine linen. It represented authority and portrayed Christ as the Head of the Church (Col. 1:18).

THE GOLDEN PLATE

This was a golden plate fitted over the mitre, and on the front of this shining gold appeared the solemn inscription: *"Holiness to the Lord."* This, of course, represented the absolute holiness of Christ.

Thus did God direct for the clothing of the high priest *"for glory and for beauty"*; and thus it typified Christ!

THE HOLY SPIRIT

"And Moses took the anointing oil, and anointed the tabernacle and all that was therein, and sanctified them.

"And he sprinkled thereof upon the altar seven times, and anointed the altar and all his vessels, both the laver and his foot, to sanctify them.

"And he poured of the anointing oil upon Aaron's head, and anointed him, to sanctify him" (Lev. 8:10-12).

- The anointing oil was applied to the tabernacle and all the vessels therein. The brazen altar was anointed seven times, with the brazen laver then anointed as well. The anointing oil, which was a type of the Holy Spirit, was then poured upon Aaron's head. All of this proclaims the fact of the absolute necessity of the Holy Spirit upon everything we do.
- Verse 14 proclaims the fact that even though Aaron stood in the place of the great high priest, which means he was called and anointed by God, still, he was a sinner and, thereby, *"laid their hands upon the head of the bullock for the sin offering."*

- This signifies that their sins were transferred to the animal that became their substitute.
- The animal then being slain testified to the death of Christ.
- The blood poured out at the bottom of the altar typified the blood of Jesus that would be shed at Calvary.
- The word *reconciliation*, as used in Verse 15, proclaims the first time it is used in the Bible and applies to the doing away of an enmity, the bridging over of a quarrel.
- It is interesting to notice that no Bible passage speaks of Christ as reconciling God to man. The stress is always on man's being reconciled to God. It is man's sin that has caused the enmity.
- This enmity in no way impacts or changes God's love. The Bible is very clear that God's love to man never varies, no matter what man may do. Indeed, the whole atoning work of Christ stems from God's great love.
- However, God's love in no way overlooks our sin. Love alone could not do away with sin. The price had to be paid for sin for the enmity to be taken away. It was paid by the death of Christ at Calvary.
- The words in Verse 17, *"without the camp,"* signified that the Lord paid for redemption of man *"without the gate"* (Heb. 13:12). Jesus was crucified outside the then city limits of Jerusalem.

THE CROSS AND THE HOLY SPIRIT

There are two things of which the modern church is greatly lacking. The first is its understanding, or rather the lack thereof, of the Cross. It has a modicum of understanding as it respects the Cross relative to salvation. However, as it regards sanctification, in other words, how we live for God and how we order our behavior—there is no understanding at all. Secondly, the church little understands the Holy Spirit. (The text will address the Cross a little later in this chapter as it refers to the blood.)

The two — the Cross and the Holy Spirit — are so directly connected or intertwined as to be inseparable. In other words, if one properly understands the Cross, one will properly understand the Holy Spirit and vice versa.

For instance, and that to which we have already alluded, Revelation 5:6 graphically displays that of which I speak.

In John's great vision of the throne of God, he saw the book held in the right hand of God the Father, who sat on the throne. A strong angel cried with a loud voice, asking, *"Who is worthy to open the book, and to loose the seals thereof?"* (Rev. 5:2).

The Scripture then tells us that no man was worthy.

John then wept because it seems that he understood the significance of this book being opened.

The Scripture then tells us that one of the elders spoke to John, telling him to weep not, and then said, *"Behold, the Lion of the tribe of Judah, the Root of David, has prevailed to open the book, and to loose the seven seals thereof"* (Rev. 5:5).

THE LION AND THE LAMB

Then John looked, but he did not really see a lion, but rather a Lamb. What does that tell us?

That tells us that we cannot have the power of the Lion, in other words, the power of the Lion of the tribe of Judah, until we first recognize Jesus as the Lamb. We can't have the *power* without first recognizing the *price* that has been paid, which refers to the Cross. Unfortunately, millions are trying to do just that! They are ignoring the Cross, while at the same time claiming the power, which, in effect, places them in the position of serving *"another Jesus"* (II Cor. 11:4).

To emphasize the fact, the Scripture says that what John saw was *"a Lamb as it had been slain,"* which signifies the Cross. This means that we cannot get to the throne unless we come through the Cross. So, those who would try to preach the Resurrection or the throne without the Cross will, in fact, never reach the throne. The answer and the key are Jesus Christ and Him crucified (I Cor. 1:23).

SEVEN HORNS AND SEVEN EYES

The Scripture then tells us that the Lamb had *"seven horns and seven eyes, which are the seven Spirits of God sent forth into all the earth"* (Rev. 5:6).

The seven horns speak of total dominion, which, in effect, is supposed to be our dominion that Jesus purchased for us at the Cross. It means total dominion over all sin. While the Bible does not teach sinless perfection, it definitely does teach that sin is not to have dominion over us, which means to dominate us in any way (Rom. 6:14).

The seven eyes speak of total illumination, meaning that without understanding the Cross, one cannot properly understand the Word.

We know that there aren't seven Holy Spirits. The idea is, the number seven speaks of total dominion, total illumination, and, as well, the total work of the Spirit. In fact, we are told what this total work is in Isaiah 11:1–2.

The point is that the slain Lamb and the Holy Spirit are both so closely intertwined that they seem to be one and the same. That's how close the Holy Spirit works within the parameters of the finished work of Christ (Rom. 8:2).

THE MOVING AND OPERATION OF THE HOLY SPIRIT

Anything and everything done by the Lord on earth is done totally and completely through the person, office, ministry, and power of the Holy Spirit. The only thing done on this earth that the Holy Spirit did not personally do was the redemption work accomplished by Christ on the Cross. Even then, the Holy Spirit superintended the conception, birth, life, ministry, death, resurrection, ascension, and exaltation of Christ (Mat. 1:18; Lk. 4:18–19). In fact, the Holy Spirit was at the Cross when Jesus died and actually told Him when to die (Heb. 9:14).

Before the preacher preaches, he should earnestly seek the Lord as to what the message ought to be, which the Holy Spirit will give to him. He should then ask the Lord to anoint him as he delivers the message, which again, the Holy Spirit will definitely do. In fact, if this doesn't happen, nothing is going to be accomplished for Christ.

The truth is, the believer — preacher or otherwise — should seek the Lord earnestly for the leading and guidance of the Holy Spirit on a continuing basis (Jn. 16:13–14). We should have the leading of the Spirit in every single thing we do and, in fact, can have if we will only seek the face of the Lord.

Regrettably, most Christians have the mistaken idea
that we are to do all that we can within our own strength
and power, and then, when we cannot do anymore, the Holy
Spirit will step in and help us. Nothing could be further from
the truth. In fact, to be sure, the Holy Spirit will have no association with that to which He does not give birth.

HOW THE HOLY SPIRIT WORKS

The Holy Spirit works totally and completely within the
confines and parameters, so to speak, of the finished work,
i.e., the Cross of Christ. That's what gives Him the legal
means to do all that He does (Rom. 8:2).

Before the Cross, the Holy Spirit could not come into the
hearts and lives of believers to abide permanently. He was
with them but not in them. In fact, the Spirit did come into
the hearts and lives of some prophets, etc., to help them do
what they were called to do. When that work was over, He
would leave. Now, since the Cross, the Holy Spirit comes
into the believer's heart and life at the moment of conversion,
there to abide forever (Jn. 14:16).

The Holy Spirit doesn't demand a lot from us, but He most
definitely does demand one thing, and upon that one thing,
He will not bend. He demands that our faith rest completely
within Christ and the Cross. In other words, the Cross of
Christ must ever be the object of our faith. When I speak of
the Cross of Christ, I am not speaking of the wooden beam
on which He died, but rather what He there accomplished.
In fact, the Cross is everything. It is the foundation of all
faith and was actually formulated in the mind of the Godhead from before the foundation of the world (I Pet. 1:18-20).

So, every false doctrine has as its beginning a false interpretation, a misunderstanding, or an outright denial of the Cross of Christ. All Bible doctrine has its foundation, its beginning, in the Cross of Christ (Rom. 6:1-14; 8:1-11; I Cor. 1:17, 18, 23; 2:2; Col. 2:10-15). Of course, if it's the Bible, then it's true.

As we have previously stated, the modern church has no idea as to the part the Cross of Christ plays in our living for God on a daily basis. To be sure, the believer cannot live a victorious life unless the believer makes the Cross of Christ the object of his faith and does so continually (Gal. 6:14).

When one looks at the Old Testament and witnesses the multitudes of sacrifices offered up, which numbered into the millions by the time of Christ, one sees that all represented Christ and what He would do for us at the Cross.

THE BAPTISM WITH THE HOLY SPIRIT

The outpouring of the Holy Spirit actually began at the turn of the 20th century and could be referred to as the *"latter rain"* (Joel 2:23). Due to the light that has presently been shed in this world as it regards the Holy Spirit, I do not personally believe that one can have the leading of the Spirit without being first baptized with the Holy Spirit. I believe the Bible teaches the following as it regards the Holy Spirit:

- While the Spirit of God definitely comes into the heart and life of the believer at conversion, that is different than what Jesus was speaking of in Acts 1:4–5. There is a vast difference in being *born of the Spirit* than being *baptized with the Spirit*.

- We believe that the Bible teaches that the baptism with the Holy Spirit is an experience different and apart from salvation. It does not make one more saved, for it's impossible to be more saved, which comes by trusting what Christ did at the Cross on our behalf. The baptism with the Holy Spirit is given to equip us for service, among other things (Mat. 3:11–12).
- We believe the Bible teaches that the baptism with the Spirit is always, and without exception, accompanied by speaking with other tongues (Acts 2:4; 10:44–48; 19:1–7).
- We believe the Bible teaches that the Holy Spirit works entirely within the confines of the sacrifice of Christ. In other words, He will do nothing outside of the price that Jesus paid (Jn. 16:13–14). This is so much a fact that it is referred to as a *law* (Rom. 8:2). This means that if the believer is to have the Holy Spirit work within his life, he is to exhibit faith in the Cross of Christ at all times, understanding that everything comes to him through the Cross (I Cor. 1:17–18, 21, 23; 2:2, 5; Rom. 6:3–14; Lk. 9:23).

With faith evidenced in the Cross constantly, the Holy Spirit will work within our lives, using the same power with which He raised Christ from the dead (Rom. 8:11).

THE PRIESTHOOD

"And Moses brought Aaron's sons, and put coats upon them, and girded them with girdles, and put bonnets upon them; as the LORD commanded Moses" (Lev. 8:13).

Aaron and his sons together represent Christ and His priestly house; Aaron alone represents Christ in His sacrificial and intercessory function; Moses and Aaron together represent Christ as king and priest.

Now, let us remember what all these chapters contain is but *"a shadow of good things to come."* In fact, the entire Mosaic economy must be put in that category (Heb. 10:1).

THE SIN OFFERING

"And he brought the bullock for the sin offering: and Aaron and his sons laid their hands upon the head of the bullock for the sin offering.

"And he slew it; and Moses took the blood, and put it upon the horns of the altar round about with his finger, and purified the altar, and poured the blood at the bottom of the altar, and sanctified it, to make reconciliation upon it" (Lev. 8:14-15).

Though duly consecrated, Aaron and his sons had first to be purged of their sins before they could commence their priestly functions in the sanctuary.

In fact, Aaron and his sons stood as penitent sinners by the side of the sin offering, which was now offered for the first time. The sin offering was called most holy because it cleansed the sinner from sin. In the whole burnt offering, Christ took His perfection and gave it to the sinner. In the sin offering, Christ took the sinner's sin and made it His own, thereby, justifying the sinner because Christ had paid the price for that sin and, in fact, all sin (I Jn. 2:2).

Let the reader understand that all of the emphasis is totally and completely on the crucifixion of Christ and very little on the resurrection, ascension, and exaltation of Christ, as important as those things actually are. However, I will remind the reader that these latter things were a foregone conclusion once the price was paid at the Cross.

THE PREACHING OF THE CROSS

So, whenever certain preachers in the Word of Faith philosophy claim that the preaching of the Cross is the preaching of death — meaning that it should not be preached — such a statement presents itself as being about as unbiblical as anything could ever be.

Paul said, *"For the preaching of the Cross is to them who perish foolishness, but to we who are saved, it is the power of God"* (I Cor. 1:18).

The laying on of hands upon the head of the bullock for the sin offering represented their sins being transferred to this innocent victim, typifying Christ taking our sins upon Himself.

Aaron then had to kill the animal, even as all had to kill the animal brought for their sacrifice. In other words, the guilty party had to personally kill the innocent animal. This, no doubt, made him very much aware of his guilt and that an innocent victim was suffering in his place.

When the throat of the animal was cut, Moses caught the blood in a basin, as all priests following him would do. He then put the blood upon the four horns of the altar and then poured the balance of the blood out at the bottom of the altar, which sanctified it.

This tells us three things:

1. LIFE'S BLOOD SHED AT CALVARY

The blood signified Christ shedding His life's blood on the Cross of Calvary. Faith in that shed blood was and is an absolute must in order for a person to be saved. The shedding of the blood signified that life had been given, for the life of the flesh is in the blood.

2. GOD'S PLAN OF REDEMPTION FOR THE ENTIRE UNIVERSE

The blood applied to the four horns of the altar signified that God's plan of redemption was for the entirety of the universe, even as the four horns pointed in all four directions of the compass.

3. THE CROSS

The brazen altar, which was but a type of the Cross, had to be sanctified, and was sanctified, by the blood being poured out at its base. This signified its purpose, and its purpose alone! The altar is the place of death, and more specifically, it was the place of the death of Christ.

Whenever you as a believing sinner trusted Christ, you were baptized into His death, buried with Him by baptism into death, and then raised with Him in newness of life (Rom. 6:3–5).

Please understand that the word *baptized* has absolutely nothing here to do with water baptism. It speaks of what Jesus did at the Cross, all on our behalf. When we evidenced faith in Him when we were originally saved, in the mind of God, we were literally baptized into His death.

This is all done by our exhibiting faith in Him. No physical act is involved, just faith, but faith in Christ and what Christ has done at the Cross (Jn. 3:16).

THE FAT

"And he took all the fat that was upon the inwards, and the caul above the liver, and the two kidneys, and their fat, and Moses burned it upon the altar.

"But the bullock, and his hide, his flesh, and his dung, he burnt with fire without the camp; as the LORD *commanded Moses"* (Lev. 8:16-17).

The fat signified that the very best animal had been offered. A sick, wasted animal would have very little fat, if any. The fat signified that God had given His best and, in a sense, represented the spiritual, physical, and material prosperity that comes from Christ.

Even though the fat was burned on the altar, the bullock itself could not be burned on the altar because it was a sin offering. In fact, of the four bloody offerings, it was only the whole burnt offering that could be burned totally upon the altar because it represented the perfection of Christ and not sin. Anything that represented sin — and we speak of the peace offering, the sin offering, and the trespass offering — had to be disposed of in other manners.

THE RAM

"And he brought the ram for the burnt offering: and Aaron and his sons laid their hands upon the head of the ram.

"And he killed it; and Moses sprinkled the blood upon the altar round about.

"And he cut the ram into pieces; and Moses burnt the head, and the pieces, and the fat.

"And he washed the inwards and the legs in water; and Moses burnt the whole ram upon the altar: it was a burnt sacrifice for a sweet savour, and an offering made by fire unto the LORD; as the LORD commanded Moses" (Lev. 8:18-21).

Whereas the bullock was offered up as a sin offering, the ram, as one of two rams, was offered up as a whole burnt offering. This means that all of it was burned on the altar because it represented the perfection of Christ.

In the sin offering, the guilt of the sinner—Aaron and his sons in this case—was transferred to Christ. Now that reconciliation has taken place, the perfection of Christ is now passed to Aaron and his sons, represented by the ram and it being offered totally on the altar.

The perfection of Christ, i.e., the righteousness of God, cannot be imputed to the believing sinner until sin has first been dealt with.

The whole burnt offering, the meat (cereal) offering, and the peace offering were all spoken of as a *sweet savour* before the Lord. They all spoke of Christ as it regarded the perfect sacrifice of His perfect self—thanksgiving for that sacrifice represented by the cereal offering, and now peace restored, represented by the peace offering.

THE RAM OF CONSECRATION

"And he brought the other ram, the ram of consecration: and Aaron and his sons laid their hands upon the head of the ram" (Lev. 8:22).

Verses 22 through 26 portray the consecration ram.

Whether we contemplate the doctrine of sacrifice or the doctrine of priesthood, we find the shedding of blood gets the same important place.

A blood-stained ear was needed to hearken to the divine communications; a blood-stained hand was needed to execute the services of the sanctuary; and a blood-stained foot was needed to tread the courts of the Lord's house. The shedding of blood was the grand foundation of all sacrifice for sin, and it stood connected with all the vessels of the ministry and with all the functions of the priesthood.

The very presence of Christ in Heaven, and we speak of His appearance at the throne of the Majesty, presents the value of all that He has accomplished on the Cross. His presence at the throne attests the worth and acceptableness of His atoning blood (Heb. 1:3).

He did it all for us.

Going back to Leviticus 8:12, as we shall see, we find Aaron being anointed alone. This was before the sacrifice of the animals with the blood applied. In this, we have a type of Christ, who, until He offered Himself upon the Cross, stood entirely alone. There could be no union between Him and His people save on the ground of death and resurrection.

The unleavened cake spoke of the perfection of the humanity of Christ.

The wave offering signified that Christ and His perfection was recognized by those who believed on Him, and thankfulness to God was offered up for the gift of His Son.

The unleavened cake, plus the oiled bread and one wafer, along with the fat and the right shoulder of the animal, were all offered up as a burnt offering, signifying Christ, who alone could satisfy the righteous demands of a thrice-holy God.

It was a sweet savour because it represented the full redemption plan, which specified the death of the Son of the living God.

LAID THEIR HANDS UPON THE HEAD OF THE RAM

The ram of consecration was the concluding sacrifice, which, in form, resembled the thank offering and the peace offering, and was designed to typify the consecration of Aaron and his sons and, in effect, all priests who would follow in their train over the many centuries. The next verse proclaims what this consecration entails.

THE BLOOD

"And he slew it; and Moses took of the blood of it, put it upon the tip of Aaron's right ear, and upon the thumb of his right hand, and upon the great toe of his right foot.

"And he brought Aaron's sons, and Moses put of the blood upon the tip of their right ear, and upon the thumbs of their right hands, and upon the great toes of their right feet, and Moses sprinkled the blood upon the altar round about" (Lev. 8:23-24).

This tells us what the consecration was.

Concerning this, Williams said: *"Cleansed, clothed, and crowned though they were, yet the moment their hands touched the sacrifice, the sinless victims were slain. Such is the nature and the doom of sin.*

"The ear, the hand, and the foot were first cleansed with blood, and then anointed with oil. The cleaning of the precious blood, and the energizing of the Holy Spirit alone fit even the noblest character for entry into God's service."

The blood of the slain ram was taken by Moses, which he first put on the tip of Aaron's right ear, and then Aaron's sons. This meant that his ear was now consecrated to God alone. He was to hear only from the Lord.

The blood was then applied to the thumb of Aaron's right hand and that of his four sons as well. This means that their *doing*, i.e., hands, would be consecrated totally to the Lord. They were to do only what He desired.

The blood was then applied to the big toe of Aaron, plus those of his sons as well, which typified their *going*. They would go only where He directed them to go. This was their consecration.

So, we have the hearing, the doing, and the walk.

THE FAT, THE UNLEAVENED BREAD, THE OILED BREAD, THE WAFER, AND THE RIGHT SHOULDER

"And he took the fat, and the rump, and all the fat that was upon the inwards, and the caul above the liver, and the two kidneys, and their fat, and the right shoulder:

"And out of the basket of unleavened bread, that was before the Lord, *he took one unleavened cake, and a cake of oiled bread, and one wafer, and put them on the fat, and upon the right shoulder:*

"And he put all upon Aaron's hands, and upon his sons' hands, and waved them for a wave offering before the Lord.

"And Moses took them from off their hands, and burnt them on the altar upon the burnt offering: they were consecrations for a sweet savour: it is an offering made by fire unto the LORD" (Lev. 8:25-28).

The unleavened bread represented the perfect humanity of Christ. The oiled bread represented His being filled with the Holy Spirit above measure (Jn. 3:34). The wafer symbolized His perfect body, which would be offered in sacrifice, as Verse 28 proclaims. The fat symbolized His prosperity in that God had given Heaven's best. The right shoulder of the ram signified the strength of this which would be offered to the Lord.

THE WAVE OFFERING

Aaron and his sons were to take these ingredients in their hands, in essence, all putting their hands on the concoction. They were then to wave it before the Lord, signifying thanksgiving unto Him and that He was the author of salvation.

THE BURNT OFFERING

Then, these things, all representing Christ, were placed upon the altar and offered up as a burnt offering, signifying that Christ would give His all on the Cross. This was a sweet savour to the Lord.

VICTORIOUS LIVING

These things done to and with the priests — including the blood being applied to the ear, etc.; their being anointed with oil, and even the sacrifices — were all symbolic. However, as should be obvious, it had to do with daily living.

Unfortunately, the modern church, little understanding the Cross and little understanding the Holy Spirit, little knows how to live for God. This is despite the fact that all true believers have the Holy Spirit. When it comes to the Cross, about all that modern believers know is, *Jesus died for me*. While that certainly is true and, in fact, the greatest statement ever made, still, that's about the gist of understanding of most Christians as it regards the Cross. In other words, they have no knowledge whatsoever of the part the Cross plays in the sanctification process, which has to do with our victory and our daily living.

As I've said many times, I think one of the main reasons for this is because the modern church little understands the Bible, and it especially little understands the Old Testament.

The consecration of the priests, as outlined in Chapter 8 of Leviticus, pertains to daily living. However, as stated, these priests could only have the symbol of what was yet to come, namely Christ. Only having the symbol, they could not actually walk in victory as modern Christians can do, that is, if modern Christians understand God's prescribed order.

THE BLOOD

Looking at these things closely, we must understand that blood was applied to the ear, thumb, and big toe. The blood was from the ram that had been killed and was to be offered up, at least in part, as a burnt offering.

The point I'm making is this: the blood applied signified that it's impossible to live the life we ought to live unless we understand the Cross, and I'm speaking of the Cross as it refers to our sanctification. The bullock as a sin offering had already been offered. Its blood was shed, and its fat was offered on the brazen altar, with the carcass of the animal taken out and *"burned with fire without the camp."*

This particular offering pertained to salvation, one might say. The two rams were offered for consecration and had to do with daily living. However, the one offering of Christ sufficed for all. The sinner must believe in Christ and what Christ has done at the Cross in order to be saved, although he understands very little about it. Likewise, the believer, after becoming a Christian, must continue to believe in the Cross, and his knowledge of this finished work will now be greatly increased.

THE CROSS

The point I'm attempting to make is that the believer cannot successfully live for the Lord and cannot walk in perpetual victory unless he understands that all of this comes through the Cross, with the Cross having given the Holy Spirit the legal means to work within our lives.

The Bible is not much on formulas; however, the little formula below will perhaps make it easier to understand. We might even refer to it as *God's prescribed order of victory:*

- Jesus Christ is the Source: This means that every single thing we receive from God, all and without exception, is made possible by the Lord Jesus Christ. We must never forget that (Jn. 1:1-3, 14, 29; Col. 2:10-15).
- The Cross is the means: This means that the Cross of Christ makes all of this possible. We are speaking

of salvation, sanctification, the baptism with the Holy Spirit, communion with the Lord, blessings of every description, gifts of the Spirit, fruit of the Spirit, etc. In other words, it is the Cross of Christ that makes it possible for the Lord Jesus Christ to give us all things (I Cor. 1:17, 18, 23; 2:2; Gal. 6:14).

- The Cross of Christ must be the object of our faith: We are not speaking of the wooden beam on which Jesus died, but rather what He there accomplished. At the Cross, He atoned for all sin — past, present, and future — at least for all who will believe. The atoning for all sin removed the legal means that Satan had to hold men captive. This means that every unsaved person in the world can accept Jesus Christ and be made perfectly clean in a moment's time if they will only do so. It means that if believers will look to Christ and the Cross, ever making the Cross of Christ the object of their faith, then the Holy Spirit will work mightily within their lives, helping them to be victorious in every capacity. Jesus must not be looked at outside of the Cross. By that, I'm speaking of what He there accomplished. Let us say it again: The Cross must be the object of our faith (Rom. 6:1-14; I Cor. 2:2; Gal., Chpt. 5; Col. 2:10-15).

- Understanding that our Lord is the Source, the Cross is the means, and that our faith is anchored in Christ and the Cross, then the Holy Spirit—who works exclusively within the parameters of the finished work of Christ—will then work mightily on our behalf. This is how the Holy Spirit works. It is the Cross of Christ that gives Him the legal means to do all that He does (Rom. 8:1-11; Eph. 2:13-18; Gal. 6:14).

THE HOLY SPIRIT

Due to what Christ did at the Cross, all believers since the Cross have the Holy Spirit living within them (Jn. 14:16–17). In fact, every single thing done in our lives, and I speak of things done for the Lord, must be done exclusively by the Holy Spirit. Anything else constitutes the flesh, which God can never honor (Rom. 8:8).

The flesh refers to our own personal strength, efforts, ability, education, motivation, talent, willpower, etc. While that within itself is not wrong, it becomes wrong if we depend on that instead of the Lord. The truth is, no matter how strong you might be, you simply cannot live for God within your own strength and ability. It cannot be done! Due to the Fall in the Garden of Eden, man and his ability have been made ineffective. However, with the Holy Spirit, all things can be done.

This is what Paul was talking about when he said, **"But if the Spirit** (Holy Spirit) **of Him** (God the Father) **who raised up Jesus from the dead dwell in you, He who raised up Christ from the dead shall also quicken your mortal bodies by His Spirit who dwells in you"** (Rom. 8:11).

Most Christians read this and think that Paul was speaking of the resurrection of the dead, which is yet to come. No, he was not! At the coming resurrection, our bodies will be instantly glorified. We shall be changed in a moment, in the twinkling of an eye (I Cor. 15:51–54). That will be the glorified body.

OUR MORTAL BODY

Paul was not speaking in Chapter 8 of Romans about the glorified body, but rather our mortal bodies. He told us that if we make the Cross of Christ the object of our faith (Rom. 8:2), the Holy Spirit, who works exclusively within the parameters of the finished work of Christ, will *"also quicken your mortal bodies."* In other words, we can then yield the members of our bodies to righteousness instead of unrighteousness (Rom. 6:13). However, we simply cannot do that, no matter how sincere we are and no matter how hard we try, if we do not maintain our faith in the finished work of Christ. This then gives the Holy Spirit the legal right to work accordingly within our daily living. This is so much circumscribed that it is referred to as a *law* (Rom. 8:2).

This is the manner in which the Holy Spirit works and, in fact, the only manner in which He works.

Christians, for the most part, don't know how the Holy Spirit works; consequently, He is by and large ignored, or else, we approach Him all wrong. It's because we do not understand the Cross and the price that Jesus paid there. Properly understanding the Cross gives the Holy Spirit latitude to work within our lives, which guarantees rest in Christ (Mat. 11:28–30) and victorious living (Rom. 6:3–14).

This is what Chapter 8 of Leviticus teaches us, as should be obvious.

THE WAVE OFFERING

"And Moses took the breast, and waved it for a wave offering before the Lord: For of the ram of consecration it was Moses' part; as the Lord commanded Moses" (Lev. 8:29).

Aaron and his sons had already been anointed with oil and had the blood applied. It was now done again, which was a fitting conclusion to their consecration. It was meant to show that the sanctification process is an ongoing process, thereby, the necessity of continued trust in the blood and the need of continued anointing with the Holy Spirit.

Beautiful and costly as was the raiment of Aaron, yet the oil and the blood were applied. This simply means that the beauty and glory of salvation, typified by the garments of Aaron, are all made possible by what Jesus did at the Cross.

That which remained of the ram of consecration was now to be eaten, along with the unleavened bread, etc. This typified the statement of Christ: *"Except you eat the flesh of the Son of Man, and drink His blood, you have no life in you"* (Jn. 6:53).

Once again, we go back to the Cross! Eating His flesh, and drinking His blood, was not meant in a literal sense, but referred to faith in Christ and what Christ would do at the Cross. It literally referred to entering into His death, burial, and resurrection (Rom. 6:3–5).

The priests were to remain in the court of the tabernacle for seven days and nights. On each of these days, the same sacrifices — the sin offering, the burnt offering, and the consecration offering — were to be repeated, along with all the other parts of the ritual. The number seven typified perfection, completion, and totality. In other words, it was a total consecration.

THE OIL AND THE BLOOD

"And Moses took of the anointing oil, and of the blood which was upon the altar, and sprinkled it upon Aaron, and upon his garments, and upon his sons, and upon his sons' garments with him; and sanctified Aaron, and his garments, and his sons, and his sons' garments with him" (Lev. 8:30).

Inasmuch as Moses was officiating that day in accordance with the directions given in Exodus 29:26, this was to be his sacrificial meal since he was divinely appointed to perform the priestly service. Ordinarily this would have been for the priests in general, but Moses was instructed by the Lord to consume it himself. This signified that even Moses had to partake of Christ, as do all. We learn from Verse 30 that there is never a time that the blood i.e., the Cross, and the oil, i.e., the Holy Spirit, aren't needed.

Aaron was outfitted in these beautiful garments, which only the high priest could wear. As well, his sons were outfitted in their garments, but still, the oil and the blood were sprinkled all over Aaron and his sons, referring to their garments, which spoke of the sanctifying process. This tells us three things:

1. It tells us that the glory and beauty of salvation, typified by these beautiful garments, cannot be ascertained by the believer without the proper application of the oil and the blood. In other words, after salvation, all the glorious and wonderful things accomplished by Christ at the Cross can be ours only by our faith in that finished work. Faith properly placed, which refers to the Cross of Christ, guarantees the help of the Holy Spirit, typified by the oil.
2. We learn from this that the sanctification process is a progressive work. In other words, it is ongoing.
3. We learn that this sanctification process can be carried out and, in fact, is carried out solely by and through the Holy Spirit, who works exclusively within the parameters of the finished work of Christ.

If it is to be noticed, the anointing oil is mentioned first. This signifies the fact that the Holy Spirit works continuously, but does so on the basis of the shed blood of the Lamb.

THE FEAST

"And Moses said unto Aaron and to his sons, Boil the flesh at the door of the tabernacle of the congregation: and there eat it with the bread that is in the basket of consecrations, as I commanded, saying, Aaron and his sons shall eat it.

"And that which remains of the flesh and of the bread shall you burn with fire" (Lev. 8:31-32).

These verses furnish a fine type of Christ and His people feeding together upon the results of the accomplished Atonement.

Feasting on Christ, which, once again, has to do with John 6:53–58, pertains to continued faith in His finished work. We are not to mistake the Lord's Supper with this feast. It is merely a symbol of this feast and points one to the sacrifice of Christ — always to the sacrifice of Christ.

It is impossible to know Christ, to understand Christ, and to enjoy the benefits of Christ without a proper understanding of the Cross of Christ. When one understands that — thereby, maintaining his faith in that finished work — that is feasting upon Christ, and that is the enjoyment of more abundant life (Jn. 10:10).

BURNED WITH FIRE

Verse 32 proclaims the fact that all which was not eaten had to then be burned with fire that nothing remain. This signifies the fact that all of Christ must be consumed. In other words, it's all of Christ, or it's none of Christ! He cannot be accepted in part, so to speak.

SEVEN DAYS

"And you shall not go out of the door of the tabernacle of the congregation in seven days, until the days of your consecration be at an end: for seven days shall he consecrate you.

"As he has done this day, so the LORD *has commanded to do, to make an atonement for you.*

"Therefore shall you abide at the door of the tabernacle of the congregation day and night seven days, and keep the charge of the LORD, *that you die not: for so I am commanded.*

"So Aaron and his sons did all things which the LORD *commanded by the hand of Moses"* (Lev. 8:33-36).

Aaron and his sons were to remain in the confines (the court) of the tabernacle for seven days and seven nights. On each of these days, the entire sacrificial ritual was to be engaged.

The number seven typifies totality and completion. In other words, that which the Lord does is perfect and is often typified by the number seven.

Then everything was done in symbolism because it was the only way it could be done. However, now, due to what Christ has done at the Cross, all of this is carried out by the Holy Spirit in reality. It is done upon the basis of our faith in Christ and what Christ has done for us in the giving of Himself on the Cross of Calvary. It is always *the Cross! The Cross! The Cross!*

"The Saviour who loves me and suffered the loss
"Of heavenly glory to die on the Cross,
"The Babe of the manger, though born without stain,
"This Jesus is coming, is coming again!"

9

The Eighth Day

CHAPTER NINE

The Eighth Day

"*AND IT CAME to pass on the eighth day, that Moses called Aaron and his sons, and the elders of Israel*" (Lev. 9:1).

This chapter describes Aaron in his role of mediation as the high priest. It symbolizes Christ in this intercessory role, which He now occupies (Heb. 7:25).

Aaron, on the eighth day, was a fore picture of Christ sanctified, anointed with the Holy Spirit, and sent into the world in order to put away its sin by the sacrifice of Himself.

The glory of the Father raised Him from the dead, thus, accepting His person and His work.

The eighth day represents the resurrection of Christ, who was raised from the dead on the first day of the week, i.e., the eighth day, which was eight days from the first Sabbath.

Aaron, although the great high priest, still was a sinner who needed the saving grace of Christ, of which the sacrifices were a type. Consequently, as he began his duties, he had to offer up a sin offering and a burnt offering for himself.

He was to then offer a sin offering, a burnt offering, a peace offering, and a meat offering for the congregation of Israel.

With the proper offerings, the promise was, *"today the Lord will appear unto you."* The only way He will appear to any degree is by and through the Cross of Christ and our faith in that finished work.

All the congregation was commanded to draw near to the tabernacle, which they did. It was meant to impress upon them that all of these ceremonies and rituals concerning the sacrifices, the blood, etc., were all done on their behalf.

THE FIRST DAY OF MARCH?

The eighth day followed the seven days of consecration. According to ancient tradition, this was the first day of March.

This corresponds with Jesus being raised from the dead, which He was, in essence, on the eighth day. He was raised on the first day of the week, which was eight days after a full Sabbath week. After the ascension and sending back the Holy Spirit, at least the Spirit coming in a new dimension, Christ would begin His high priestly work, of which Chapter 9 is a type.

Some have placed this into the second coming of Christ when He will come back to redeem Israel, in which His glory at that time will then cover the earth. While it certainly could lean toward that, it is my thought that the second coming, which will be followed by the millennium, little needs shadows and types for its portrayal. So, I think the heavier meaning deals with the resurrection of Christ after He had redeemed lost humanity, in which He would now begin His high priestly work, which, in fact, continues unto the hour.

THE SIN OFFERING AND THE BURNT OFFERING

"And he said unto Aaron, you take a young calf for a sin offering, and a ram for a burnt offering, without blemish, and offer them before the LORD*"* (Lev. 9:2).

As stated, even though Aaron was the great high priest, thereby, a type of Christ, still, he was a poor mortal in need of a Saviour, which meant that he was a sinner. Sin, sin, sin — in everything, there is remembrance made of sin as man's great, ever-present, and crushing burden, and of the bloody sacrifice of Christ Jesus as its only remedy.

Concerning this, Seiss said: *"Everywhere, even in our holiest moods and most sacred doings, there still flashes out the stern and humiliating accusation—'O man, you are a sinner! All your goodness is but abomination apart from Christ! Your only hope is in Him whose body was broken and whose blood was shed for the remission of sins!'"*

MERCY STREAMING IN BLOOD

All of this means that our hand must be ever kept on the brow of the atoning Lamb. We must never cease to rest upon Jesus and His offering of Himself for us. We must ever look to the Cross.

The songwriter said:

"Sit, forever viewing,
"Mercy streaming in His blood."

This — His sacrificial and atoning death, the shedding of His blood — and this alone underlies everything else. There is no heavenly consecration, at least that which God will recognize, that does not take in this. It is the beginning, the middle, and the end of all human sanctification. Without resting upon Christ as the sin offering, we can never come to the high honors of the priesthood of saints. We are no longer our own; we are bought with a price — *"with the precious blood of Christ as of a lamb without blemish and without spot."*

Oh dear reader, can you not sense the presence of God even as we utter these words? Can you not sense the total reliance we must place upon Him, who has paid for all of our sins?

Even though Aaron and his sons were called of God, robed in beautiful garments, and, thereby, stood as leaders of the people — they were poor, frail, flawed, sinful mortals and, thereby, must have the same sacrifice as the worst sinners in Israel.

SIN

If one has a proper view of the Cross, then one will have a proper view of sin.

It is true that we are new creations in Christ Jesus, with old things having passed away and all things having become new (II Cor. 5:17). As well, we are definitely *kings and priests* (Rev. 1:6) and, in fact, are perfect in Christ. However, we must at the same time properly understand what all of that means.

Yes, we are all of this in Christ, which refers to what He did for us at the Cross. In other words, when God looks at us, He can do so only as He looks at Christ. Every victory won by Christ, every price paid by Christ, and every sacrifice made by Christ — all and in totality were developed and carried out strictly for us — for sinners. He did none of that for Himself, not at all for His Father in Heaven, and neither for angels, but altogether for us.

The idea is this: what He is, I am, but all because of the Cross and my faith in His Cross (Rom. 6:3–14; 8:1–2, 11; I Cor. 1:17–18, 21, 23; 2:2; Gal. 5:1–6; 6:14; Eph. 2:13–18; Col. 2:14–15).

CHRIST

That's what I am in Christ because of Christ, and solely because of Christ, which again refers to His Cross.

Despite all of this, I must recognize the fact that the sin nature is ever present within me (Rom. 6:1–2, 6–7, 12–18, 20, 22–23). For those who would claim that the believer no longer has a sin nature, I would counter by saying, if that is so, the Holy Spirit wasted a lot of time through Paul, explaining something that didn't exist.

Find the holiest man or woman on earth, whomever that might be, and through that individual, enough evil thoughts and evil passions will arise in that heart in one day, and sometimes even one hour, to doom that soul forever and forever. Such is the horror and the power of sin. Were it not so powerful, such a great price would not have needed to be paid.

To the believer who will not admit his personal frailty, faults, and failures, deception has become the rule. John said, *"If we say that we have no sin, we deceive ourselves, and the truth is not in us"* (I Jn. 1:8).

That being the case, and it most definitely is, even among the best of us, what then is our hope?

THE BLESSED HOPE

Our hope from beginning to end and from the first to the last is altogether in Christ, but it is in Christ according to the sacrifice of Himself on the Cross. He must never be separated from the Cross as it regards its benefits. Through the Cross, Jesus opened up the way to the Holy of Holies. Without the Cross, man would never have been able to bridge that great gulf, but the Cross bridged it, which means that Jesus became our sin offering. This means that He became the Sin-Bearer, the penalty-taker, if you will, the sin offering, and in this, He was *most holy* (Lev. 2:3, 10; 6:17–18, 25, 29; 7:1).

THE BURNT OFFERING

The sin offering was offered first, with the burnt offering following.

The sin offering proclaims Christ as the victim, and a perfect victim at that, taking the sins of the sinner upon Himself, in effect, becoming the Sin-Bearer, suffering its penalty, which was death.

The burnt offering typified the perfect Christ giving His perfection — righteousness — to the sinner, who, within himself, had no righteousness. In fact, it took five offerings to properly portray the one offering of Christ.

Now that all sin had been atoned, and done so by the sin offering, the perfect righteousness (typified by the burnt offering), could be lavished upon Aaron and, in fact, all who trust Christ.

THE SACRIFICES FOR THE PEOPLE

"And unto the children of Israel you shall speak, say-ing, Take you a kid of the goats for a sin offering; and a calf and a lamb, both of the first year, without blemish, for a burnt offering;

"Also a bullock and a ram for peace offerings to sacrifice before the LORD*; and a meat offering mingled with oil: for today the* LORD *will appear unto you.*

"And they brought that which Moses commanded before the tabernacle of the congregation; and all the congregation drew near and stood before the LORD*.*

"And Moses said, This is the thing which the LORD *com-manded that you should do: and the glory of the* LORD *shall appear unto you"* (Lev. 9:3-6).

On the eighth day Aaron, robed in linen and anointed, came forth out of the tabernacle to offer up the four great sac-rifices for the people: the sin offering, the burnt offering, the meal offering, and the peace offering. A public proclamation was made that God would accept him and his sacrifice by a special manifestation of His glory. This came to pass.

All of Israel was commanded to bring forth the specified sacrifices, which, no doubt, the elders of Verse 1 did on behalf of all the people.

THE LORD WILL APPEAR

There were six sacrifices in all regarding Israel (two burnt offerings, two peace offerings, plus one sin offering) five of them bloody sacrifices (Lev. 9:3–4).

It was promised that the Lord would appear unto them that day, that is, would manifest Himself in some way, which He did! However, it must be remembered without fail that the Lord could not manifest Himself until the proper sacrifices could be offered.

Likewise, if the Lord is in some way to appear among us presently, again to manifest Himself in some way, He will not do so unless Christ and what He has done at the Cross be given the proper place as it regards our faith. Regrettably, the flesh parades itself, and Christians by the untold thousands, who know little of the Word of God, think it's the Lord when it's not!

Worse than that, Satan with his ministers parade themselves under the guise of angels of light, and much of the church doesn't know the difference (II Cor. 11:13–15).

Why?

How?

Christ and His glory cannot at all manifest Himself unless we go through the Cross. There is no other way. Preachers who would try to tell you of other ways are only speaking of manufactured ways, which are the ways of man and not of God. The only way to the Holy of Holies is through the blood of Christ. Concerning this, Paul said: *"Having therefore, brethren, boldness to enter into the holiest by the blood of Jesus,*

"By a new and living way, which He has consecrated for us, through the veil, that is to say, His flesh" (Heb. 10:19–20).

I think what Paul said speaks for itself. We can go into the Holiest only by the precious blood of Jesus, and in the shedding of His blood, He gave His life, i.e., His flesh, i.e., the Cross.

ALL THE CONGREGATION

The entirety of Israel drawing near and standing before the Lord means that they were standing before the tabernacle. There were at least 3 million of these people, so many of them could little see the tabernacle, if at all, but, no doubt, exactly what was taking place was related to them by others who were closer. It would have been an awesome sight!

The cloudy pillar, with its awesome presence, would have rested above the tabernacle. They knew this was God and that He dwelt between the mercy seat and the cherubim in the Holy of Holies.

They were told that with the proper sacrifices offered, which they were, the *"glory of the Lord would appear unto them,"* and that He did, which we will study at the close of this chapter.

ATONEMENT

"And Moses said unto Aaron, Go unto the altar, and offer your sin offering, and your burnt offering, and make an atonement for yourself, and for the people: and offer the offering of the people, and make an atonement for them; as the LORD commanded" (Lev. 9:7).

Atonement is mentioned over and over in the Old Testament, while it is mentioned only once in the New; and then, it should have been translated reconciliation (Rom. 5:11). As stated, it refers to and means that man has been reconciled to God through the atoning, sacrificial death of the Lord Jesus Christ. That being the case, and as important as it is, why is the word *atonement* mentioned only once in the New Testament?

In the Old Testament, atonement was something that had to be done over and over again because the blood of animals was not sufficient to take away sins (Heb. 10:4). So, inasmuch as the ritual of sacrifice had to be repeated over and over, in fact, unceasing and unending, it was necessary that the word *atonement* be used, as well, over and over.

Also, the atonement effected in the Old Testament was in reality only a stopgap measure. It was, one might say, atonement on credit. In fact, it was a very incomplete atonement.

THE TRUE ATONEMENT

The Four Gospels record the true Atonement in the sacrificial, atoning death of Jesus Christ on the Cross of Calvary, to which all the animal sacrifices had pointed. When it was done, once for all, it was a completed work and, therefore, didn't have to be mentioned again and again. It was mentioned again and again in the Old Testament, as stated, because, in reality, the work was actually never done, demanding repeated sacrifices.

However, the Apostle Paul explained over and over again in all of his 14 epistles the results of the completed atonement in Christ. *Jesus died for me*, in essence, explains the Atonement. He died as my substitute, taking my place, thereby, reconciling me to God. However, there remains the results of the Atonement, which Paul graphically explained, and which we have attempted to explain over and over again, even in this volume.

If it is to be noticed, the results of atonement were never explained in the Old Testament because Old Testament atonement was never actually complete. The results were alluded to, but only in passing. The Lord spoke through the Prophet Ezekiel, saying: *"And I will give them one heart, and I will put a new spirit within you; and I will take the stony heart out of their flesh, and will give them an heart of flesh:*

"That they may walk in My statutes, and keep Mine ordinances, and do them: and they shall be My people, and I will be their God" (Ezek. 11:19–20).

If it is to be noticed, these passages speak of a future tense when Christ would come, effecting a completed atonement.

So, to sum up, the word *atonement* was used over and over in the Old Testament simply because the work was never done. It was used only one time in the New Testament because the work was completed in the death, which was the sacrifice of Christ.

THE BLOOD

"Aaron therefore went unto the altar, and slew the calf of the sin offering, which was for himself.

"And the sons of Aaron brought the blood unto him, and he dipped his finger in the blood, and put it upon the horns of the altar, and poured out the blood at the bottom of the altar" (Lev. 9:8-9).

Why was blood so important?

It was vastly important because it spoke of Christ who would give His own life, and do so by shedding His blood. As the Scripture says, *"the life of the flesh is in the blood"* (Lev. 17:11).

God is not flesh and blood, but rather Spirit. For Him to pay the price for dying humanity, He would have to become man, which means that the Creator, in a sense, would have to become a creation, which is beyond our comprehension. In doing so, which was a necessity, that is, if man was to be redeemed, He would have to become flesh, blood, and bone.

God cannot die, and death was required if man was to be redeemed. So, God would have to become man.

Why would He have to become man?

When God created Adam, He gave Adam latitude and discretion, which, it seems, were not given even to the angels. It seems from Genesis 1:26–27 that tremendous dominion was given to man. In fact, Psalms 8:4–6 implies that this dominion included all of God's creation.

Psalms 8:5 says, *"For You have made him a little lower than the angels, and have crowned him with glory and honour."*

The word *angels* in this verse is an improper translation. The actual Hebrew reads, *"For you have made him a little lower than the Godhead."* That means that man was originally created superior to the angels, which means that man was and is God's highest creation.

The tragedy is that man is a fallen creature. This means that he fell from total God-consciousness down to the far lower level of total self-consciousness. So, we do not see man now (which includes redeemed man) as God originally made him. In fact, Jesus Christ was the perfect man, the man that God originally intended; however, Jesus was God manifested in the flesh, which refers to the Incarnation.

THE FIRST ADAM AND THE LAST ADAM

Everything that God gave to the original Adam, in a sense, was lost in the Fall. Death became the mainstay instead of life.

Darkness became the emphasis instead of light. Inasmuch as God had created man in this fashion, in effect, making him the image of God, man could not be redeemed by mere fiat or decree. In other words, the righteousness of God demanded satisfaction. While God has the power to do anything, His power is always subjected to His nature and His righteousness. So, for man to be properly redeemed, another Adam would have to be sent into the world. He would do what the first Adam didn't do, which pertained to perfect obedience, and to undo, in fact, what the first Adam had done, which was to allow sin into this world, i.e., Satan. Jesus came to destroy the works of the Devil (I John 3:8). That second man, whom Paul referred to as the *last Adam*, was and is the Lord Jesus Christ (I Cor. 15:45–50).

He is referred to as the last Adam simply because the term means that there will never be the need for another. So, what would the last Adam do in order to redeem humanity?

THE CROSS

From before the foundation of the world, God through foreknowledge knew that He would create man and that man would fall. Foreknowledge, as well, knew the manner in which man would be redeemed. Love created man, and love would have to redeem man.

Concerning this, Peter said: **"Forasmuch as you know that you were not redeemed with corruptible things, as silver and gold, from your vain conversation** (lifestyle) **received by tradition from your fathers;**

"But with the precious blood of Christ, as of a lamb without blemish and without spot:

"Who verily was foreordained before the foundation of the world, but was manifest in these last times for you" (I Pet. 1:18–20).

So, from this passage and others similar, we know that the Cross was not an incident, an execution, an assassination, or an accident. In fact, we know that Jesus came to this world not only to live but, as well, as a sacrifice to die. Furthermore, He specifically came to die on a Cross.

WHY A CROSS?

In Israel of old, the Law (the Law of God) stated that if a man *"committed a sin worthy of death,"* and this speaks of a heinous sin, he was to be put to death. As a sign of his terrible sin, which means that he was cursed by God, his body was to be hung on a tree. He was to be placed accordingly to serve as a spectacle of his terrible crime.

However, his body was not to remain on the tree into the night but, before dark, was to be taken down and buried (Deut. 21: 22–23).

In other words, we are speaking of the worst type of sin. This means that the Cross was demanded because Jesus died not only for sin in general, but the worst type of sin that man could imagine, even the very root of sin. So, His death had to include the worst among the worst, and, to be sure, it did. This means that He atoned for all sin, irrespective of its nature or degree. This is why the Cross was demanded.

In fact, the Holy Spirit through Peter said, *"Who His own self bare our sins in His own body on the tree, that we, being dead to sins, should live unto righteousness: by whose stripes you were healed"* (I Pet. 2:24).

Paul said, *"Christ has redeemed us from the curse of the law, being made a curse for us: for it is written, Cursed is every one who hangs on a tree"* (Gal. 3:13).

So, the Cross was a necessity because Jesus had to atone for all sin, even the most hideous of sins.

THE PRICE

The price for that redemption was high. In fact, it was so high that no man could pay the price. If the Lord had left it there, demanding that man pay the price, man possibly might have an argument; however, due to the fact that God paid the price Himself, then man is left with no argument.

To redeem fallen man, a perfect life would have to be given. As should be understood, due to original sin, no man could supply that perfect life. Therefore, as stated, God would have to become man, which He did, *"the second man"* (I Cor. 15:45–50).

Christ would live a perfect life, not even sinning one time and not even failing one time, which meant that He did what the first Adam did not do. He rendered a perfect obedience.

THE SIN DEBT

However, there remained the terrible sin debt that had to be addressed. His perfect life could not address that sin debt, only His perfect death. Therefore, as the perfect sacrifice, He offered up Himself on the tree, i.e., Cross, shedding His life's blood, which was untainted by sin and, thereby, God readily accepted it. This means that by pouring out His life's blood, Christ gave His life, which atoned for all sin, hence, the constant application of the blood respecting the Old Testament sacrifices (Eph. 2:13–18).

We were not purchased with such corruptible things as silver and gold, even as Peter said, which are the most valuable commodities in the world, but which were insufficient. We were rather purchased by His precious blood — perfect blood, incidentally — which no other individual had (I Pet. 1:18–20). For life to be regained, a perfect life would have to be given, which was the price that the nature and righteousness of God demanded. Jesus paid that price, and that's the reason that Paul said, *"But God forbid that I should glory, save in the Cross of our Lord Jesus Christ, by whom the world is crucified unto me, and I unto the world"* (Gal. 6:14).

WHY WAS BLOOD PUT ON THE HORNS OF THE ALTAR?

The brazen altar was the first vessel of all the sacred vessels. It sat outside of the tabernacle in the court. One other sacred vessel stood between it and the tabernacle, which was the brazen laver.

On each of the four corners of the brazen altar was a horn. Each one pointed outward — north, south, east, and west.

This referred to the fact that God's redemption plan was one plan and was for the entirety of mankind all over the world. This means that every other supposed plan of redemption, whatever it might be, was not acceptable by God and, in fact, was cursed by God (Gal. 1:8–9). Furthermore, this plan, which was symbolized by all of these sacred vessels, all and without exception, pointed to Jesus Christ as the Saviour of the world. That's the reason that Jesus said, *"I* am the way, the truth, and the life: no man comes unto the Father, but by Me" (Jn. 14:6).

He also said, "I am the door: by Me if any man enter in, he shall be saved, and shall go in and out, and find pasture" (Jn. 10:9).

REDEMPTION

The Lord commanding Aaron, and all priests who would follow after him, to apply blood from the sin offering (at least in this type of sacrifice) to the four horns of the altar was done in order to proclaim the way and the manner in which this plan of redemption would be put into force. The blood coming from the slain victim, and part of that victim being burned on the altar, specified that Christ would effect redemption by and through the Cross, and by and through the Cross alone!

This means that man can be saved only by trusting in Christ and what Christ has done for us at the Cross.

The balance of the blood was then poured out at the bottom of the altar, which signified that Jesus would die on an altar, i.e., a Cross. The altar was always a place of death!

WITHOUT THE CAMP

"But the fat, and the kidneys, and the caul above the liver of the sin offering, he burnt upon the altar; as the LORD commanded Moses.

"And the flesh and the hide he burnt with fire without the camp" (Lev. 9:10-11).

As is obvious here, only a part of the carcass of the sin offering was burned on the altar, that being the fat and certain other organs, while the balance was taken *without the camp* and there burnt with fire. This says two things:

1. The carcass being taken without the camp and there completely burned proclaims the fact that all sin would be completely expiated in the death of Christ, which means to do away with the guilt incurred. The whole curse fell upon the substitute. The atonement was not completed until the whole sacrifice was consumed. In fact, the sin offering was to be burned in a clean place, actually, *"where the ashes are poured out"* (Lev. 4:12).

2. The majority of the sin offering being burned outside of the camp coincides with the statement as given by Paul, *"Wherefore Jesus also, that He might sanctify the people with His own blood, suffered without the gate,"* meaning outside of the city limits of Jerusalem, so to speak (Heb. 13:12).

THE BURNT OFFERING

"And he slew the burnt offering; and Aaron's sons presented unto him the blood, which he sprinkled round about upon the altar.

"And they presented the burnt offering unto him, with the pieces thereof, and the head: and he burnt them upon the altar.

"And he did wash the inwards and the legs, and burnt them upon the burnt offering on the altar" (Lev. 9:12-14).

As we have stated, the sin offering was most holy and symbolized Christ taking the guilt of the sinner and making it His own. The burnt offering symbolized the perfection of Christ and Him giving that perfection to the sinner.

The process of cutting up the carcass is not mentioned here because it is implied in the fact that the ritual on this occasion was exactly the same as in the offerings made by Moses.

Aaron's sons handed the dismembered victim to him piece by piece, which was done in this manner for a reason.

The idea is twofold:

First of all, it pointed to the great price paid by Christ, especially His separation from the Father from noon to 3 p.m., when He was on the Cross. During this time, the earth, or at least that part of the world, turned black because a thrice-holy God couldn't look upon His Son as He did bear the sin penalty of mankind. During that time, He was separated from the Father, at least as it regarded the union He had always known.

As well, the dismemberment of the victim is also meant to portray the terrible ravages of sin upon the human heart and life. That's why Jesus said of Satan that he steals, kills, and destroys (Jn. 10:10).

WASH THE INWARDS

All of the burnt offering was consumed on the brazen altar — all, that is, with the exception of the hide.

But yet, certain parts of the physical organs were washed and then placed on the altar along with the carcass.

This was meant to show the veracity of the Atonement. In other words, what Christ would do at the Cross would be far more than a mere external application. It would go to the very vitals — the very soul and spirit of the individual — hence, the *inwards being washed.*

This is the reason that man's solutions never work. He can only deal with externals. He tries to deal with the internals through humanistic psychology, but such is a fruitless effort. In fact, it is worse than useless! When the person comes to Christ, he or she is born again, which means that the person has become a new creation, and done so both inwardly and outwardly (II Cor. 5:17).

THE PEOPLE'S OFFERING

"And he brought the people's offering, and took the goat, which was the sin offering for the people, and slew it, and offered it for sin, as the first.

"And he brought the burnt offering, and offered it according to the manner.

"And he brought the meat offering, and took an handful thereof, and burnt it upon the altar, beside the burnt sacrifice of the morning.

"He slew also the bullock and the ram for a sacrifice of peace offerings, which was for the people: and Aaron's sons presented unto him the blood, which he sprinkled upon the altar round about" (Lev. 9:15-18).

Four different offerings at this time were offered for the people (in fact, this was the very first time that this was done):

1. It was the sin offering for Israel's atonement.
2. It was the burnt offering, which gave to Israel the perfection of Christ.

3. It was the meat offering, which was to render thanks for God accepting the offerings that had been presented.
4. It was the peace offering, which signified that due to God accepting the offerings, the people now had peace with God.

Verses 22 and 23 proclaim the blessing of the people. The lifting up of hands became a custom of priests in blessing the people when completing their duties for them in the rituals.

Exactly what Moses said would happen did happen: *"The glory of the Lord appeared unto all the people."*

How did this happen?

Verse 24 tells us: *"And there came a fire out from before the Lord, and consumed upon the altar the burnt offering and the fat."*

REDEMPTION BY BLOOD

As we have previously stated, it took five great offerings to properly portray the one sacrifice of Christ. As Aaron and his sons offered up sacrifices for the people for the very first time, four of these offerings were presented, leaving out the trespass offering. This was left out because the offerings were general instead of personal. While they definitely had a personal result, they were, in fact, offered for the entirety of the nation.

The trespass offering mostly concerned itself with differences or wrongs done to a neighbor. After the sacrifices were properly explained to the people, trespass offerings were no doubt presented, beginning at that time. However, for now, the four sacrifices mentioned here dealt with the entire nation in general.

Most surely, we find in the description of all these offerings, plus the entirety of the Bible for that matter, that redemption by blood is the great theme of the Scriptures from beginning to end. This may be repulsive to some and, no doubt, is; however, it is only because they do not understand the terrible ravages of sin, even though sin is even at that moment destroying them.

We must ever remember that we're not dealing here merely with this life but for eternity. The sin is great. The price was high for cleansing as it regards this terrible malady, but God paid the price when He became man and gave Himself on the Cross of Calvary. Paul said, *"Who gave Himself for our sins, that He might deliver us from this present evil world, according to the will of God and our Father"* (Gal. 1:4).

Had that not occurred, of which all of these sacrifices were types and shadows, we would have died in our sins, forever lost. To be sure, the thought of eternal darkness is beyond comprehension!

THE WAVE OFFERING

"And the fat of the bullock and of the ram, the rump, and that which covered the inwards, and the kidneys, and the caul above the liver:

"And they put the fat upon the breasts, and he burnt the fat upon the altar:

"And the breasts and the right shoulder Aaron waved for a wave offering before the LORD; as Moses commanded" (Lev. 9:19-21).

For the sin offering, a goat was offered. For the burnt offering, a calf and a lamb were offered (Lev. 9:3). For the peace offerings, the bullock and the ram were sacrificed.

What did the different animals mean?

In this instance, the goat represented sin more than any of these other animals, which Christ took upon Himself.

The lamb and the calf are the most docile of the animals, representing the humility of Christ in the offering up of Himself as an offering to God.

The bullock typified sin forgiven, and done so because of Christ, while the ram specified the high priestly work of Christ, with both proclaiming that peace had been restored. Regarding the peace offerings, the fat of the bullock and the ram, as well as other parts, were burnt upon the altar, signifying that all blessings come from God, of which these things were a type.

Aaron then took the breasts and the right shoulder of both the bullock and the ram, lifted them up, and waved them for a *"wave offering before the Lord."*

The wave offering signified that all blessings came from above, which means that redemption would come from above and would do so in the form of the Lord Jesus Christ, of which these sacrifices were types.

THE BLESSING

"And Aaron lifted up his hand toward the people, and blessed them, and came down from offering of the sin offering, and the burnt offering, and peace offerings" (Lev. 9:22).

As stated, the lifting up of the hands of the priests became a custom in blessing the people when completing their duties for them in the rituals. What the priests said to them on this occasion is not stated, but it could have been what was established for priests in Numbers 6:24–26:

"The LORD *bless you, and keep you:*

"The LORD *make His face shine upon you, and be gracious unto you:*

"The LORD *lift up His countenance upon you, and give you peace."*

THE APPEARANCE OF THE GLORY OF THE LORD

"And Moses and Aaron went into the tabernacle of the congregation, and came out, and blessed the people: and the glory of the LORD *appeared unto all the people.*

"And there came a fire out from before the LORD, *and consumed upon the altar the burnt offering and the fat; which when all the people saw, they shouted, and fell on their faces"* (Lev. 9:23-24).

Concerning this, Ellicott said: *"The sacrifices being ended, there still remained the burning of the incense on the golden altar which stood in the Holy Place of the tabernacle. Hence Aaron, conducted by Moses, left the court where the altar of burnt offering stood, and where the sacrifices had been offered, and went into the Holy Place where the altar of incense stood to perform this last act of the ritual (Ex. 30:7).*

"Having already delivered to Aaron the charge of all the things connected with the sacrifices in the court, Moses now also committed to him the care of the things within the sanctuary, showing him at the same time, how to offer the incense, how to arrange the shewbread on the table, how to light and trim the lamps of the lampstand, all of which were in the sanctuary."

This being done, both of them came out, after which they had, no doubt, prayed and asked the Lord for His guidance, and then they blessed the people.

AND THEN IT HAPPENED!

The fire did not come directly from Heaven, but rather came from God, who dwelt between the mercy seat and the cherubim. A literal tongue of flame came from the Holy of Holies through the veil without burning it, and struck the brazen altar and consumed the burnt offering and the fat. In fact, it was visible to all of Israel, at least after a fashion.

When the people saw this, they shouted and fell on their faces, which, of course, is understandable!

Some claim that this particular fire was the first fire on the altar; however, according to Leviticus 8:16 and 9:10, this is not correct. Fire had already been kindled on the altar in order for Aaron to offer up sacrifices for himself and his sons.

This being the case, fire from God manifested His divine presence and showed that He had accepted the sacrifice, which He consumed with the tongue of flame.

This means that what the Lord had commanded had been faithfully obeyed by Moses as he instructed Aaron and Aaron's sons. All was complete. There was nothing lacking and, therefore, the divine glory appeared, and the whole assembly fell prostrate in adoring worship.

THE GLORY OF GOD

However, let us not forget that the glory of God, represented by the tongue of flame that came from the Holy of Holies, was the result of the proper sacrifice. In other words, it was the Cross, which the altar and the sacrifices represented, that God acknowledged and honored. More particularly, it was His Son, who would die on that Cross, which guaranteed atonement and brought about the manifestation.

How important it is that we understand these things! This is the reason that we preach the Cross! This is why Paul said that nothing must be emphasized to the extent that the Cross of Christ is made of none effect (I Cor. 1:17).

We see here Israel brought into the full enjoyment of the results of accomplished atonement, at least as much as could be done at that particular time. They shouted because God had accepted the atonement. Unfortunately, we are all too often shouting over other things that have little significance.

Let me say it again: It is ever *the Cross! The Cross! The Cross!*

"Lo, He comes, with clouds descending,
"Once for our salvation sinners slain;
"Thousand, angel hosts saints attending,
"Swell the triumph of His train."

"Every eye shall then behold Him,
"Robed in mighty majesty;
"Those who set at naught and sold Him,
"Pierced, and nailed Him to the tree."

"Now redemption, long expected,
"See in solemn pomp appear:
"All His saints, by man rejected,
"Now shall meet Him in the air:"

"Yea, amen! Let all adore You,
"High on Your eternal throne;
"Saviour, take the power and glory;
"Claim the kingdom for Your own."

Bibliography

CHAPTER 1

H.D.M. Spence, *The Pulpit Commentary: Leviticus 1:3*, Grand Rapids, Eerdmans Publishing Company, 1978.

C.H. Mackintosh, *Notes on the Book of Leviticus*, New York, Loizeaux Brothers, 1880, Pg. 6.

Ibid., pg. 16.

Ibid., pg. 24.

CHAPTER 2

C.H. Mackintosh, *Notes on the Book of Leviticus*, New York, Loizeaux Brothers, 1880, Pg. 3.

H.D.M. Spence, *The Pulpit Commentary: Leviticus 2:3*, Grand Rapids, Eerdmans Publishing Company, 1978.

CHAPTER 3

C.H. Mackintosh, *Notes on the Book of Leviticus*, New York, Loizeaux Brothers, 1880, Pg. 101.

George Williams, *Williams' Complete Bible Commentary*, Grand Rapids, Kregel Publications, 1994, Pg. 65.

C.H. Mackintosh, *Notes on the Book of Leviticus*, New York, Loizeaux Brothers, 1880, Pg. 79.

CHAPTER 4

C.H. Mackintosh, *Notes on the Book of Leviticus*, New York, Loizeaux Brothers, 1880, Pg. 106.

Ibid., pg. 115.

George Williams, *Williams' Complete Bible Commentary*, Grand Rapids, Kregel Publications, 1994, Pg. 66.

C.H. Mackintosh, *Notes on the Book of Leviticus*, New York, Loizeaux Brothers, 1880, Pg. 129.

CHAPTER 5

Joseph A. Seiss, *Holy Types*, Smith, English & Co., New York, 1866, Page 83.

Ibid., pg. 84.

C.H. Mackintosh, *Notes on the Book of Leviticus*, New York, Loizeaux Brothers, 1880, Pg. 138.

CHAPTER 6

Ellicott's Commentary on the Whole Bible, Zondervan Publishing House, New York, 1880.

C.H. Mackintosh, *Notes on the Book of Leviticus*, New York, Loizeaux Brothers, 1880, pg. 149.

Ibid., pg. 150.

CHAPTER 7

Joseph A. Seiss, *Holy Types*, Smith, English & Co., New York, 1866, Page 102.

George Williams, *Williams' Complete Bible Commentary*, Grand Rapids, Kregel Publications, 1994, pg. 68.

Ibid., pg. 68.

CHAPTER 8

George Williams, *Williams' Complete Bible Commentary*, Grand Rapids, Kregel Publications, 1994, pg. 68.

C.H. Mackintosh, *Notes on the Book of Leviticus*, New York, Loizeaux Brothers, 1880, Pg. 153.

Joseph A. Seiss, *Holy Types*, Smith, English & Co., New York, 1866, Page 119.

Ibid.

George Williams, *Williams' Complete Bible Commentary*, Grand Rapids, Kregel Publications, 1994, pg. 69.

CHAPTER 9

Joseph A. Seiss, *Holy Types*, Smith, English & Co., New York, 1866, pg. 148.

Ellicott's Commentary on the Whole Bible, Zondervan Publishing House, New York, 1880.

The Rev. Jimmy Swaggart is a Pentecostal evangelist whose anointed preaching and teaching has drawn multitudes to the Cross of Christ since 1956.

As an author, he has written more than 50 books, commentaries, study guides, and The Expositor's Study Bible, which has sold more than 1.5 million copies.

As an award-winning musician and singer, Brother Swaggart has recorded more than 50 Gospel albums and sold nearly 16 million recordings worldwide.

For nearly six decades, Brother Swaggart has channeled his preaching and music ministry through multiple media venues including print, radio, television and the Internet.

In 2010, Jimmy Swaggart Ministries launched its own cable channel, SonLife Broadcasting Network, which airs 24 hours a day to a potential viewing audience of more than 1 billion people around the globe.

Brother Swaggart also pastors Family Worship Center in Baton Rouge, Louisiana, the church home and headquarters of Jimmy Swaggart Ministries.

Jimmy Swaggart Ministries materials can be found at **www.jsm.org**.

NOTES